Check the Gs

The True Story of an Eclectic American Family and Their Wacky Family Business

RAY SHASHO

iUniverse, Inc.
Bloomington

Check the Gs
The True Story of an Eclectic American Family
and Their Wacky Family Business

iUniverse books may be ordered through booksellers or by contacting:

iUniverse
1663 Liberty Drive
Bloomington, IN 47403
www.iuniverse.com
1-800-Authors (1-800-288-4677)

Gary W. Sweetman Photography and Digital Imaging 800-226-4004

ISBN: 978-1-4502-9860-5 (pbk)
ISBN: 978-1-4502-9858-2 (clth)
ISBN: 978-1-4502-9859-9 (ebk)

Library of Congress Control Number: 2011903061

Printed in the United States of America

iUniverse rev. date: 3/16/11

To my beautiful wife, Sharon, who always believed in me, especially during those tough and challenging moments in our lives together. I learned to fall in love and stay in love because of you.

My daughter, Michelle, and my son, Ray Ray, I'm very proud of each of your own personal conquests and continued perseverance in this difficult and complicated world. Thank you for being incredible kids.

Thanks, Mom and Dad, for giving me the most wonderful childhood a son could have.

For Uncle Moey, Cousin David, and Cousin Teri, who left us much too early, thanks for the wonderful memories; we'll meet again in the next life.

But most of all, thanks for the love we all continue to share together.

> I think Carly Simon's lyrics say it best:
> And tomorrow we might not be together
> I'm no prophet and I don't know nature's ways
> So I'll try and see into your eyes right now
> And stay right here 'cause these are the good old days

Contents

Chapter 1	Chin Lung Art Gallery	1
Chapter 2	Change the Luck	10
Chapter 3	Saff Their Brains Out!	21
Chapter 4	Johnnycake Road	31
Chapter 5	Bye-Bye, Baltimore	45
Chapter 6	Dark Days … "By and By"	59
Chapter 7	Visiting Bensonhurst	68
Chapter 8	Psychedelic Days	84
Chapter 9	The Basement	94
Chapter 10	The Newport-Miami Beach	104
Chapter 11	Long Live the King of the Jungle!	112
Chapter 12	Who's Going to Make the Next Ale-say?	121
Chapter 13	"Rock" Raymond	138
Chapter 14	That's My Cousin, You Asshole!	149
Chapter 15	Brown Institute of Broadcasting	160
Chapter 16	"This Is Ray Richards on 1340 WSEB"	174
Chapter 17	Worldwide Electronics	184
Chapter 18	Throwing Tomatoes for Justice	198
Chapter 19	Do You Want to Meet My Friends?	209
Chapter 20	Is the Grass Really Blue?	218

Chapter 21   Hail to Mr. and Mrs. Shashow … and the
             Redskins   228

Chapter 22   Sight & Sound Camera and Electronics   238

Chapter 23   Farewell to a Friend   250

Chapter 24   Celebrity Gs and Almost the Pope   259

Chapter 25   Everything Was Sold to the Bare Walls …
             Even the Toilet   267

Chapter One

Chin Lung Art Gallery

It was 1962 when Dad and his twin brother, Joey, opened their retail store on the corner of Thirteenth and F Street in Washington DC. The three-story building had the best show windows in town. Only three blocks away was 1600 Pennsylvania Avenue NW and its very famous house. Inside the house was a man named Kennedy, who was busy dealing with an incident called the Cuban missile crisis.

Three years later on a Saturday in April, my father insisted that I go downtown with him and work at the store. I was six years old. The only time I had visited Washington DC was when I straddled my dad's shoulder's and witnessed beautiful white horses pulling President Kennedy's coffin draped with an American flag down Pennsylvania Avenue. It was a sad day; so many people cried. Mom dressed me up in a white long sleeve shirt with a red bow tie and a red vest that had some kind of emblem printed on the left side. My pants were perfectly ironed, and my shoes were shined. My head didn't have a hair out of place thanks to Dad's Vitalis.

Yesterday, Mom had taken me to the barbershop on Edmondson Avenue. That place was neat; they had real monkeys in their windows. My older brother Howard had always shared his experiences of working at the store and how it felt to break the ice, to make your first sale. I guessed it was going to be my time to share now. After I got dressed, I started thinking about the day to come and got really antsy. It was the first time that I'd get to see dad's store in the city. I was excited. I sat down at the kitchen table with Dad while Abuela, my grandmother, served the both of us bagels with cream cheese. Abuela was intelligent, sweet, and soft. Her hair had always been gray since I could remember. She wore 1950s prescription glasses attached to a chain that dangled down. Even with the chain attached around her neck, she'd still sometimes wonder where her glasses were.

My cousin Tony arrived at our home at 7:45. He should have been here at 7:30, but he was late after he decided to cook a big Saturday morning breakfast for his kids. Tony stood at six foot two, but I always imagined him to be much taller. Tony was one of the camera experts at my dad's store on F Street. He and his wife, Gigi, were definitely my oldest cousins and were old enough to be my aunt and uncle. He had the heaviest Cuban accent I had ever heard; it took me years to finally understand what the heck he was talking about. He was the type of person who would do anything in the world for you, without hesitation. He was a good soul and funny as shit, or as Tony would say, "chit." He had a great sense of humor, and when he told a funny joke or story, it was even funnier because of his accent.

I finished my breakfast and then sat quietly watching Dad as he got in his last cup of coffee. Dad made more of a slurping sound than a sip, and after every slurp he'd swallow and let out a euphoric "Ah." While holding his coffee mug by his mouth, he glanced at the wall clock and then said in his best Sergeant Joe Friday impersonation, "Let's go!" I immediately sat up from my chair and ran into Mom's bedroom to kiss her good-bye. She was resting in bed with Terry, our black and white terrier. She wished me good luck as she hugged and kissed me.

I ran back into the kitchen to say good-bye to Abuela. She wasn't wearing her glasses, so she fumbled around her upper chest area looking for them. When she couldn't find them easily, she cried out in her nervous Cuban accent, *"Donde estan mis espeuelos?"* (Where are my glasses?) I laughingly explain to her, "Abuela, they're around your neck." She'd look down and see them dangling below her chest and then burst into a quiet laughter. Our charming skit would be performed frequently over the years to come. My brother Howard was still sleeping; he had plans and wasn't coming downtown with us today.

We marched out the front door to a beautiful summer day, walking down cement stairs and to the driveway where Dad's navy blue Oldsmobile 98 parked. I gazed over to the middle of our front yard where Howard and I had planted sunflowers. We had a contest to see who could grow the biggest sunflower. Howard's flower looked to be around six inches taller than mine. He always beat me at everything, but then he was seven years older than me. Tony climbed into the driver's seat, Dad sat up front with him, and I sat in the back seat. I was one of the men now. We pulled out of our driveway onto Johnnycake Road. Ten minutes later, Tony pulled into a Shell gasoline station. He asked for ten dollars of gas, but the attendant pumped in only eight dollars. Poor Tony always had a hard time asking for gas at the service station; attendants always pumped in the wrong amount of gas because they never understood him.

We finally got on the interstate and headed south for Washington DC. We passed by the Carling Brewery as we left Baltimore. After about an hour or so, we were getting closer to the downtown Washington area. We were moving slowly in a lot of traffic, and it seemed like we were always stopping at a traffic light. Then I saw these really old, rundown buildings and groups of black men hanging out on a street corner laughing. I looked ahead through the windshield window and spotted the Washington Monument. I hoped that we were almost there.

After fidgeting in the backseat of my dad's Oldsmobile for an hour and inhaling massive amounts of cigar smoke from both Dad and Tony during the trip, we finally turned into the Twelfth Street parking garage. My clothes reeked of cigar smoke, and I desperately needed to get out of the car. When the car came to a complete stop inside the parking garage, I was the first one to jump out. I felt kind of puny from the smoke and the long car ride. I needed fresh air. The windows were completely shut during the entire trip because the air-conditioning was on. I could see thick black soot lying on top of the dashboard from all the cigar-smoked trips that Dad and Tony had made into downtown; all the ashtrays contained a pyramid of ashes. I didn't want to complain about the smoke and seem wimpy, so I kept quiet and watched the scenery out my window. I wanted to be a tough guy like my dad and Tony. A black man handed dad a parking stub and quickly drove his car away. We walked on the city sidewalk toward the end of the block. We couldn't cross the street because a blinking sign at the end of the block told us not to walk. I walked behind Dad and Tony the whole time since coming out of the parking garage, but when we stopped to wait for the light to change, all of us stood close together. It actually gave me a break because their cigar smoke kept drifting back toward my face.

I took a minute to take my first good look at downtown. The first thing I noticed was a man throwing food scraps at a group of pigeons. I never got a chance to watch pigeons. They don't seem like very smart birds and always hung out in the city for some reason. They looked kind of fat and clumsy and seemed to want to walk rather than fly. I got bored watching the pigeons eating, so I focused my attention on all the different kinds of people wearing serious faces as they marched up and down the street. It was a bright and sunny day when I left Johnnycake Road, but now everything kind of looked old and gray; I guessed the sun was hiding behind one of those big buildings. The cars and busses looked like they weren't sure what lane they wanted to stay in, and I heard engines revving and horns beeping. With every step I took, I smelled bus fumes. We crossed the street when the sign finally said walk. The next light also said walk, so we kept crossing streets. Then we headed up a really steep sidewalk. I felt like I was leaning over like one of those ski jumpers in the Olympics. We passed by a hamburger place called Little Tavern Shops. I smelled the burgers as we walked by, and it was a refreshing odor; it gave me a nice break from inhaling all those crappy bus fumes. The scenery quickly turned into old and dirty brick walls with huge metal doors. Sitting on stoops outside the metal doors were scary-looking bums staring back at us. Some of the tramps focused their attention to what was inside their crinkly brown paper bags. One of them stared right at me, and I sped up and walked in between Dad and Tony. I tried to concentrate on looking straight ahead so that I wouldn't see anymore bums, but I just had to turn my head one last time to see if they were still staring at us. They weren't, so I concentrated next on a glass window that took up almost half of the block. It was part of Dad's corner store. Two green signs that crossed each other with white lettering stood tall on the corner and read, "13th St NW/F Street NW." We rounded the corner to another glass window loaded with merchandise and prepared to enter the corner building.

Dad, Tony, and I walked into the store lobby and entered the opened double doors; I could hear the Supremes song "Stop! In the Name of Love" playing through an outside lobby speaker. We all walked in, and I led the way. I immediately heard Uncle Moey shouting at me, "Wow, look, my nephew Ray-Ray is here!"

Bernadette's face was all smiles, she was a fantastic salesgirl. "Aw Raymond, you look like a little man."

I saw Uncle Joey in the distance sneering at me. "Are you ready to work, sonny boy?"

Then Fat Bobby walked over to shake hands. Fat Bobby had a baseball bat–sized cigar in his mouth, and his stomach was really huge. When he walked over to shake my hand, I could only stare at his fat stomach. When Bobby came to a complete stop, I actually felt his stomach touching me. Somehow he was able to talk with me with that cigar in his mouth/ "Ray-Ray, nice to see you again." I always thought of him as an uncle, but he wasn't related to me. Fat Bobby was a really nice man and was fun to talk with, but his gigantic stomach was a bit scary. I thought it would open up and swallow me whole.

I started to walk around my dad's store, checking out all the great stuff like I owned the place. All the merchandise was lined up like soldiers and filled every available space inside the lit glass showcases and wall cases. Even the walls were crowded with hanging merchandise. I saw chandeliers with hanging price tags for sale on the ceilings. There were expensive table clothes that were kept in a curtained-off secret back room, figurines of hobos and clowns that scared the crap out of me, and oil paintings of landscapes that stood perfect and slanted in rows above the wall cases. Rows of suitcases filled the open spaces above the wall cases, and each wall case was devoted to a certain line of merchandise. There were transistor and shortwave radios loaded with batteries and ready for demo, reel-to-reel tape recorders, portable record players, binoculars, travel clocks, and clock radios, mini black-and-white television sets, Princess style rotary telephones, and all kinds of cameras.

The showcases were stocked with carefully lined-up watches, rings, sunglasses, knives, fancy cigarette holders, and lighters. Sitting on top of the glass showcases stood ashtrays for people that smoked and a round mirror for trying on sunglasses. There was a revolving display of Washington DC slides for sale, a smaller revolving display case containing charms of Washington DC, and a spinning display of postcards.

Souvenirs of the nation's capital that said "Made in Hong Kong" and an assortment of smaller gift items sat orderly on large open show bins running down the middle of the store. One of their fastest selling items was displayed in one of those bins: a personal massager. A handwritten sign sat on top of the display that read, "One Thousand and One Uses." The item came in pink or white and in three different sizes, medium, large, and extra large. I actually watched a pretty lady buy one. Everyone in the store seemed to make a big deal about it too, especially when the lady bought the extra large personal massager.

All the stuff for sale had to look clean and spotless to try and lure the customers into buying. Showcases were squirted down with Windex and wiped down for a sparkling clear invisible shine every twenty minutes or when smudges were noticed. Everyone used the feather duster to keep the dust off an item until it was sold.

I walked over to stand next to my dad, behind the showcase filled with rows and rows of sunglasses. I was proud to be with him—my father and me, finally working together at his store. There he was, with his perfectly combed, curly, oiled hair; white short sleeves; and skinny black tie. He looked down at me with a strange look on his face and said, "I'm not your father." Oh no! Could I have mistaken Uncle Joey for Dad? They were identical twins, so I really shouldn't feel too stupid. But I did feel stupid, so I snuck over behind the register counter and hid. The register counter was really tall; no one could see me because I was so little. It felt like a place that I really shouldn't be hanging around because I think all the money was kept back there. I started looking around and saw an old-fashioned cash register with a large safety pin taped to it. I asked Uncle Joey what the safety pin was for, and he said it was for good luck. I started to realize that they were really superstitious, especially when it came to making money. I noticed later that if business was slow, they would try and change the luck by walking outside or standing in different spots around the store. The biggest unthinkable was folding your arms; it was considered a jinx. I got hollered at twice the first day for folding my arms.

Other neat stuff behind the register counter was a really loud adding machine used to ring up lots of items at one time. Below the register in very special slots was an assortment of brown paper bags that included the sizes of very small, small, medium, large, and a shopping bag with handles. If a customer bought a lot of stuff, Dad would wrap the merchandise up in brown paper and tie it with twine, so it would be easier to carry out the door. Dad liked wrapping up packages; he took his time and made sure the twine was tied extra tight and perfect so that a customer would be able to carry their stuff home comfortably. There were other things behind the tall register counter, like a stubborn credit card swipe machine (I knew it was stubborn because I tried playing with it), a black rotary telephone hung on the wall, tissue paper to wrap up the Washington DC souvenirs, and a bell. It was the kind of bell you might see ringing during Christmas at a Salvation Army stand. Dad said that the bell was used to stir up excitement during a lull period. Dad or Uncle Joey would ring the bell and shout out, "All right, second shift now reporting for duty!"

Handwritten signs on brown paper bags were everywhere. My dad claimed to be the inventor of writing sales signs on brown paper bags. The signs shouted out messages to bring in business, like "Look" (with eyes drawn in the *O*s). Other paper bag sales signs were "Sale, Lowest Prices in Town," "Clearance," "Save, Save, Save," "Buy Now and Save," and my favorite, "Going Out for Business. There were smaller handwritten signs inside the outside show windows too.

I had fun exploring around my dad's store. Something else that really caught my attention was a colorful selection of paper money from all over the world. Dad said that foreign customers would donate a sample of their money to be displayed up on the wall. I didn't realize that there were that many countries in the world. There must have been over a hundred different types of paper money. It was really something to see.

After I stared at the money on the wall for about twenty minutes, Dad told me to go upstairs and look around at the rest of the store. I didn't even know there was a rest of the store. He showed me the steps that led upstairs to another floor. I was a little nervous going upstairs all by myself, but I wanted to be tough like everyone else, so I didn't say anything. I counted fifteen carpeted stairs to the second floor. On the way up I noticed a really old, dusty gray hanging lamp. It must have been really old because it wasn't working. I could kind of tip the lamp when I tried to reach for it. When I took a closer look at the lamp, I noticed that someone wrote their initials into the dust. I thought it was pretty cool that someone had thought of doing that. I finally left the lamp alone and continued my trek to the second floor. I peeked inside three small rooms that looked like closets, where they kept all the stuff that wouldn't fit above the wall cases downstairs. Dad called it inventory. There was a huge desk up there too, so I started to peek inside the drawers.

For some reason, anytime I'd start sneaking around somewhere without anybody else knowing, it made me feel like I was going to crap in my pants. I quickly hunted for a bathroom. I walked around a large stack of brand-new portable record players and saw another room that led to some more steps. I walked inside the room and found a really old bathroom. It had a pull-down chain for flushing the toilet and a window on the ceiling. Because I found the bathroom, I decided to use it fast; being sneaky made me have to go. I almost needed a stepstool to climb up on the giant toilet. I always hated using strange bathrooms. It was disgusting! Sitting there all by myself, on that huge disgusting toilet, it felt like I was in the olden times. I could have fallen off that disgusting toilet and broken my neck, and nobody would hear me screaming for help. It was a scary ordeal for a little kid, so I did my business fast and got out of there.

I was still a little nervous from the olden bathroom, but I decided to check out the third floor anyway. Steeper, uncarpeted stairs led me to the third floor. The third floor was the scariest place of all. I heard the rattling noises of dishes from the Blue Mirror Grill below us. The third floor had hundreds and hundreds of stacked boxes and Washington DC souvenirs everywhere. The third floor felt like hanging out at a haunted warehouse. I just didn't want to be there alone. It was like someone or something was always watching me. At any minute, I could be startled by something, maybe a giant rat or perhaps a psycho killer in hiding. Then all of a sudden I got really scared and ran all the way down to the sales floor. I calmed down once I saw Dad smoking his cigar behind a showcase. Nobody was going to see me scared! But I sure wasn't going back upstairs to the third floor again … not alone anyway.

Chapter Two

Change the Luck

I walked toward the front of the store and saw Uncle Moey leaning on the very first showcase. He looked like a lion getting ready to pounce on its prey. He was my favorite uncle because he always played with us kids. He'd drop by our house on a Sunday with my girl cousins, Caren, Elana, and Linda. We'd all play baseball or pickle together across the street at the ball fields behind the school. Uncle Moey had a big stomach and usually wore an untucked short sleeved dress shirt with an undone button around his belly area. His face looked like he was going to break you in two pieces, but he was really a big teddy bear. Grandma Shashow nicknamed him Mershey when he was just a kid growing up in Brooklyn. While I watched him, he quickly jumped up from the showcase and roared, "Can I help you?" Two very black men had walked into the store wearing outfits that looked like pajamas. Their shirt, pants, and hats all matched; one man wore all green and the other wore tan. Their outfits looked to be very comfortable, and both men wore sandals. I looked at their faces and noticed that both men had light beards, a mustache, and very white teeth. I became nervous when I saw the scratches that looked carved into their faces. I'd never seen anything like that before.

Uncle Moey addressed the strange looking visitors again. "What can I help you find today my friends?"

The really black man with the scratched face started to speak, "*Parle vous francais?*"

My eager uncle squinted and answered, "*Un peu* ... very little."

"We are from Nigeria and looking for some presents to bring back to Africa," the customer said. It looked like the lion had found his prey. The African men followed my strong-willed uncle over to the wall case loaded with all types of radios. Uncle Moey started to talk with them as if they were from another planet or something. "I have shortwave radio ... you know shortwave? Many bands; you can listen all over the world, like BBC." The African men with scratches on their faces began to smile and nodded their heads up and down with approval. My uncle seemed to communicate the exact words that the African men wanted to hear; it was like he had read their minds or something. Uncle Moey unlocked the wall case with his key and slid the case door open. He laid the lock with the key inside down on the showcase, and then he reached in and pulled out two monster radios and sat them both on the showcase side by side. They were probably the best radios in the whole store. All three of the men spent some time talking about how the radios worked, and then my uncle started to read a pull-out map chart that was attached to one of the monster radios, to see what stations would be broadcasting at that time. Uncle Moey turned on one of the giant radios, and we heard lots of static. He turned the large radio dial slowly, waiting for the sound of a foreign language. All of a sudden, as clear as it could possibly get, we heard a news report from the BBC. My uncle kept a determined look, "Listen to BBC ... *très bien!*" Uncle Moey continued to tune in and began to pick up stations from all over Africa. He carefully turned the shortwave radio dial and found stations from Cameroon, Ivory Coast, and then finally Nigeria, "Ah, I found your country."Magnifique!"

The African men looked as happy as my uncle did. "*Ah, très bon* ... Will the voltage work in our country?"

My uncle shouted, "All over the world; 110 and 220 voltage!" He emphasized the word voltage in his best French accent.

The African men grinned from ear to ear. "Okay, we take the both."

Uncle Moey yelled over to Dad, "I need a Zenith 3000 Transoceanic and a Grundig Satellite 205 shortwave radio!" The hunt was over, and now my uncle prepared for the kill.

Dad nodded his head with approval. "Yes, sir, coming right up, kid!" I followed Dad upstairs as he quickly walked to the second floor to get two brand-new shortwave radios sealed in their boxes. We located several stacks of shortwave radios in one of the smaller stock rooms. Dad found a new-in-box Zenith 3000, but we only found an empty box to the Grundig 205—the last piece was the display model on the shelf. He picked up the empty box and handed it to me. "Here, cookie, carry this empty box downstairs and take it to your Uncle Mershey." Dad picked up the other box with the merchandise inside and lifted it up on his shoulder, and then we headed back downstairs. As we stepped onto the sales floor, he yelled over to Uncle Moey, "The Grundig is the last *on-way,* put it in an *ox-bay* and *ell-say* it! *Yallah* already, let's go, chop-chop!" I never knew Dad could talk Pig Latin. Howard and I talked to each other in Pig Latin sometimes, and I thought only kids knew how to speak it. Anyway, I walked over to my Uncle Moey and sat the empty Grundig 205 box in front of him on top of the showcase. I was happy that I could help with his sale, but I never realized that you needed to know all kinds of secret languages to work at Dad's store.

While the African men stopped to look at the watches in the showcase, Uncle Moey discretely placed the model Grundig Satellit 205 shortwave radio in the box. He placed the boxed-up radio on the register counter alongside the Zenith 3000 and then hurried to sell the African men an assortment of the flashiest wristwatches. After twenty minutes, each of the African men picked out eight ladies watches, which were very fancy and looked really expensive. They were covered with colored rhinestones, and you had to open up a little door to tell the time.

Then Uncle Moey ran over to the rings showcase on the other side of the store; he moved really fast for a man with a big stomach. He unlocked the case, reached inside, and pulled out four wedding band sets, slipping them on each of his fingers. He displayed the rings on his hand and said, "Take a look, my friends, beautiful wedding band sets for your wives or girlfriends." The African men examined the rings and believed them to be real, but I knew they weren't. I asked Dad earlier in the day about the rings, and he said they were only a sketch. The rings were cheap imitations that looked like the real thing. I heard Dad use the word "sketch" before at home; he'd use it to describe a person that was a liar or a hustler too. The African customers bought several wedding band sets at four hundred dollars each. Bernadette took me to the side later and whispered that the rings only cost twenty-five dollars each to buy from the wholesaler. She said that's how you make good PR, which she said was a slang word for profit. Then she told me that when one made double the profit on one sale, it was called, "Saff your brains out." She started to laugh when she told me that. Wow, there sure was a lot to learn in becoming a salesman. I could tell that everyone was really trying hard to teach me things, though.

Uncle Moey then took the African men over to the very back wall case. I slowly walked over to watch what they were doing. He pulled something out of one of the wall case drawers. The three men huddled and were viewing whatever he had pulled out of the drawer. The African men seemed to be excited, and there was plenty of laughter. Whatever they were looking at, they bought really fast. They were kind of hush-hush, so I couldn't get a glimpse of what they bought. Meanwhile, there was a stack of merchandise piled up on top of the register counter. It was all the neat stuff that my uncle had sold to his customers so far. Then the African men pointed up at the suitcases that were stacked at the very top of the wall cases. I watched Uncle Moey reaching up high to get one of the suitcases for the Africans, and his pants fell all the way down to the ground. My eyes were now focused on a pair of baggy striped boxers. I couldn't believe it! Bernadette and I looked at each other and busted out laughing. Bernadette laughed the hardest, and as her eyes filled up with tears, she practically begged me, "Please stop laughing, Raymond ... I can't take it anymore." When she said that, I really lost it and laughed even harder, with then tears rolling down my cheeks. Bernadette held her hand to her chest and cried, "My chest hurts ... I'm gonna have a heart attack." She started walking away from me with a strange look on her face, and again she cried out, "Oh no, now I got to go to the bathroom." She flew up all fifteen stairs toward the olden times bathroom with one hand between her legs.

Uncle Moey didn't appear to be embarrassed over his pants falling down. I remember Dad telling Mom sometimes when he got home from work that Mershey's pants fell down again today, but I never knew what that meant. Now I do. I guess it happened so often that he didn't get embarrassed about it anymore. Uncle Moey just said, "Whoops" and then proceeded to pull up his pants. The African men didn't think too much about his pants falling down either and just continued to inspect the suitcases. I had noticed my uncle stopping to tighten his belt many times during the day; he did wear his pants kind of loose. Uncle Moey laid each of the wristwatches that were selected by the African men on cotton-filled jewelry gift boxes. Then he placed each of the sketch engagement ring sets in fancy ring boxes. He had already rung up all the items on the adding machine. The African men picked out two really large brown suitcases, and Uncle Joey added them up on the adding machine too.

The African men looked like they were all done shopping. Uncle Moey walked over to the register counter and told Uncle Joey, "Check line; they're finished." Meanwhile, Dad took the wristwatches in their white gift boxes, the rings in their fancy ring boxes, and the shortwave radios to wrap them up in brown paper. He bundled them in two separate piles for each of the customers. I walked over to watch Dad wrap up the packages, and I spotted a strange item in the bundle. There were several square-like boxes with pictures of naked people on them. I pretended not to see them. So that's why the African men were so happy earlier at the back of the store. My cousin Tony told me later that they were 8mm movies. I asked Tony what check line meant. He said it meant ring up the sale, get the money. Dad tied twine around each bundle after he wrapped them up in brown paper, and then he placed the bundles in the two large suitcases. I watched Uncle Joey take their money. They had something called traveler's checks, and Uncle Joey had to look at their passports.

The two men picked up their suitcases and said, "*Merci beaucoup!*"

Uncle Moey shook their hands and said, "*Merci,* come back and see me again, my friends."

Then Dad yelled, "Thank you! Have a nice trip back to Africa."

Uncle Joey bounced his head up and down and quietly said, "Thank you … Thank you." Everyone in the store seemed to be frozen as they watched the Africa men leave the store. My eyes were still fixed on my Uncle Moey. I was excited over the way he convinced the African customers to buy things. They barely spoke English, and yet they spent thousands of dollars. He truly was the king of his jungle.

My first day of work was mostly an adventure for me. I'd stop by each showcase or wall case and stare through the freshly polished glass, and then I boldly unlocked the cases one by one with the key that Dad gave to me. I'd remove a transistor radio or a reel-to-reel tape recorder from the shelf, and I'd start pushing buttons to see how they worked. Dad encouraged me to take out the instructions from inside their boxes. Then I was startled by Uncle Joey. "Ray-Ray! Come over here! While you're looking inside the cases, get the Windex, paper towels, and the feather duster, and then clean all the shelves and dust off all the merchandise. Let's go, chop-chop!"

I had a job to do, and I'd have something interesting to tell everyone at home now. What I really wanted to do was sell something, but I didn't know how yet. I started cleaning inside each wall case and made my way all around the store. I was going to work hard and do a great job; I'd make Dad and Uncle Joey proud of me. Bernadette brought over a small step ladder so I'd be able to reach the top shelf, and then she helped me take out all the clock radios. She started dusting off one of the radios with the feather duster while I started to clean the glass shelf with the Windex and paper towels. She had a cigarette burning inside the ashtray that sat on the showcase next to her. We worked together cleaning the entire clock radio wall case.

A man dressed in a gray suit walked over to me and asked the price of one of the clock radios that was sitting on top of the showcase. I froze. With all the salesmen around, I was surprised that he picked me to answer his question. Bernadette glanced down at the radio. There was sticker with a number on it that read, "9509." She told the man in the suit, "That's a very nice clock radio; it's a General Electric model on sale today for only $49.99. I've got one brand-new in a box for you today, sir. Do you want me to plug it in for you?" Then she winked at me.

"Sure, why not," he said.

I stopped cleaning to watch Bernadette help the customer. She quickly grabbed the radio and plugged it in behind her. There were lots of electric outlets behind all the showcases. She turned the radio on and started to tune it. She stopped tuning when she heard the Temptations song "My Girl." Bernadette started snapping her fingers and moving her hips side to side with the music. Then she smiled at me and started singing. "I've got sunshine on a cloudy day." I smiled back at Bernadette. I thought she was really cool.

The man in the gray suit smiled. "Yeah, I like that song too; I'll take it."

Bernadette climbed up on the step ladder and reached on top of the wall case for a new one. "Anything else today, sir? How about a wristwatch, or maybe a nice camera? We carry all the latest makes and models."

"No thanks, just the clock radio today."

"You can pay right up here, sir. Joey, check line $49.99 plus tax. Thank you very much, sir; come back to see me again, okay?"

After Bernadette's sale was over, she helped me to put all the clock radios back in the wall case. At the rate I was going, there was no way I was going to clean all the wall cases like I had planned. Suddenly, I heard Dad's voice: "Raymond, let's go get a sandwich next door." It was around lunchtime and I was starving. I followed Dad next door to the Blue Mirror Grill. The restaurant had a really long lunch counter with swivel stools. Other parts of the restaurant had booths, but the counter definitely stood out the most. I could see them making the food in the kitchen. The restaurant really was blue and had mirrors all over. When I walked into the front door, there were stairs that led down to another floor called the champagne room. I saw signs with half naked ladies and huge boobs. I heard Dad and Tony laughing about the champagne room earlier in the car.

Dad and I walked up to the really long counter. A man with oily curly hair and a really thin mustache walked over. "How are you today, gentlemen?"

"Hello Sal, this is my son, Raymond."

"Hello, Raymond, are you going to start helping your father out at the store from now on?"

"I think so."

"Good for you, young man. What can I get the both of you today?"

"Get us a couple of foot-long hot dogs to go; put mine on a hard roll with mustard."

"Okay. Anything to drink today, gentlemen?" I told him I wanted a Coke. "Okay, coming up, my friends."

Then a really tall man with white hair, a large face, thick black bushy eyebrows, and a dark blue suit slowly walked over to us. "Hello, Mr. David," Dad said. "I'd like you to meet my son, Raymond."

17

The man took out the big black framed glasses from inside his suit pocket and then slid them on his huge face. "Hello, young man." My little hand disappeared into his huge grip when we shook hands. "Sal, give this nice young man a free Coke on the house."

I thanked Mr. David. He was the boss of the Blue Mirror Grill and the Champagne room. He acted like a big shot but was really a very nice man. Dad said the Blue Mirror was famous in Washington DC for their delicious strawberry cheese cake, and he sometimes brought home one that Mr. David gave to him for free. Sal handed us a brown bag with our lunches inside. He appeared a bit grouchy to me, but that was probably just the way he was. Dad pulled out a wad of cash from his side trouser pocket and paid the cashier. I thanked Mr. David again for the free soda, and then we walked back to the store to eat our lunch.

Dad said, "Let's eat upstairs; it's nice and quiet there." Dad and I climbed the fifteen carpeted stairs to the second floor and spread out our lunches on the large metal desk. My foot-long hot dog came with tiny individual paper cups, each filled with relish, mustard, ketchup, and chili, and the French fries were extra thick. While I ate my lunch, I noticed several large statues of President John F. Kennedy. I asked Dad why they were sitting there in a corner by the desk. He said that after President Kennedy was killed, he and Uncle Joey had an idea to sell the statues as souvenirs. Dad said the statues were handmade by Aunt Sophia's brother, Adam. I had always thought Adam was an uncle. He drove a new Ford Thunderbird, and when he came to visit us on Johnnycake Road, he always brought me a toy replica of his car. Anyway, Adam had finished molding about thirty life-size busts of the president, but it turned out that they were too heavy for the customers to carry out of the store and too much work to make. Dad said that their souvenir bust idea had turned into a real bust!

After lunch was over, Uncle Joey hunted me down. "Go get the feather duster and start dusting off all the souvenirs. Let's go, chop-chop!" Everyone liked using that phrase "chop-chop" for some reason. After I dusted off the souvenirs, I stood over by Bernadette, and Uncle Joey barked at me again, "Don't fold your arms; it's bad luck!" Twenty minutes later and for most of the rest of the day, he'd holler out, "Raymond, get the showcases." The feather duster, Windex, and a roll of paper towels added up to become a big part of my day at Dad's corner store on F Street.

Everyone took turns cleaning the showcases and feather dusting the merchandise. If the store got busy after the last person cleaned the showcases, then that person would have to do them again. That meant the person was lucky. If you cleaned the cases and business all of a sudden got quiet, then someone else needed to clean the cases—and fast. Business was kind of slow, with not many big sales since Uncle Moey sold the African men all that stuff. Dad looked kind of mad. "Someone get the showcases and change the luck; let's go, look alive already—it's payday!"

Bernadette volunteered. "Ok Mister S., I'm going to change the luck; I got the magic touch, you'll see." She hurriedly grabbed the paper towels and Windex and started to clean the showcases in lightning speed. Right after Bernadette said she'd change the luck, I sneezed really loud. Everyone looked at me and then all at once, everybody screamed, "Blesh!" They scared the crap out of me. Later in the day a customer sneezed inside the store. Everyone stopped what they were doing and screamed, "Blesh!" He got so scared that he stumbled and fell onto the souvenir table. Bernadette was right, though: she did change the luck. More and more customers found their way into the store, and even the lobby filled up with lookers. Dad in his excitement rang the bell behind the register counter and started shouting, "Buy now and save … Everything must be sold to the bare walls … There's plenty of room for everybody—don't push that lady." The customers smiled when Dad made his speech, but a few of them looked startled and confused. Dad looked happy again after Bernadette changed the luck, and he said, "Good girl that Bernadette. I'm gonna give you a big raise." Bernadette smiled, rolled her eyes, and said, "That'll be the day."

All of the salespeople were waiting on customers when a crazy looking guy with tattered clothing made his way in through the crowd of shoppers. He was really dirty, stank, and was arguing loudly to himself. Dad walked over to him. "What do you want, *mejnoon*?" I knew that word; a *mejnoon* was a crazy person. The filthy *mejnoon* ignored Dad and got much louder. Then Dad screamed at him, "Ball four! Take a walk already!" The *mejnoon* snickered and then turned around and made his way out the front door, but he left an odor trail much like a skunk. Dad started laughing. "What a psycho … no use."

Bernadette covered her nose and mouth with her hands. "What an ell-smay, Mister S.! I got to go and find the Lysol spray quick … *Khara … Mejnoon!*" It was funny to hear Bernadette use the word *khara*. It was a Syrian word that meant shit. After the *mejnoon* and his ell-smay left the store, I walked over to watch my cousin Tony for awhile.

Chapter Three

Saff Their Brains Out!

Tony was talking with a man wearing a hat that looked like an upside down ice bucket with a long tassel that hung to the side. I sure had seen a lot of strange people today. Tony looked like he was getting ready to pull out a camera from the glass case. It was fun listening to Tony speak in his Cuban accent. I moved closer so I could hear their conversation. Dad had always told Howard and me that Tony was a fantastic camera salesman. When I watched him, he looked like a magician preparing for his magic act. He took out a camera from the wall case and held it in his hands. "This is the Canonet QL 19 35mm; it's a brand-new camera from Canon. You can use manual or automatic exposure. If you want something easy to use, then this is a good one. It's on sale for $249.95 today; I sell the flash and the case for it, too." The customer looked really interested as Tony slipped the camera into his hands. Tony took out an electronic flash and slid it on the camera while the customer continued holding it. He watched the customer examining the camera. "If you want a bigger lens, they make the same camera with an f 1.7 lens for fifty dollars more." The customer seemed to be really happy with Tony's suggestion. It was almost like when someone picked a card from a magician's deck, and the magician guessed the right card.

The customer with the funny hat asked Tony if he could get a better price. Tony threw his hands up in the air and said, "I'll try to ask the boss and see what he says." Tony walked over to Dad and talked in a hushed voice, "My G wants a better deal." I walked over closer to see what was going on, and I heard Tony explaining, "The camera is lot 300. The flash is lot 50, and the case is lot 20." He was talking in some kind of top secret code. I was starting to think everyone that worked here were spies or something. Tony received his final instructions; Dad wrote it on a brown paper bag. Then Dad hollered, "*Yallah* … check line already!" Tony walked over to his customer. He grabbed the Canon camera with the bigger lens, a camera case in the box, an electronic flash in the box, two rolls of film, and some batteries. He piled up everything nice and neat on top of the showcase in front of his customer with the funny hat. Tony looked sure of himself. "I'm going to give you the camera with the better lens … the case and flash … free film and batteries—all for $350.00 plus the tax." Tony the magician just pulled a rabbit out of his hat.

"Okay, wrap it up." I could almost hear his customer clapping in the audience after his magic trick. Tony asked his customer if he wanted him to load the camera up with film and batteries. He showed him how to load the film and advanced the roll to number one, and then he loaded the penlight batteries into the electronic flash. Tony brought the camera outfit to the register counter, where Dad bagged the merchandise and checked line. Tony was a great camera salesman; it didn't matter how bad his English was because Tony was confident about selling what he knew best, and he definitely knew all about camera equipment. Tony told his customer in his Cuban accent, "*Zank* you. If you have any other question about the camera, call me; here's my business card."

It was late in the afternoon. I decided to sit on the stairs for awhile to take a break. I watched a hip looking black guy walk inside the store and make his way toward the showcase filled with sunglasses. I got up quickly and walked over to behind the showcase. All the salesmen were either waiting on customers or not on the sales floor. I stood at the showcase while the customer stared at the sunglasses in the case. You could barely see my head above the showcase. I was really nervous but wanted to make my first sale. Then all of a sudden, I got really brave and said, "Can I help you, sir?"

I noticed Uncle Joey was leaning behind the register counter. I couldn't see him when I was resting on the stairs before. I thought for sure he'd be mad at me for trying to wait on a customer, because I was just a little kid. But he just watched me and said, "Go ahead …check the G." Uncle Joey watched but left me alone to handle my first big sale.

The customer didn't laugh or make fun of me because of my age, either; he took me seriously. He stooped over to get a better look at the wide selection of sunglasses in the showcase. "My man, let me check out those shades on the back row." I guessed that shades meant sunglasses, so I unlatched the lock and slid open the showcase door, and then I got on my hands and knees to look inside the case. I reached all the way inside for the sunglasses and pulled them out gently. He tried them on. "You got a mirror, man?" The mirror was usually there, but Uncle Joey had taken it behind the register counter to watch himself shaving with a Ronson electric razor. Uncle Joey grabbed the mirror and stood it up for my customer. As he tried the shades on, he took out a strange looking comb out of his back pocket to puff up his hair. He bounced his head from side to side as he got closer to the mirror. "How much they cost?" He continued to fix himself up while looking in the mirror.

I said, "It's $3.88, sir."

The man started to chuckle., "Is that your best price, my man?" I was surprised by the question, so I didn't say anything. "You gonna clean 'em up for me, right?"

"Yes, sir." I proudly peeled off the sticker from the lens and then cleaned them off with Windex. The sticker wouldn't come off cleanly, and I started to panic.

I quickly walked the sunglasses over to Dad and showed him the sticker imprint on the lens. He said, "Squirt a little lighter fluid on it … Here, try this." He handed me a yellow and blue metal can of fluid. I squirted a drop on the lens, and it magically came right off. Then I shined it up again with Windex and a paper towel. I wanted everything to be perfect; after all, it was my first sale.

My customer tried the sunglasses on again after I had cleaned and shined them up for him. "Yeah, they look all right."

Then I looked over at Uncle Joey behind the register counter and announced in my high-pitched, six-year-old voice, "Check line, Uncle Joey … $3.88 plus tax."

Uncle Joey gave me a half smile and said, "Yes, sir, Mister S., you got it."

I thanked my customer a bunch of times; I was really happy. We shook hands, and he said, "No problem, and thank you, little man; you're a good salesman." I had broken the ice, and like my customer said, I was a salesman. Afterward, everyone congratulated me on my first sale. I felt like I could compete against the star salesmen now.

As I continued to enjoy the moment, I was startled by Dad's voice: "Raymond! Get the showcases … *Yallah,* you're lucky." And just like that, my moment was over.

While I was cleaning the showcase, a couple of tourists walked in. They looked lost and confused. One of the two men approached Uncle Moey, who was leaning on his favorite spot at the front of the store. He had a soldering iron out and an earphone in his ear while he tinkered with several broken transistor radios and tried to get them working again. The tourist asked him, "Do you fix cameras?" Dad heard their question from the other side of the store and shouted, "Saff their brains out!"

Uncle Moey looked up at the foreign tourists and then pointed over to Tony. "Go see the tall man over there; he's is the camera expert." The two men hurried to the other side of the store where Tony stood puffing away on his cigar. Everyone at the store smoked constantly.

Dad, Tony, and Fat Bobby smoked their cigars while Joey and Bernadette inhaled their cigarettes.

The foreign customer showed Tony his camera and said, "I have a Nikon F SLR 35mm camera, and the shutter is stuck."

Tony grabbed the camera from the man's hand. "Let me take a look." He held the camera in his right hand and walked quickly to the back of the store and through the hanging curtain door that led to the back room, filled with linen tablecloths for sale. The tourists followed him to the curtain door and waited. I followed Tony through the curtain door, to watch and learn how he'd fix the camera. I wondered what else Tony the magician could have up his sleeves. Tony inspected the camera, opened the battery compartment with a quarter, and took the batteries out. He scraped the contacts with a tiny screwdriver and replaced the batteries with new ones. He tried snapping a few photos to see if it worked. Then he looked at me and said, "It works! Okay cover your ears." Then without any further warning, Tony took out a hammer and started to bang really loud on one of the counters that the tablecloths had laid on. He kept banging and banging for several minutes. I wasn't sure why he was banging on the table because it didn't seem to accomplish anything. I'm pretty sure he got the attention of the foreign tourists, though. Tony popped out from behind the curtain with the repaired camera in his hand. Tony the Great had done it again! As he handed them their camera back, he told the tourists, "I had to replace the *ridicates* and the *saphinolio,* but luckily we had the parts; it works perfect now."

One of the foreign men grabbed the camera and snapped a quick photo to make sure that it worked. *"Ah, wunderbare!"* he said.

"You can pay up front at the register." Tony hollered at Uncle Joey, who was leaning on the register counter, "Check line ... Lot eighty!"

Uncle Joey sneered and shook his head up and down at the same time. "That'll be forty dollars." The German tourists paid without hesitating.

Tony called me over after his customers had completely left the store. "*Oye,* Raymond! Let me teach you how to saff a Gs brains out." Tony the Magician was about to reveal one of his magic trick secrets to me. He said, "It only cost four dollars apiece for the new batteries that I put in their camera. I charge the customer forty dollars and make a profit of thirty-two, so I saff their brains out." Tony had a big grin on his face while he told me his secret. I asked him why he was banging on the table with a hammer. "I made believe that I was working hard to fix their camera, but all I did was to replace the batteries. I told them that I replaced some parts; we use phony words like *ridicates* and *saphinolio* to describe something that's not real; it's all make believe, but I still fixed his camera anyway." Tony put his unlit cigar into his mouth and then started to laugh really hard. He had a funny laugh. I don't think there is anyone in the whole world who could laugh like Tony. His laugh sounded a little bit like a Chimpanzee squealing.

I watched Uncle Joey for awhile straightening the souvenirs. He'd straighten, feather dust, and replenish the souvenir stock for most of the day. Then the phone rang, and Uncle Joey answered, "Chin Lung Art Gallery." He listened for a response and yelled at the phone, "Hold the wire!" Then he laid the receiver on the register counter. He called out, "Bernadette! I think it's your husband. Should I tell him you're banging someone else?"

Bernadette walked over to the phone and replied in an excitable voice, "Are you crazy, Joey? You know one thing, I'm going to tell everybody who you banging; you're a sick man." Uncle Joey laid his head down on the register counter and started laughing really hard.

Bernadette picked up the phone, and I could barely hear her conversation. "Hello … uh-huh … No-no … Okay, bye." That was all she said. When Bernadette got off the phone, she stared at Uncle

Joey like she was really angry and shook her head. Uncle Joey was still laughing, but he picked up his head to look at her. Then she started to laugh and said, "You know, you're something else. I'm not going to let you drive me crazy, because as long as I have my health and strength, you don't bother me. Maybe you need to go home and bang your wife, Sophia, tonight."

When Bernadette wasn't waiting on a customer, she was constantly writing down numbers on a brown paper bag. I asked her what she was doing, and she'd tell me that she was adding up all of her bills. When business was slow, Bernadette turned on a display model TV to catch a glimpse of her favorite soap opera, which she called her stories.

It got to be late in the day. Bernadette started to get her scarf and coat on. She said, "Okay, Mister S., I need to go and catch my ride." She had to walk five blocks to the Greyhound station and grab a bus back to Baltimore. Then Uncle Joey called her over with a "Psst," which leaked out from the corner of his mouth. Bernadette walked behind the register counter. Uncle Joey peeked at her, and then he slowly turned his back to her and slipped something into the palm of her hand, so no one else could see or notice. She smiled and kind of sang, "Thank you." Then as she headed slowly for the front door, she hollered, "Bye, everybody, have a good weekend. It was good to see you, Raymond; tell your mother I said hello." And off she went, running down the street.

Next, Uncle Joey called for the rest of the salesmen, one by one, to meet with him behind the register counter. "Fat Bobby!" Bobby walked slowly to the counter still puffing away at his bat-sized cigar. Joey turned his back again and handed Bobby something down low. Fat Bobby grabbed the mysterious item and slowly made his way toward the back of the store. The top secret ritual continued for Uncle Moey and then again for Cousin Tony. Suddenly I heard, "Ray-Ray! Come over here … hurry up!" I jumped up from sitting on a drawer attached to the wall case. I almost crapped in my pants; was I going to be included in the top secret ritual in honor of breaking the ice today? I imitated everyone else's move and met Uncle Joey behind the register counter. He turned his back on me and handed me a small brown paper bag down low. After I grabbed the tiny bag, he smiled at me and said, "Good boy." It was the first time all day long that he actually smiled at me. I clutched the tiny bag in my hand and then walked over to behind the rings counter, without sneaking a peek at what was inside. I held the brown paper bag in both of my hands and noticed that it had my name written on it. Finally, I looked inside the bag and pulled out a twenty-dollar bill; it was my first payday. I had no idea that I'd be paid like the other salesmen on my first day of work, but I did get a lot of commands hollered at me today, so I felt I deserved it.

It was six o'clock in the evening, and it felt like the day had slammed on its brakes. I walked outside and stood in the store lobby to watch what was left of the city traffic. It was still light outside, but the streets were almost empty. The Four Tops song "I Can't Help Myself" played on the radio through the outside lobby speaker. Then I heard Uncle Joey calling for me again. "Raymond! Come over here!"

I thought to myself, "I got paid and just cleaned all the showcases, what else could he want?" Uncle Joey had a mean-looking face most of the time, but I don't think he really meant it. He looked kind of like how a dog growled when someone tried to take his bone away.

I walked over and stood in front of him behind the register counter, and he told me in a hushed voice, "Go next door and get me a cup with ice." He glared at me with his sly smile. "Are you sure that you can handle it all by yourself, sonny?"

I said, "I'm not afraid, I can do it." I felt like a grown-up today. After all, I was on the payroll now. When I came back from my solo adventure with the cup of ice in hand, it felt as if I had just climbed Mount Everest and was really proud of myself. Uncle Joey took the cup from my hand and snapped at me, "Okay, now beat it!" In a blink of an eye, he jumped up on top of the register counter. He looked like a parrot sitting on its perch. Then he started rattling his cup of ice. His mood quickly changed after a few sips from inside the cup. He smiled and laughed and acted like he wanted to stay at the store for a really long time, even though it was getting close to closing time. I watched Uncle Joey pouring something into his cup with ice. I saw the letters "J&B" on the outside of the bottle. Dad had the same bottle sitting on the bar in our basement at home.

About twenty minutes later, Dad and Uncle Joey walked outside and just disappeared. No customers had walked in for a long time. I walked back outside to the lobby and saw them standing next to each other by the street, talking. Dad had one of his hands on his hip and took a drag off his cigarette with the other hand. Uncle Joey had both of his hands behind his back, and his burning cigarette was hidden. I could tell that they were in serious thought. Then they both finished their cigarettes and flicked them into the street. Dad and Joey turned around and walked back toward the store. I knew they were coming, so I ran inside. As soon as Uncle Joey walked through the doorway, he shouted, "Let's get out of here! Start locking up." It would be his final command for the day. Everyone gathered their coats and headed slowly for the door. I followed Dad, but he told me to wait up front with everyone else. Dad walked to the very back of the store, opened a metal panel door, and flicked each breaker one by one to turn out all the lights. Uncle Joey hid behind a paneled door at the very front of the store and waited for the lights to close. The paneled door was covered by souvenir pictures of John F. Kennedy and dangling Kennedy half dollar key rings. Dad walked back up to the front, and we all waited there quietly in the dark. Uncle Joey asked, "Everybody ready?" Then he set the alarm code, which made a long beep. "Okay, let's go!" We filed out the front door like a small army of soldiers. Dad closed the front door and turned his key to lock it. Then he grabbed both of the front door handles and shook them hard. The store was closed and my first day at work was finally over. We walked together in a small group back to the parking garage. But first, we'd have to pass by the bums that stared at us. Once we got past them, I knew we'd be safe. Wait a minute, what was I thinking, I was surrounded by tough guys; it was them that better watch out. The bums weren't there when we walked by. I kind of wondered where they all went to. It felt good to walk down that steep hill, I was really tired.

When we finally arrived at the parking garage, dad, Uncle Joey, and Fat Bobby gave the parking guy their ticket stubs. Two black guys in matching shirts ran over to a conveyerlike elevator, stepped on it, and mysteriously disappeared. A few minutes later, two cars followed each other to the exit at the front of the parking garage. Fat Bobby walked over to his Cadillac and tipped the parking guy. Dad shouted, "See you Monday, kid!"

Fat Bobby said, "Goodbye, everybody," and still with the cigar in his mouth, he made his red Cadillac sprint out of the parking garage.

Uncle Joey and Moey got into their black Cadillac next and gave another tip for a different parking guy. I got a quick "See you later" from Uncle Joey.

Uncle Moey smiled. "Bye, Ray-Ray; you did good today." He climbed into the passenger side of the Cadillac, and they slowly pulled away from us.

Meanwhile, the first parking guy was still looking for our car. I stood there waiting, quiet and tired from the long day. I heard screeching brakes from a car as it made its way down from an upper level. Finally our car raced in to a hard stop. Dad tipped the parking guy fifty cents, and we all piled into the navy blue Oldsmobile and headed back to Johnnycake Road. It was the longest day of my six years of life. I was exhausted from cleaning so many showcases, and I slept all the way home.

Chapter Four

Johnnycake Road

Abuela had dinner waiting for us when we got home from work. She made one of my favorite meals, *picadillo*. It was ground beef mixed with chopped onions, tomato sauce, raisins, garlic, and olives, on top of some white rice. I couldn't wait to eat it. Howard and I battled to see who would get to eat the *raspa*. When the rice was overcooked and slightly burned at the bottom of the pot, it formed brownish hard crunchy rice, called *raspa*. It seemed like forever since I ate my foot-long hot dog with Dad up on the second floor. Tony came inside for a little while and spoke Spanish with Mom and Abuela. It was the first time that I had seen him all day without a cigar in his mouth. It was already almost eight o'clock. Tony said good-bye to everyone and headed home to his wife, Gigi, and their four kids, Teri, Bebe, Sonia, and Henry.

My routine had been all changed around today. I didn't get a chance to play with any of my friends, look at my baseball cards, or even play with my dog, Terry. I liked lying down behind the sofa with my dog. We'd lay there together staring out the window, and nobody ever knew we were back there.

When Dad usually came home from work, he'd drink that same J&B stuff that Uncle Joey drank in the store, only he wouldn't make me get him a cup with ice first. When I was a little kid and Dad came home from work, he'd put me on his lap while he sat in his favorite chair. Then we'd both watch TV for awhile before he ate his dinner. After he drank a few J&Bs, he'd ask me to gather up all my toys and then line them up in one very long row. It usually took me about an hour or so. Most of my toys didn't cost a lot of money, so it appeared that I had lots of toys after lining them up one after another. When I had them all lined up perfectly, Dad would get out the Polaroid camera and snap a few photos. After the picture was developed, Dad let me roll on this special stick to make the photo look shinier. The stick had a really strong smell, and if I inhaled too much of it, I'd get lightheaded.

While I sat and ate my dinner with Dad, Mom walked in and sat down with us at the kitchen table. "Ray-Ray, tell me about your first day at work today." My mom had a Cuban accent, but I never really noticed. Her red hair was always kept perfect. When Mom had lived in Cuba, she was a model. I told her, "It was a really long day. I helped to clean the shelves and the showcases, and I made my very first sale."

"Congratulations, son, that's fantastic!"

Then my brother Howard walked into the kitchen and said, "So you survived your first day of work in Washington DC? How did it go little brother?" Howard was definitely a husky kid, but his weight problem never seemed to bother him. He was a go-getter and never quit at anything, except for trying to lose weight. He loved eating, and always ate his food really fast. When Howard or I would get a stomachache, Mom's cure was always a tablespoon of Paregoric, an over-the-counter remedy that just happened to be made with opium. If Paregoric hadn't cured us, a last resort would be the enema bag. I despised the enema bag; I'd run away from her screaming, "I don't need no enema!"

I responded to Howard's question. "Yeah, I broke the ice today."

"Really? What did you sell?"

"I sold a pair of sunglasses to a really cool black guy, and nobody helped me."

"Good job. Before you know it, you'll be selling record players, radios, and TVs like your big brother."

Howard always made sure that I knew that he was better than me. One would think he wouldn't act like that because he was seven years older.

"I saw a dirty crazy man yelling at himself inside the store, and Dad had to tell him to get out."

Howard started laughing and then said, "So you saw your first *mejnoon* today."

"Yeah, it was a little scary, but I was more scared of the bums on the way to work that stared at me. Why do they hang out so close to Dad's store, anyway?"

Dad looked over at me while he was eating and said, "The bums are there because of the hamburger joint, Little Tavern. I think they feed them during the day."

I said, "I learned a lot today at the store. Bernadette taught me about making PR, and Tony told me about the saff brains."

Dad and Howard started laughing really hard. "You mean saff their brains out, right son?" Dad said.

"Yeah, that's it." I felt kind of embarrassed when I didn't get that right.

Howard said, "All right, I'm going to listen to the new Beatles album that I bought today. Oh, by the way; my sunflower is almost twice as big as yours, Raymond."

"I know; I'm going to try and make mine grow bigger tomorrow."

Howard and I shared the same bedroom. I was really getting tired, so I decided that I'd go to my room and listen to Howard's new Beatles album with him until I fell asleep. We both liked the Beatles. I remember when we first heard their album *Meet the Beatles;* it was around my birthday in January of last year. Then the following month, we all sat around the TV and watched them on *The Ed Sullivan Show.* Even Dad and Mom liked them. I got really interested in music. I listened to WCAO on my transistor radio and watched *Shindig, Hullaballoo* and *The Ed Sullivan Show* on TV. I also listened to whatever Howard listened to. When I was little, I liked listening to songs like "The Purple People Eater" and "The Twist." I really liked it when we all sat in the living room together and listened to an Allen and Rossi comedy album. Sometimes we listened to an album called *The First Family.* It was kind of funny hearing actors pretending to be President Kennedy and his family. I was even listening to records when I was just a baby. Mom said the only way she could get me to go to sleep when I was a baby was to play a song called "Oh My Papa" by Eddie Fisher. If that wouldn't work, she said I liked listening to the vacuum cleaner.

I woke up Sunday morning at ten o'clock. All I remembered from the night before was lying in my bed and listening to John Lennon singing "Eight Days a Week." I started to get dressed and noticed that Howard was already out of his bed. I walked into the kitchen and watched Mom and Abuela at the kitchen table, chatting in Spanish and drinking coffee. Mom was smoking one of her Parliaments. They both wore their robes and scarves around their head. I could tell they had just woken up because they were talking a lot slower than normal, and Mom's voice sounded deeper.

"Well good morning, working man," Mom said.

"Good morning, Mom … Buenos dias, Abuelita." I always tried to impress my grandmother with the few Spanish words that I knew.

"Ay, que bueno … good morning, Ray-Ray."

Mom said, "Do you want me to make you some breakfast, sweetie?"

"Isn't Dad going to make us all a big Sunday breakfast today?"

"No, your father is still sleeping."

"I'll get my own; all I want is some cereal and orange juice anyway. Where's Howard?"

Mom said, "I saw him outside watering his sunflower earlier."

"I'll be right back." I ran out the front door and on to our front yard. Howard must have just finished watering his sunflower because the hose was still lying on the ground. I looked down Johnnycake Road and saw him talking with his best friend, Ronnie Abernathy. The Abernathys had a huge German shepherd named Major that ran loose inside their house. The dog was almost bigger than me. Major bit my ear once, so I was scared to get near him again. Anytime I'd go over to the Abernathys' house, they'd have to put Major in the garage till I was gone.

Howard and Ronnie started a skateboard club together called "The Rat Finks" after Ed "Big Daddy" Roth's monster character. The initiation to the Rat Finks was to skate full speed down a really big, steep hill across the street without wiping out. I asked Howard if I could be in their club, but he said I couldn't because of my age. I did just about everything by myself because of our age difference. Mom would toss the baseball around with me in the back yard, but mostly I'd play all by myself. Our backyard was all fenced in and pretty large. I'd set it up like a baseball diamond using patio chair cushions and trash can tops for the bases. I used an old sneaker for the rubber on top of the pitching mound. Then I played an imaginary big league game. I mimicked the great Orioles announcer Chuck Thompson calling the play-by-play, and I'd pretend to be the Baltimore Orioles battling their foes: Boog Powell at the plate hitting an imaginary baseball into the upper deck for a home run, or Brooks Robinson at third base diving for a baseball hit by Tony Oliva and throwing him out in the nick of time at first base. I'd be Paul Blair running back toward the fence near the warning track and leaping to catch an invisible ball hit by Harmon Killebrew, right before it left the park for a homer, and then I'd be Dave McNally winding up on the mound and throwing a perfect pitch to strike out slugger Rocky Colavito. While all this was going on, I'd be imitating the roar of the crowd at Memorial Stadium. Sometimes I had to move my imaginary baseball game to inside our living room, especially when I'd notice the neighbors watching me and shaking their heads. I think they thought I was some kind of a nut.

I ran over to turn the hose back on and soaked my sunflower really good. Howard stuck a stick next to his sunflower to keep it nice and straight. His sunflower was clobbering mine; it looked more than twice as big. I was kind of surprised that he hadn't watered my sunflower after he watered his. I'm sure he had to realize by now that he would win the contest. I walked back inside my house and started to wonder, what was I going to do for the rest of the day? Dad was up now, walking around the house in his robe and slippers and holding a Schlitz in his hand. I wished he'd gather us all up in Mom's aqua colored Desoto and drive us to the Enchanted Forest. I loved going there. There was a serpentlike creature sitting on top of a castle that led you inside the park. Once inside, there were fairy tale buildings and characters. I got to take a boat ride on "Little Toot" and slide down a huge sliding board from up on top of a mountain at the end of the park. "Dad," I said, "what are you going to do today?"

"Not much, cookie, maybe listen to the ballgame while I take a nap on the hammock; it looks like a beautiful day outside."

Mom walked into the living room where Dad and I were standing. "Teddy, I put some hamburgers and hot dogs out so you can barbeque later; I'll make the baked potatoes and the salad." I was always happy when Dad barbequed. Sometimes Howard would invite Ronnie over, and they would let me play Pickle with them. Pickle is a game with two people playing catch. There are two bases and one or two runners. The two runners try and run to the other base without getting tagged out. Howard and Ronnie would always dare me into running by missing the ball on purpose. I was pretty fast and was good at sliding into the base. It was probably the only time they let me play with them.

"What time do want me to start the fire, Jenny?" Dad made a funny face at Mom while saying that.

Mom said, "What do you think … 5:30?"

"Yeah, yeah, okay … I'm going to put on my bathing suit, drink a couple of beers, and take a nap outside. .I'll see you later, sweetie."

Mom looked down at me with one hand on her hip and said, "This is the story of my life." Sundays were always kind of exciting for me because it was Dad's only day off from working at his store. We never went to church on Sundays because Dad was Jewish, and we never went to a synagogue because Mom was Catholic. But we always had a Christmas tree and a menorah during the holidays.

Every Sunday morning since I was little, dad played his sound effects album with famous bugle calls on it. He turned up the volume on the record player really loud and began shouting out famous battle cries like, "Charge!" and "We shall never surrender!" and "Don't fire until you see the whites of their eyes!" and "Don't give up the ship!" Dad got really into it and wound me up. I'd start running around the house with my fake sword and toy gun yelling, "Charge!"

I decided to go into the bedroom and bring out my box of Topps baseball cards. I liked to look at them while watching TV in the living room. I kept my cards in a big white shoe box. I sorted each team separately and then carefully stacked them in neat bundles with rubber bands wrapped around each bundle. Howard was still outside with Ronnie Abernathy, so I decided to sneak into his bottom left desk drawer. It's where Howard kept all of his baseball cards. He had a huge collection that included much older cards. It really bothered me that he threw his baseball cards in that bottom drawer; they were all loose and mixed up. But Howard's collection was really cool. I loved sneaking into that drawer. I dug deep into the drawer and pulled out bunches of cards to look at. Then I sat quietly on the floor and whispered each players name to myself, "The 1960 Mickey Mantle … 1957 Willie Mays … 1963 Sandy Koufax … Wow, a 1955 Hank Aaron." He even had most of the Orioles since moving to Baltimore from St. Louis. And I saw some of the old St. Louis Browns cards in there too. Keeping his baseball cards messy was one thing, but Howard would actually put them on his bicycle spokes to make a flapping noise, or he'd flip them with his friends, with the chance of losing them forever. Howard would sometimes ask me nicely if I wanted to flip baseball cards with him. I was just excited that he even wanted to play with me, so I'd say yes. He would flip his doubles against my most cherished cards and beat me just about every time. I was so upset that I'd run over to Mom crying. She'd ask Howard nicely to give me back my baseball cards. At first he'd say no, he had won them fair and square. But later in the day, he'd finally give them back to me. One time he waited until the very next day.

There was one other game that I played with Howard that he invented. We'd set up a baseball diamond on the floor using our favorite baseball cards. Then we'd use a fork and a penny as the bat and ball. We'd put the penny on the skinny part of the fork and then bang down hard on the fork part with our fist. The penny would go sailing in the air like a baseball. If it touched any one of your baseball cards, then it was an out. If it didn't hit any of the cards it could be a single, double, or triple, depending on how far it flew. If it flew over all the outfielder cards, it was a homerun. Howard got a lot of homeruns in that game and always beat me. I found out later he'd secretly bend the fork when it was his turn up. Then he'd bend it back to normal when it was my turn. It was much easier to get a homerun when the fork was bent up.

I finished looking through Howard's baseball cards; he'd never know I was in there because they were all messy anyway. I headed for the bathroom—anytime I felt sneaky, I'd always have to go. Afterward, I sat on the floor in our living room and turned on the TV set while looking at my cards. After I got home from kindergarten during the week, our maid, Thelma, always stacked her chairs in the living room while she cleaned the kitchen floor. Then I could hide underneath those chairs, look at my cards, and watch TV all at the same time. I removed the top from the shoebox that my baseball cards were in. Because the Orioles game was about to start soon, I decided to take a look at my Orioles cards first. Then all of a sudden, I heard singing at my front door. "Ray ... mond! Ray ... mond!" It was my friends. Anytime we visited one of our friends' homes, we wouldn't knock or ring the door bell; we'd harmonize their name outside until they finally opened the door. We all sounded like a bunch of alley cats begging for food. I put away my cards and walked over to see what they wanted. It was Mary Jane from next door and my best friend, Johnny from down the street. Johnny's mom was crippled from giving birth to him and was always in a wheelchair. When I was little, I'd ride my bike down to Johnny's house in my baseball uniform. I wasn't a real little leaguer, but Mom bought me the uniform anyway. Mary Jane and I were always in stiff competition over something, especially when it came to who would be the first to ride their bikes without their training wheels. I fumed when l saw her riding around without them on one day. All I could think about was that a girl had beaten me. I don't think I would have minded it as much if it were any other girl besides Mary Jane. She had a way of making you feel inferior when she beat you at something, and I hated that feeling. Last winter, she and Ronnie Abernathy rode a sled together down the big hill across the street, near the ball fields. They wiped out and hit a tree. Mary Jane broke her arm and Ronnie broke his leg. It was big news on Johnnycake Road for quite a long time. I think it was bigger news than the time our kitchen oven caught on fire and the fire engines came.

My friends wanted to ride bikes across the street at Johnnycake Junior High's parking lot. They said they went exploring and found tons of chalk in all kinds of different colors, just lying there by a dumpster. I ran to the garage and jumped on my bike, and then the three of us headed for the big discovery. I parked my bike near the dumpster in front of the school. We all acted like finding that chalk was like discovering gold or something. We weren't sure why it was there, but it felt kind of sneaky taking it. I bet those teachers would get new chalk after they come back from their summer vacation. We all took some and shoved it in our pockets. Then all of a sudden, we heard the ice cream truck coming near our street. We started screaming, "Ice cream man!"

I said, "Follow me to my house; my mom will give us all money." We rode our bikes back to my house, and I ran inside. "Mom, Mom, I need money for the ice cream man … hurry! I'll need money for Johnny and Mary Jane, too." Mom quickly reached into her purse, pulled out a dollar, and handed it to me. "Thanks, Mom!" She never minded when I asked her to pay for my friends. I'd even promise all my friends that Mom would make them all peanut butter and jelly sandwiches, and she'd always do it without getting mad. I ran back outside and met my friends in front of our house. "Hey guys, I got a dollar for all of us." I heard the bells from the ice cream truck getting closer and closer. It was definitely the Good Humor man. If it were the Mr. Softee truck, we'd hear it playing a song. The bells got louder; it was going to come down our street. The three of us were practically standing in the middle of Johnnycake Road; none of us wanted to take the chance of missing the ice cream man. Then, I saw the white Good Humor truck turning on to our street. It pulled to a stop right next to us. I glanced down the road and saw other kids waiting for him to stop in front of their homes. I asked for a Good Humor bar, Mary Jane got a strawberry shortcake bar, and Johnny got a chocolate éclair bar. We sat on our metal lawn furniture in front of my house and quietly ate our ice creams.

I watched our neighbor Mr. Hopkins in the front yard hitting plastic golf balls with one hand and drinking a glass of whiskey in the other hand. I knew it was whiskey because Dad told me. I looked over at him, and he noticed me. "Hello dere!" He'd never say there, it was always Dere. I think he got that from Allen and Rossi.

"Hello, Mr. Hopkins!" Mrs. Hopkins always let me play with her children's old toys. My favorite was a jet airliner that worked on batteries. It would move around all by itself making a sound like a jet engine and then pretended to takeoff. The wing lights also blinked.

But the neatest thing was when the inside cabin lit up, you could see a stewardess moving up and down the aisle serving the passengers. I'd lie on the floor staring at that stewardess go back and forth, over and over again, until the batteries ran out. Mrs. Hopkins was a really nice lady. She'd always say, "How boot that" instead of saying, "How about that." I think they mispronounced words on purpose just to be different.

Mrs. Hopkins felt really sorry for me when I was sick. I had spent a week in an oxygen tent at St. Agnes hospital. Mom said I had bronchial pneumonia. One day at school I had a really high fever. My teacher didn't know that I was sick, so I stayed in school for the whole day. I got even sicker and then fell asleep on the school bus on the way home. The bus driver had to carry me inside my house. Mom took my temperature and then called Doctor Coon Coon. His real name was Doctor Borden, but I liked to call him "Coon Coon." I remember him coming into my bedroom with his bald head and big black bag and telling Mom that I'd have to go into the hospital. I was so upset; I jumped up and down on the bed in front of the both of them and screamed, "I'm not going to any hospital!" I sometimes think about being inside that plastic oxygen tent, and I can still hear the nurses pouring the ice behind me. When Mom came to visit me, she'd hold my hand through a zippered pocket. I went back and forth to the hospital three times until I finally got better.

The Hopkins house was sort of a red color, and ours was green. Their kids were older than Howard. Denise and Rhonda had been my regular babysitters before Abuela came to live with us. They were both a lot fun. Denise played board games with me and drove us to the five and ten store, where I was allowed to pick out a toy. Rhonda was really pretty. She'd always ask Mom if she could give me a bath before they left me with her. I didn't mind that too much, but she'd sprinkle way too much talcum powder on me, especially on my private area. One day I caught Howard looking up her dress as she walked up the stairs. Mr. and Mrs. Hopkins' son, Skipper, mostly liked to pitch tents in their backyard.

I played with Johnny and Mary Jane for awhile after we ate our ice creams. Then I headed home to watch what was left of the Orioles game. Dad was snoring on the hammock in the backyard. He had just his bathing suit on, and the baseball game was tuned in on his radio. Mom was in the kitchen with Abuela slicing cucumbers for the salad while Abuela was seasoning the hamburgers for the barbeque. Howard walked through the front door with his skateboard under one arm. Mom heard him walking in. "Howard! Come here in the kitchen." I pulled out a pitcher filled with iced tea from out of the ice box and poured a drink for myself. Mom turned to me and said, "Ray-Ray, stay here for a minute." I sat down at the kitchen table. Mom said, "Your father and me have something very important to tell you after dinner, so stay home for the rest of the day."

Howard and I just stared at each other. We both looked a little worried. Then Howard said, "What is it, Mom? Go ahead and tell us now, is there anything wrong?"

"No … I want to tell you with your father; there's nothing wrong."

"I can't wait till then," I said.

"We're going to eat pretty soon, so you won't have too much longer to wait. Raymond, go wake up your father and tell him to start the fire; the hamburgers are ready." I ran outside to the backyard, but Dad was already sitting up in his hammock drinking a Schlitz beer. "Hi, Dad, Mom wants you to start the fire. Can I squirt the fluid on the charcoal?"

"Go ahead." The charcoal was already sitting on top of aluminum foil inside the barbeque. I picked up the can and started squirting. "You want to light it too, son?" he asked.

"Sure." Dad handed me the matches. I'd never lit anything with matches before. I'd tried lighters, especially at Dad's store. Dad pulled out one of the matchsticks from the matchbook. Then he lined up the red part with the part that you strike. Dad said, "Here, hold the matchstick here and strike it hard on this part. When it's lit, throw it on the charcoal and run."

42

I was kind of nervous when he said I should run. I struck the match on the part that looked like sandpaper, and nothing happened. I tried again and saw a spark, so I threw it into the barbeque and ran. Dad started laughing. "You've got to wait till the match is lit before you throw it in, butch." I tried it again. This time the match was lit, but when I tossed it onto the charcoal it must have gone out. I was getting anxious and frustrated, but I wanted to show Dad that I could do it. I tried again, and this time the match was lit. I tossed it onto the charcoal, and whoosh! It was like an explosion. The heat singed my eyebrows. Dad looked at me and said, "Are you okay son? I told you to run after you threw the match; you got too close to the fire."

"I think I'm all right. Wow, that was something!"

I wanted to ask Mom if I could invite Johnny over to eat with us, but she didn't want anybody over because of what she and Dad were going to tell us. We all ate outside on the picnic table. Our dog, Terry, was circling around the table looking for food. I decided I'd like to try and catch some lightning bugs later after Mom and Dad's big news.

After dinner was over, Mom and Abuela cleared all the dishes from the picnic table. There weren't too many things to clean afterward because we ate on paper plates. After everything was put away, Dad called everyone into the living room. Here it came … I was starting to get worried and scared. "Your mother and I have an announcement to make," he said. Howard and I looked like frightened mice. Abuela looked calm, so I figured she already knew. The big announcement would surely be for just us kids. Then Dad said it. "We're moving out of Baltimore."

Howard and I asked the same question at the same time: "Where are we moving to, Dad?"

"A place called Silver Hill, Maryland, not far from Washington DC. And … we're going to live in apartments for awhile. The drive in to work, six days a week, is too much. Hadje already! We'll live in an apartment for awhile until I can save enough money for another house. Well … that's it, I guess." I think the news was more exciting than sad. I was going to miss my friends, but I'd be starting first grade at a new school anyway. And it would be a much shorter drive for when I went to work with Dad at his corner store on F Street. I'd still be able to follow the Orioles and Colts; after all, we were still going to be living in Maryland.

Chapter Five

Bye-Bye, Baltimore

A gigantic moving truck came to our house and picked up all of our furniture. Mom and Dad gave a lot of our furniture away to Thelma because it wouldn't fit in our new apartment. The moving truck followed us all the way to Holly Hill Apartments in Silver Hill. We'd be only twenty minutes away from Dad's store on F Street. It took me a long time to get over not having my dog anymore; we had to give her away because the apartments didn't allow pets. I was really mad about that and I wondered if we would have had to give Mike, our parakeet, away too—if he hadn't flown away out of our bedroom window before the move. We had a baby chick once, but it got loose and fell into the toilet. Ever since that had happened, I couldn't eat chicken anymore.

While I sat there in the backseat of Mom's Desoto, I started daydreaming about my kindergarten class in Baltimore. I played Hansel in my kindergarten's stage show of *Hansel and Gretel*. I remember the large school auditorium being completely sold-out that evening. I was really nervous before the show started, but I said all my lines without making any mistakes. And I got to share the stage with Judy, who played Gretel. I had a huge crush on Judy that entire school year. I guessed I'd never see her again.

I thought about how it was really cool when Mrs. Crouch, our kindergarten teacher, took us all on that field trip to the WMAR-TV studios to be on the *Bozo the Clown Show*. The whole time I was in the audience, I kept waving at myself on the TV monitor. Bozo never picked me to play any of the games, but I did get to watch myself on television when it aired later. Mom and I were really excited, waiting to see my big showbiz moment. When the show finally aired, I looked like a yo-yo. I was the only one in the audience who seemed to be waving at nothing for the entire show. Then I wondered if they'd even have the *Bozo Show* on TV in Silver Hill. And what about my other favorite shows like *Lorenzo* or *Pete the Pirate*? I wasn't sure if I was ready for that many changes yet. Then I thought about mine and Howard's sunflowers. We left Howard's sunflower tied to that stick. Howard said if nobody bought our home for a long time, then maybe his sunflower would grow taller than the house. He said he would call Ronnie Abernathy after a while to see if his sunflower was still there and growing. I tore my sunflower out of the ground before we left. Howard won the contest, and the tallest sunflower got to stay planted.

We arrived at the apartments, and they looked all right, I guess. Our home was on the very bottom floor. It was going to be strange having so many families living in one building. Mom told me before we left Baltimore that there was a huge playground behind our building and a community swimming pool. I couldn't wait to check out the playground. I was really happy that Cousin Tony and Gigi had decided to leave Baltimore at the same time we had. They moved to a different apartment complex about ten minutes away. If I had trouble making any friends, I could always get Mom to drive me over there to play with Teri and Bebe, Tony's kids.

The movers finished unloading everything. It would take us about a month to get all settled in. My first experiences of living in Silver Hill weren't so great. As soon as we were all unpacked, I ended up in the hospital again. This time, I had to get my tonsils and adenoids removed. I had no clue what those were; all I knew was that I didn't get nearly as much ice cream as they said I would after my operation, so I was disappointed. I wasn't in the hospital very long, but Mom and Dad bought me some really neat toys. Then my first grade teacher made a big stink about how I was talking to another classmate while she was teaching us. I was only talking with Tracey, and besides, she was the one talking; I was just listening. I always just listened when I tried talking to Tracey. She loved horses, and it was the only thing she ever talked about. She'd get mad at me if I acted like I wasn't interested. And man was I sick and tired of listening to her talk about horses.

I was normally a model student. My teacher even picked me to represent the whole first grade class in the student council. But without blinking an eye that day, my teacher replaced me on the council when she caught me and Tracey talking. She never even gave me a second chance to redeem myself. That was the very first time that I had even been told not to talk in class; it just didn't make any sense to me. But the student council was kind of boring anyway. We did plant and dedicate a tree once, but that was the only thing I found interesting. After every meeting, my teacher made me stand up in front of the whole class and tell them all the latest student council news. I was a really good talker, so I didn't mind that too much. The kid they replaced me with was pretty shy and never had much to say. A girl named Bonnie replaced him later in the school year. I don't want to sound mean or anything, but I was glad when he got the boot.

During that first year Mom hurt her back and got surgery. She was stuck in bed for awhile and was in a lot of pain. She cried a lot too, and it really bothered me to watch her suffer like that. We all had to pitch in and help around the apartment. I was really glad that Abuela was living with us. I'm not sure how we all would have managed otherwise.

My best friend at Holly Hill was Susan Madison. She was a few years older than me. I really liked hanging out with her because she played like a boy, but she was really pretty. Her favorite game was red light, green light. We'd play outside in front of our building until it started to get dark. Susan had really long straight blonde hair and pretty blue eyes. She was kind of like a Scandinavian beauty. She was several inches taller than me, and for some reason I was glad that she was. It was late Sunday morning, and I told Mom that I was going to the playground. I didn't really care if no one else was out there; I spent lots of hours alone on that playground. I always climbed the huge jungle gym. When you reached the very top, there was a bird's head with a big nose wearing a hat. I liked sitting on his hat alone and just thinking about stuff. There was a really long bike path that circled the entire playground. I was about to cross over the bike path when *wham!* A little kid ran right into my left knee with his bike. He was going really fast. It seemed like he came from out of nowhere because I never saw him coming. I felt an instant stinging sensation, but it didn't hurt as much as I thought it would. Then I looked down at me knee and saw blood gushing out everywhere. It scared the crap out of me, so I ran all the way back home. Abuela cleaned it up and wrapped it with a bandage. She liked to take care of everyone and always knew just what to do. Mom said she had been a gynecologist in Havana, Cuba. She actually brought Howard into the world. Mom said that Abuela was a very sympathetic woman and refused to collect money from anyone who even hinted at being poor. Mom said she'd also hide people on the roof of her building who were members of a secret anti-Machado organization. Poor Abuela lost everything she ever had because of Fidel Castro. When she was at the airport and ready to leave Cuba to live in America, she was only allowed to leave with the clothes she was wearing. They took her purse away and all of her money.

I ran back to the playground and went looking for that little kid. He didn't even say he was sorry when he ran into my leg; he just kept on riding his bike. Then I spotted him: he was still down there on his bike like nothing had ever happened. I ran over to him and pointed at my leg. "See what you did, you dumb little kid!" He looked at me like he just didn't give a crap. When he saw how mad my face looked, he started to get scared. He quickly turned his bike around and started pedaling really fast. I stood there and kept watching him for a minute. He skidded to a stop in front of two adults. Then I watched him pointing his finger at me. I guessed that they were probably his parents. The both of them turned their heads toward me. When I noticed them trying to focus in on me, I started walking really fast toward the swings. I thought about telling his parents what had happened, but some parents are always sticking up for their kids no matter how bad they were.

And besides, I saw Susan walking toward the swings. "Ray, come on over and sit with me!" I sat on the empty swing next to her. We both sat without swinging. Our legs were limp, dangling while both of us stared down at the ground. We didn't say a word for about a minute. And then she spoke, "Ray … do you have a girlfriend?"

I was immature, nervous, and totally surprised by the question, so I replied, "Nope."

Susan looked up at me with those beautiful blue eyes and hinted, "You really should, ya know."

I said, "Okay, I guess so … I don't know, I guess." That was all I could say to her. I had much better words in my head, but they refused to travel to my mouth. It felt like I was Charlie Brown or something. I really liked her a lot, but I just didn't know what to say or do. Pretty girls made me nervous. I had felt the same way about Judy, too. Susan and I remained only friends. I wouldn't have known what to do with a girlfriend anyway. All I knew is that I had a mushy feeling inside of me when I was around her.

The following week was my birthday. Mom planned a big party for me with about twenty-five kids. It was a great chance for me to have fun with some new Silver Hill buddies. Besides Susan, I didn't really have any other close friends. The party was set for Sunday, January 30, at 1:00. My real birthday was Thursday, but that was a school day. Early Saturday morning it started to snow really hard. Howard and I listened for the weather report on WPGC while we started to decorate the apartment for the party. WPGC Good Guys Radio was our favorite radio station. Dad and Uncle Joey even played WPGC through the outside lobby speaker at their store. We'd fall asleep every night with it playing on the radio in our room. Howard and I slept in bunk beds; I was on top because he was older. I fell out of the top bunk a few times. One time I bumped my head really hard. Mom and Dad had to buy a wooden bar to help keep me in.

While decorating for the party, Howard blew up a bunch of balloons and stuck them to the walls by rubbing them on his sweater. It was like magic. Sometimes after rubbing his sweater, he'd stick his finger on my earlobe, and I'd get an electrical shock. He really zapped me good a couple of times; I even saw a huge spark at the side of my face.

We finished decorating the apartment Saturday afternoon. On Sunday morning, almost twenty inches of snow had fallen, and there were wind gusts up to fifty miles per hour. The newsman on TV called it "the blizzard of '66." Our phone started to ring like crazy. All the moms of my friends called and cancelled. Everyone was stuck in their homes and couldn't get out. I think Mom was more disappointed than I was. I was kind of happy it snowed. School would probably be canceled for most of the week, and I could build forts and go sledding. I knew I'd eventually get my birthday presents from everyone anyway. But Mom was determined to have a party for me. All the buildings at Holly Hill had a basement floor that connected with each other. The basement floor was where the laundry rooms and trash cans were. You could walk through all the apartment buildings without going outside. Mom called just the parents back who lived at Holly Hill. She convinced most of the moms into letting their kids come. Mom asked Howard to escort each one of my friends through the basement floor and to my party. Eight kids made it, and we got to go outside and play in the snow after the party was over.

Mostly it was a really good year. We said good-bye to Mom's aqua Desoto when Dad bought her a new navy blue Pontiac Bonneville station wagon. The Baltimore Orioles beat the Los Angeles Dodgers in four straight games and captured their first World Series championship, and I never grew tired of talking about my Oriole heroes, Brooks, Frank, and Boog. The Beatles came to town on August 15 and performed at DC stadium. I became a Monkees fan after hearing their first single on WPGC called "Last Train to Clarksville." But I was completely blown away by a TV show about a superhero who fought crime alongside his sidekick, Robin the Boy Wonder. The caped crusader wore a utility belt, and when he fought villains, the fight scenes spelled out "POW! BAM! ZOKK!" Batman was my new idol. I collected the entire series of Batman trading cards that year. Then I traded them all for a shopping bag full of really old baseball cards. Mom was kind of mad at me when I got home and showed her my really great trade, probably because it took us so long to complete the Batman set. Mom and I worked hard as a team, searching all over town for Batman cards to complete that set. We'd usually take a break and eat at this really long lunch counter in the S. S. Kresge's store, at the Pen-Mar Shopping Plaza. They always had a contest going on to win a free soda or something. I got to pop one of the balloons that were hanging up around the lunch counter, and inside was a free prize. The last time me and Mom ate there, I won a free banana split.

We moved again the following year to another apartment called Hickory Hills, just a few miles away. Tony and Gigi moved again to Surrey Squares Apartments, in Forestville. I think there were a couple reasons for us moving again, but I believed the one that clinched it was because of our fat, noisy upstairs neighbor. When the lady walked around her apartment, it sounded like a sonic boom. There were marks all over our living room ceiling from Howard banging the broom handle up and down in retaliation. Mom and Dad just couldn't take it anymore, and neither could I.

Hickory Hills was brand-new and was still under construction; we were the first ones to move into the building. We'd have to walk on wooden planks to get into the building because they hadn't poured cement for the stairs yet. We really weren't supposed to be moving in yet, but Mom convinced the landlord to let us move in anyway. Sometimes Mom and I ate lunch with the construction workers when the chuck wagon parked outside our building. And Howard and I finally got our own bedrooms; I was glad because we were starting to get on each other's nerves.

My first grade year was at Forestville Elementary, but I needed to change schools after we moved, to Silver Hill Elementary. I didn't have a lot of white friends at that school, but I was invited to a ton of birthday parties from black friends. Silver Hill had two separate buildings, a newer main building and a really old white building that was probably built in the 1920s. There were only a few classes taught in the ancient white building. There were also classes held in the portables, which were modular classrooms behind the main building. I had the most fun in that old white building, though, because there seemed to be a lot less supervision by any of the teachers.

All the boys played kickball during recess. There was this older kid who always dressed up during recess as the Green Hornet. He eventually found an Asian kid to play his sidekick, Kato. They'd always zoom around the playground together attracting lots of girls. When I first started going to Silver Hill, I noticed right away that there weren't many black students at all. And you could probably count all the Asian students in the whole school on one hand. I'd say most kids had a problem making friends with kids that were different than they were. I don't think I ever had that problem, as long as the kid was nice to me. When I worked at Dad's corner store on F Street, I was around people from all over the world—including bums, hushos (which is our word for thieves) and *mejnoons*. I guess I had kind of an advantage over most kids when it came to dealing with different people.

I started to find my own identity at Silver Hill. I wore my favorite tight beige slacks and a paisley shirt with a dickey underneath. A dickey was basically a half or fake turtleneck, and they looked really cool underneath shirts. I had a bunch of them in all sorts of colors. I wore Beatle boots too. They were really narrow and hard to walk in, but they looked really cool, and that's all that mattered. I thought the zipper on the side of the boot was out of sight! When I wasn't wearing my Beatle boots, I'd wear these Clarks desert boots; it was usually the choice for Mods, which was what I was calling myself nowadays. My haircut was kind of like a Beatle mop top. But I wasn't really a diehard Beatles fan or anything like that; most of the bands that I liked wore hair styles that resembled a Beatles mop top, like Paul Revere and the Raiders and The Buckinghams. I was hip and followed all the cool bands, thanks to WPGC.

I really liked school, mainly because of my favorite teacher, Mrs. Gentry. She was my second and fourth grade teacher. I was a good student and loved to write really long stories. But the one thing that created a special teacher-student bond between us was Orioles baseball. Mrs. Gentry loved the Orioles as much as I did. We were always outnumbered; it seemed like everyone around us was a Washington Senators fan. So every morning, before we were seated for the start of class, we'd huddle around her desk and quietly talk about last night's ballgame. Sometimes she even showed up to watch me play at one of my baseball games, and it was great to have my mom and teacher both cheering me on in the stands. I played third base with a baseball team for the Silver Hill boys club, and I mimicked every move that Orioles great Brooks Robinson had made on the field. I was really good in my first year of playing organized baseball; in fact I was going to make the all-star team until I broke my finger. During a game one sunny afternoon, I got into position to catch an infield pop fly, and the ball landed directly on my right index finger. I was in the worst pain that I ever felt in my whole life and collapsed to the ground. I tried not to cry, but I couldn't help it. One of my coaches was also an ambulance driver and knew right away that it was broken. He raced me and Mom to the emergency room, where the doctor set it and put on a splint. Before the doctor set my finger, he gave me a shot with this really big needle to numb it. Then he actually bent my finger all the way back ... and it stayed there! It looked horrible, but I really didn't feel anything. I couldn't play in the all-star game and missed the rest of the season. It was already the second time that I had broken a bone. When I was three years old, I broke my clavicle sliding down a board into a blow-up pool.

It was Monday at school, and everyone was excited over our class field trip to the Naval Academy in Annapolis. Mom drove me to school this morning because she volunteered to be a chaperone on the trip. I usually walked to school every day. Mom had been a chaperone before, and I never minded it. You would think most guys wouldn't want their moms anywhere near them at school. But Mom never embarrassed me or anything like that, and she and Mrs. Gentry always seemed to hit it off.

This really cute girl named Sandy agreed to be my trip buddy. I was really glad because I had a huge crush on her. She had long dark brown hair and a big ol' smile that showed much of her teeth; I really liked that. I felt kind of mushy inside when she spoke too. I was sorta figuring out that I liked girls that smiled big and talked kind of babyish. Our school bus driver drove us to a pier, and then we all boarded a boat to the Naval Academy. Sandy and I sat together, and Mom gave us our privacy and sat somewhere else. I excused myself and walked over toward Mom for a second. "Mom, can I have some money to buy Sandy some candy?" There was a snack bar on the boat, and everybody was buying stuff.

She handed me two dollars and said, "You really like her, don't you?" I was kind of embarrassed to admit that to my mother, so I nodded my head and just smiled. "She's adorable, Ray-Ray," she said.

After buying the candy, I returned to my seat next to Sandy. "Here, I bought this for you." She was all smiles but kind of acted like she expected it. We sat closely together and giggled for the entire boat ride. We got off the boat and then spent the entire walking tour through the academy together. I really wanted to hold her hand at the crypt of John Paul Jones, but I chickened out. On the way back to the boat, our class stopped at a gift shop. I spent all of my souvenir money on a stuffed navy mascot goat and then gave it to Sandy. She was all smiles again, but this time she was really excited and started jumping up and down. She stuck to me like glue all the way back to the boat. We sat really close together on one of the bench seats on the boat. She said she was going to name her goat Raymond. I felt all warm inside when she said that. Then the knucklehead inside of me came out again. About ten minutes before the boat reached the dock, for some idiotic reason I began talking about my best friend Michael and how great he was. I kept saying really cool things about him and how funny he was. For the entire trip back, it was all I could talk about.

When we got on the school bus for the ride home, she acted differently toward me. To make things even worse, the next day at school recess, I introduced them to each other. Michael wasn't even in our class, but Sandy had an immediate crush on Michael. No kidding, especially after all the cool and funny things I said about him. She even started ignoring me at school. Why was I such an idiot! It was like someone else was in my brain and was preventing me from growing up.

On the Christmas Eve in '67, Dad drove us all to Tony and Gigi's apartment to spend our traditional Christmas with them. I never wanted the evening to end, and it always went by so quickly. I'd never get bored; Gigi always suggested something for us kids to do. She and Tony always went all-out in decorating their apartment for the holidays. But the two things that I always liked the most were her traditional bubble lights on the Christmas tree and their fake fireplace made out of cardboard with the flickering artificial flames. I don't know why, but I really liked that cardboard fireplace a lot. Tony had grown a really big beard. Uncle Joey would jokingly call him Castro while they worked together at the store, but I don't think Tony liked it very much.

It was exciting for me to be spending Christmas with all my cousins. The oldest was Teri. She was three months older than me. The grownups called her *Teresita*. Her parents sometimes called her *Teté*, a nickname I believed she hated with a passion. She was a really pretty girl but a real scaredy-cat. She threw a fit when her dad tried to pull out her loose tooth. She screamed, laughed, and cried all at the same time. When the tooth was finally out, she felt really silly about all the fuss she had made. We all had a good laugh about it afterward. Teri was a lot of fun, and I really liked hanging around her, but she'd clobber me if I'd ever made fun of her, like those times when she'd wet her bed when she was little.

I guess I'm not completely innocent when it came to being a scaredy-cat, though. On the Fourth of July, Gigi and Tony invited me to go with them to see the fireworks near the Washington Monument. After the show was over, Tony left us to go and get the car. He didn't come back for hours. We were left there in the middle of the night, standing all alone in the middle of Washington DC without anyone around. I didn't even see any cops. So … I may have gotten somewhat panicky. I asked Gigi a couple of hundred times when was Tony coming back, and I probably came within minutes of a nervous breakdown.

Bebe on the other hand, always acted like nothing ever bothered her. But she and her sister did have some heated arguments. She was a bit clumsy and messy at times, while Teri was just the opposite. Bebe's nickname was "Bebe-Chong." I was never sure how they came up with that one. Bebe always seemed to call attention to herself at the strangest times. Once we were all in Miami together visiting my Aunt Terry, and Bebe accidentally stepped on a baby chick. The tiny legs of the chick were broken, so my Aunt Terry grabbed the baby chick and rung its neck to put it out of its misery before tossing it in a dumpster. We stood there with our mouths wide open and watched in outright horror and disbelief. We couldn't believe our Aunt Terry would do such a thing, and poor Bebe felt so guilty afterward. On that same trip, Aunt Terry took us to Monkey Jungle. The concept at Monkey Jungle was that the humans were in the cage and the monkeys were all running around loose. We walked by a spider monkey that was chained but open to the public. When Bebe walked by, the monkey lunged at her and grabbed her hair and pulled on it really hard. It took several minutes for the monkey to let go, and it created quite a stir. Of course Bebe was in tears over the senseless attack. Strange things like that were always happening to her.

Sonia and Henry were the youngest. My mom liked calling Sonia "*Sony-Que.*" There was a huge playground with a giant fort at Tony and Gigi's apartment complex. One day Sonia ran off with another kid and got totally lost in their neighborhood. When they finally found her, she was being led away by some crazy woman. Henry was nicknamed, "*Henriquito.*" Cubans always created cutesy nicknames for their family members. Gigi always called Henry "My son, my son," imitating the doggie daddy on the cartoon Augie Doggie."

That Christmas Eve we were all really excited about opening presents. The first thing Dad did was to call Teri and Bebe over. He said, "Okay girls, say I'm a Cuban refugee, and I'll give you each a dollar." In harmony, they both said it really loud, "I'm a Cuban refugee!" Dad handed them each a dollar bill. But then he walked over to Sonia and Henry and gave them each one too.

Then Gigi yelled out, "Okay everybody,… let's eat!" Gigi always sat us kids together in a separate dinner table, totally blocked off from seeing the grownups. She served us pork, a large bowl of black beans and rice with plantains on the side and Cuban bread with olive oil. Then she brought us all a *café con leche.* Her kids loved them. I only got to drink them at Tony and Gigi's place. After me and my cousins finished eating, we all spread out on the living room floor until the grownups were done. The grownups were always slower eaters than us kids. The TV was already turned on to a Christmas special with Bing Crosby on *The Hollywood Palace.* I enjoyed the show but couldn't wait to open presents.

After the grown-ups were finally done, Tony gave Dad one of his new cigars. Dad poked a whole at the end of it with a special tool that Tony gave to him. Tony lit up Dad's cigar and then lit up one for himself. For a second, it felt like I was back at Dad's store again. Mom and Abuela were helping Gigi clean up in the kitchen. Teri gathered Bebe and me together and then whispered, "Let's get them to hurry up so we can open our presents already. On the count of three, let's all run in there and yell, 'Let's open presents.' Ready? One … two … three … go!"

We all ran into the kitchen and screamed, "Let's open presents!" Then we all started laughing because we scared the crap out of them.

Gigi held one hand to her chest while the other hand held a cooking pot. The pot wasn't completely dry, so water was dripping on the floor. She was breathing kind of hard and looked straight down at the floor when she said, "You scared the living bejesus out of me!" But it worked. After she finally recovered, she said, "Okay, I get the message, we're finished. Everyone into the living room."

As soon as she said that, Howard brought out a huge present and handed it to Gigi. "Wow, what could this be, I'm speechless." Gigi had a picturesque smile. I guess she got plenty of practice posing because they were always snapping family photos. When Gigi posed for pictures, you would almost swear that she was a mannequin. She always had a determined look on her face that made her look like something was on her mind. Sometimes I thought that she believed she was meant for a life of glamour and wealth, and somehow she got crossed up with someone else's life. Gigi unwrapped the huge present, and there was a smaller box inside. She peeled off the paper on the second box, and there was yet another smaller box inside of it. She started laughing really hard and said, "That is hysterical," and then she tore the paper from the final box and pulled out a 45 record. The label read, "Woman Woman" by Gary Puckett and the Union Gap—it was Gigi's favorite song.

Chapter Six

Dark Days ... "By and By"

On Thursday, April 4, 1968, I rode downtown to work at the store with Dad, Howard, and Tony. It was our spring break at school. At 6:01 in the evening that day, Dr. Martin Luther King was assassinated, which sparked rioting all over Washington DC. Dad and Uncle Joey had taken a walk down the street after they heard the news to see what was going on. They both had a keen sense and knew that DC would have its share of troublemakers. They walked down to Ninth Street and had to turn around when it started to get dangerous. Gangs of angry black youths started breaking windows, throwing rocks, and screaming. A young black man purposely pushed dad and angrily cried out, "Get out of my way, whitey!"

Dad replied, "Sorry, sir, it's my fault." Dad didn't want any trouble and knew he was outnumbered. He was only a businessman. My father understood why the black population was so outraged; he said to me, "After all, King was their leader." Smoke was in the air, police and fire sirens blared, and people of all color headed home nervously. If there was trouble ahead, Dad and Uncle Joey would always investigate, and nothing ever fazed them. They were never scared of anything or anyone. Dad and Joey lived through the toughest of times in Brooklyn; they fought the Japanese in World War II, but I think what was more important during the riots was that they had street smarts.

The brothers arrived back at 1300 F Street. When they walked into the store, all of us were huddled around a Zenith display model television set, watching the latest news events unfold. Bernadette had already left the store to catch her bus back to Baltimore. Uncle Moey's eyes were glued to the breaking news, and he remarked, "The *Abeed* are going to burn the city down." *Abeed* was a Syrian slang word for blacks.

Dad added, "When we were out walking, we saw signs in store windows that said, 'We are black—don't burn our store.'" I stood there and watched the news broadcast images of Marines with machine guns, sent by President Johnson to guard the capitol, and army troops positioned to protect the White House only three blocks away.

Tony had a worried look on his face. He said, "We should empty out all the windows and get the fuck out of here." Tony didn't take crap from anybody, but it made good sense to pack up and leave. By this time, Mayor Washington had told all the merchants to close their stores and leave the city anyway. I wasn't nervous until Tony made his comment.

They all knew it might take hours to get all the merchandise out of the windows, so Uncle Joey locked the front doors so no one could get in. We all lined up in a row and passed one another each piece of merchandise from out of the show windows, like passing buckets to put out a fire. The windows were packed, and there were a lot of expensive goods. If the angered mobs had marched by Chin Lung Art Gallery, they would have definitely broken all the windows and emptied them out. Even though there was an alarm system in place, no one would have paid any attention to it on that day. We finished emptying the windows in record pace. Dad and Tony blocked the access door, which led from the windows into the store, with an iron gate so none of the looters would be able to get inside. Dad commanded, "Take all the merchandise downstairs into the basement," We never used the basement for anything; it was like an old dark dungeon. This would be a good spot to hide the merchandise from looters. Uncle Joey ransacked the cash register and left only the coins. Dad shouted over at me, "Call your mother and tell her we're leaving in about fifteen minutes."

Back home, Mom and Abuela watched the news on TV and were getting worried. Abuela had dinner waiting for us on the stove. The phone rang. Mom reached for the phone that sat on a small end table next to the couch in the den. She picked up the phone and looked at the wall clock; it said 7:30. The store usually closed later on Thursday nights, so she wasn't panicky yet. "Mom, we're leaving the store in about fifteen minutes," I said. "We had to stay and empty out all the windows."

Mom nervously replied, "I was so worried, *Ramonsito*. I'm watching the news with Abuelita, and they said there's going to be a lot of trouble downtown. Please be careful. Is your father and Howard all right?"

"We'll be real careful, don't worry ... Everybody's fine. Dad says to tell Abuela to have the dinner ready, he's starving. I'll see you soon ... I love you, Mom. Bye." After I called Mom, everyone else decided that they had better call home too. Uncle Joey called Aunt Sophia, Uncle Moey telephoned Aunt Faye, Tony informed Gigi, and Fat Bobby instructed his wife that they were all leaving soon to come home. Dad shut off all the lights, and everyone waited for Uncle Joey to set the alarm code. We slowly marched out the front door together and cautiously walked down the street, heading for the parking garage. It was an eerie feeling walking the streets that evening; it was fear of the unknown. Dad, Tony, Howard, and I climbed into the Oldsmobile 98, and I was relieved that we had arrived without an incident. Still, I was scared and sat at the edge of my seat for the entire trip home. The routine thirty-minute drive turned into hours. Many of the roads driving home closed down, and we were rerouted by police and national guardsman. There were army vehicles everywhere. It was like the entire city was under attack. We finally walked through the front door at around ten o'clock at night. Tony drove off quickly to see his family after Dad parked the car. Mom and Abuela were so happy and relieved to see us. Then for the next twenty minutes, Howard and I described to them all the events that had unfolded for the day. At the dinner table, Dad discussed with me and Howard how we would have to go back to work the next morning with normal business hours. Dad said, "Even if the store is not busy tomorrow, we still need to protect it. The store is our bread and butter, our livelihood. Do you understand?"

I said, "Protect the store from the hushos, right, Dad?"

Mom didn't want me to go with them on Friday, but Dad insisted, "He'll be all right. Raymond can handle himself; he does very good around the hushos.

The rioting had spread throughout the city by eleven o'clock on Thursday night. Mayor Washington ordered the damage to be cleaned up by morning. Activist Stokely Carmichael addressed a rally the next morning. After the rally, violent confrontations with the police erupted; the rioters tossed Molotov cocktails into buildings and threw bottles, bricks, and rocks at firefighters who tried to put out the blazes.

For the entire day on Friday, all of us stood guard and protected the store. Dad called Bernadette and Fat Bobby very early that morning and told them both to stay home. The store windows were left completely empty. People were scared to come downtown, and so there was no business. Only a handful of foreign tourists that hadn't seen the news came into the store. All day long we left on a Sony portable TV to listen for the latest news updates. We watched and listened for the rioters' next move, what streets they were going to target next. At one point, rioting had reached within two blocks of the White House before the rioters retreated. I was edgy for the entire day and relieved when it was finally time to close. When we left the city, I was shocked to see army tanks readied for battle.

Saturday, April 6, was a repeat of Friday. Soldiers with rifles were on every street corner. On Sunday, April 7, the city appeared much quieter, and so Dad and Uncle Joey decided to close the store.

By Monday DC was on a normal, back-to-work schedule, and we loaded the windows back up with merchandise. There were still soldiers around. The occupation of Washington DC was the largest of any American city since the Civil War. Later that week, Dad and Uncle Joey installed strong metal pull-down gates with heavy padlocks to protect the store windows.

In June that year, I laid in my bed half asleep, listening to WPGC like I always did. I barely heard the DJ, Jack Alix, break away for a special news bulletin: "Senator Robert F. Kennedy has been shot." The next night, I was almost asleep again when a news bulletin announced that he was dead. I just laid there with a sick feeling in the pit of my stomach. For the very first time, I was worried for our country. Too many bad things were happening. When President Kennedy was killed, I was sad like everyone else, but I never felt scared for our country like I did now. I guess I was too young to understand everything then, but in school they had led me to believe that our country was invincible. Now I wasn't so sure anymore.

It was a Thursday evening. The doorbell rang, and I ran over to answer it. It was Bill the laundry man. "Hi, Bill," I said.

"Hi. Raymond, how's life in the little league? Are you smacking that ball hard?"

"Yea, I got a double last week. but we still lost the game."

"Hey. you still got a hit; you'll bounce back next week." I always looked forward to talking with Bill. He was always so happy. He came to our house every week to pick up all of our clothes that needed to be dry cleaned. Bill was a middle-aged Italian man. He had a big nose and wore big, black-framed eyeglasses. He always had a huge smile on his face, which made it hard to see his thin mustache. We all loved Bill; he was like part of our family. He'd even stop by Tony and Gigi's place to pick up their clothes.

"Mom, Bill is here!" I yelled.

Mom and Abuela walked over to the front door and greeted Bill. Mom said, "Hi, Bill!"

"Hi, Jenny. Hi Mama, how are you feeling?" He always called Abuela "Mama."

Abuela said in her heavy Cuban accent, "Oh, so-so, Bill; the arthritis is very bad in the nighttime."

"Oh I'm so sorry to hear that, Mama. Maybe a little wine before you go to sleep… *Un poco vino.*"

"Tss tss tss … Yes, perhaps." Abuela's laughter was like a hissing sound. Mom already had a pile of clothes ready at the front door. Bill stuffed them in a big white bag that looked like a giant pillowcase and tied it shut at the very top.

"Give my best to Ted when he gets home. I'll see you next week, family!"

"Bye, Bill!" I shouted.

Mom said, "See ya, Bill."

Abuela said, "Okay, Bill, see you soon."

Thirty minutes later I heard the front door opening. I ran to the front door and saw Dad hanging up his coat. "Hi, Dad, how was work today?"

"Uh, same old shit." Then he started laughing. Dad never liked talking about work when he was home. Mom walked over by him. Dad turned his face toward her so she could give him a kiss, and then he made that face. He always made a face when someone kissed him on his cheek; it almost looked like the kiss was hurting him or something. Dad headed for the bathroom to wash his hands for a good thirty seconds or so; it was part of his coming-home ritual. I always knew his hands were really clean when he got out, because they were really red and I could smell the soap. Sometimes I'd break up his ritual by hiding in the closet and scaring him when he tried to hang up his coat. It would be in retaliation for all those times he'd scared the crap out of me. I always knew when I scared the crap out of him, too, because he'd look at me with that serious Uncle Joey glare on his face and say, "Are you finished or what … Now I'm going to get you back two times." I have to admit he scared me pretty good over the years. He'd sneak up on me from out of nowhere, stick his finger in my ear, and then calmly shout, "And now …!" Sometimes he'd scare me so bad that I retaliated with my little fists of fury.

After washing his hands, Dad walked into the kitchen to see what was for dinner. He lifted the top off, stared into the cooking pot on the stove, and hollered, *"Bueno Bueno,* Cruzey!" ("Cruzey" was Dad's nickname for Abuela's last name, Cruz) He reached into the kitchen cabinet and grabbed a tall glass before opening the freezer door and taking out an ice tray. He popped out about four ice cubes and dropped them into his glass. Then he left the kitchen and headed for the den. It was his sanctuary from working at his corner store on F Street. While in the den, he reached for the J&B bottle that stood on the bar and poured scotch into the tall glass with ice. Then he sat in his comfy reclining chair. Dad usually had several strong glasses of scotch every night. He slowly untied the laces from each of his shoes and removed them. Feeling a bit more comfortable, he lit up a Viceroy cigarette in the dim room. On a different day he might smoke a cigar instead. Then he picked up the television remote control box and pressed the on button. It was Thursday night, so Dad clicked the channel to *The Dean Martin Show.*

Abuela relaxed in bed after cooking dinner, and Mom walked into her room to chat and pray together. In Abuela's room there were three rows of shelves loaded with statues of saints. Howard and I started watching *The Dean Martin Show* with Dad, and after twenty minutes, he sat up out of his chair and announced, "I'm starvin'. It's time to eat." Dad walked into the kitchen with the unfinished glass of scotch in his hand. He stuck a ladle into the cooking pot, scooping up Abuela's delicious chicken with rice, and then placed it on a dish. He carried his dinner to the kitchen table and sat alone, because everyone else had already eaten. But there was a portable black-and-white Sony TV that sat on the kitchen table, and so Dad turned on the second half of the show while he ate his dinner.

After he finished his dinner, Dad retired to the den with a second glass of scotch in his hand. Howard and I were still in the den laughing about a comedy skit with Phil Silvers. It was a school night, and I normally went to bed by ten o'clock, but I'd gotten away with waiting till the start of *The Tonight Show Starring Johnny Carson*. After *The Dean Martin Show* was over, Howard snuck into his bedroom and called up one of his girlfriends.

It was 11:00, and Dad started to watch the news on TV. Mom walked out and said in a concerned tone, *"Ramonsito,* it's late, and you have school tomorrow."

"I know … I was just watching TV with Dad for awhile."

I got up off the couch to give Dad a hug. "Goodnight, Dada, love you." Howard and I always called our father "Dada" when we were in a playful mood.

"Goodnight, butch, I love you too."

I walked down the hallway and knocked on Howard's locked bedroom door. "Goodnight Howard!" I heard him talking on the phone, but there was no reply, so I stopped in to give Abuela a kiss goodnight. She was also watching the news while lying in her bed. She gave me a kiss on the cheek and said, *"Que sueno con los angelitos"* (sleep with the angels).

Mom watched me in Abuela's room, and then she followed me to my bedroom and waited for me to get under the covers. She kissed my cheek and said, "Goodnight, sweetie." After she left the room, I remembered that I forgot to turn on my radio, so I jumped out of bed and turned on the power switch, it was already set to WPGC. Mom walked back to her room to read a magazine for awhile before finally going to sleep. Dad stayed in the den alone. After he finished his second scotch, he pulled out some pistachios to nosh on. He'd eventually get up from his recliner to fall asleep on the couch and then make his way into the bedroom. This was a routine that we all knew too well.

We all knew Dad had a drinking problem. I remember Mom getting really mad at him because he drank so much, and she poured all of his scotch down the kitchen sink. Dad was always a lot of fun until he reached the point of no return, and it always bothered me when I couldn't communicate with him after he finished that first drink. But he never missed a day of work. Sometimes after he was almost finished with his first drink, Dad made a detour into Abuela's room, where he'd sit and ask questions about her religion. Dad respected Abuela very much; he often sat at the end of her bed while she lay there, and they'd discuss their religious beliefs and the similarities. Dad always liked repeating Abuela's favorite saying, "By and by." Abuela was a very calm person who always took one step at a time. When anyone in our home got nervous, upset, or stressed out, she'd always try and calm us down by repeating the words, "By and by." Dad was a very loving father, and he provided me with just about anything I needed. I think Dad's way of teaching Howard and me about life was making us work at his store. He'd call it "the school of hard knocks."

Chapter Seven

Visiting Bensonhurst

It was kind of a sad time for me later in '68. Tony and Gigi, along with all my favorite second cousins, moved down to Miami, Florida. Gigi said she was fed up with the cold winters in DC. But more important, Tony's heart wasn't into working at Dad's store anymore; he had talked about moving to Florida for quite awhile. They spent their final few days in Maryland living with us at Hickory Hills. Then one early morning, their brown Dodge station wagon and a U-Haul trailer packed with furniture were gone.

I still had my buddies at Hickory Hills to hang out with. Max lived one floor above, and Travis and his older sister Deanna lived one floor below us. Two floors up were Gerry, Billy, little brother Mark, and their older sister Cheryl. On the very top floor lived Gus and his older sister. I think Howard was on a mission to date all the older sisters in the building. Mission accomplished! We all lived together in one apartment building, and everyone had offbeat personalities. Each one of them played a certain role for me. I usually played war with Travis. He had red hair and freckles and was about my height, but he was several years older than me. Travis and I invented a cool game called "the lonely lieutenants." Our war adventure was based on hiding under a bridge that led to the entranceway of our apartment building. We waited there for hours, with rifles and hand grenades in hand, for the German tanks and infantry to cross that bridge, and then *fire!* It was always a complete surprise attack. We invented a second game that required us to paint our rifles in animal camouflage. I painted my weapon in zebra, and Travis painted his in leopard skin. We were African hunters that stalked big game around our apartment complex. Travis and I were the dreamers of the bunch.

His dad, Travis Senior, worked for the State Department, so he got to grow up in places like Kenya, Africa, and Ankara, Turkey. Travis's favorite adventure story was when his dad took him on safari, and they were chased by a crazed bull elephant. His parents were really good friends with Mom and Dad, and they visited our apartment frequently to play poker. I think Mom and Dad had more friends than Howard or I ever had. Mom always initiated the effort of hosting, and she always made friends with the parents of my friends. Dad always acted like he never cared about making friends, not wanting strange people in his space. He always said, "All I want is to come home from work, have a couple of drinks, and relax." I noticed that the older Dad got, the harder it was for my mom to establish any kind of social life. She'd always have to be clever. Mom would usually introduce him to a neighbor after he was already relaxed in his recliner and had tasted a few sips from his first glass of scotch. Once that was accomplished, Dad was a great host and even treasured the companionship.

My chum Mitch from upstairs was a husky kid. We played sports together and had sleepovers. Mitch and I created a game much like the Marco Polo swimming pool romp. One of us was blindfolded and had to feel around and try to find the other guy, who evaded but also had to constantly speak or make noises. When the blindfolded player sensed he was within range, he'd have to tag him to win the game. One day I was blindfolded and in hot pursuit of Mitch's presence, and I accidently knocked over a very expensive nude sculpture. The statue broke in two pieces, and his dad was livid. He screamed at us and chased the both of us into Mitch's bedroom and then slammed the door. I had never been scolded by anyone who wasn't a family member before, so I was worried, but Mitch eased my anguish when he broke out into laughter. Mitch was a bit of a rabble-rouser and never took anything seriously. Thanks to him, I got a look at my first *Playboy* magazine. He also initiated roughhousing. Mitch always wanted to wrestle, box, or tackle me. I never liked it because I didn't like anyone touching me.

Mitch and I were both huge sports fanatics. He liked the Senators and I liked the Orioles. He was a Redskins fan and I was a Colts fan. His dad was a radio announcer and knew a lot of Washington DC sports celebrities. Back in '67, his father invited me over to their apartment to meet Pete Richert, a pitcher for the Washington Senators. I shook Pete's hand and then handed him a baseball to sign. I had autographed the ball myself with phony Oriole signatures. I never met anyone famous before, so I created sketch autographs. (I liked using that word, "sketch," ever since Uncle Moey sold those Nigerians the sketch diamond rings.) Pete stared at my baseball and sarcastically said, "There's a bunch of Oriole signatures on this ball; are you sure you want mine?" Then he laughed and signed it anyway. Afterward, Mitch and I were playing on the floor with a loaded toy that shot arrows, and I accidently shot one over Pete Richert's crew cut. He looked over at me with a disturbed look on his face and said, "You really are an Orioles fan, aren't you." It was kind of ironic because Pete got traded to the Orioles that same year.

Billy and Gerry from two floors up were the brothers that I hung out with. Gerry was the older brother, and Billy was around my age. We rode bikes just about everywhere, hung out, and acted cool. Oh yeah, and we talked about girls … a lot. These two were the tough guys in the group. Billy kind of reminded me of how Elvis might have been in his childhood years. Billy was tough but also a nice guy. I couldn't be tough at any time like he could. I'd have to prepare for toughness, kind of like an actor. For Billy, it always came naturally, and he lived his life by one rule: "There's only three types of social groups in society today, and you need to decide which one you fit into. You either gotta be a Mod, a block, or a collegian. And you have to live your life according to their rules." Then he explained to me that Mods were modern-day hipsters and hippies, the blocks resembled the Greasers of the 1950s, and collegians were the do-gooders headed for college. Billy and Gerry were blocks, and Billy definitely knew that I was a Mod. Maybe that's why I couldn't be tough like he was, but he did try teaching me things. I'd listen to him but wouldn't commit to anything. I remember Billy talking about looking for moons on the ground with Gerry one day. He learned the lingo from Gus, who lived on the very top floor. Gus was older than all the rest of us and influenced Billy. I finally learned that looking for moons on the ground meant looking for cigarette butts; they would smoke a butt that still had some life left to it. I never tried one but enjoyed talking about it. I was still not ready to cross that line and become a bad ass.

Gerry wasn't tough like Billy was. He was constantly being tormented at school because his ears were so big. The mean-spirited kids called him "Dumbo ears." One day his mom asked me to come upstairs and visit with him. When I got there I was surprised to see his head wrapped up in bandages. He had his ears surgically altered. The mocking was way too much for him to handle and had finally taken its toll.

I was alone with Mom after school on a Friday, and I decided to walk outside onto our balcony. I looked down and saw a drunken black guy trying to climb up on the drain spout while he held a liquor bottle in the other hand. He reminded me of one of those bums that hung out near Dad's store, and I hated those bums. He was muttering obscenities as he struggled to climb up to our second-floor balcony. Mom was getting ready to call the police, when suddenly a powerful inner strength came pouring out of me. "Hey you down there, get the hell out of here … Let's go, move it now!" I sounded like I was twenty years older. The drunken bum didn't even look up at me. He jumped off the drain spout and took off running. Guess I had stored up enough courage from throwing out all the hushos at Dad's store.

On Saturday evening, I was hanging out in front of our apartment building around seven o'clock. It seemed like the whole neighborhood was outside that evening. There were kids riding bikes on the huge parking lot in front of our apartments, teens were working on their muscle cars, and parents were mingling and sharing gossip. Mom was out there too, sitting on the steps that led to our apartment building with Mitch's mother. They were really good friends; I'd always see the both of them sitting at our kitchen table in the morning, yakking away and drinking coffee while smoking their cigarettes. I decided to sit down next to Mom for a minute. I listened to Mom telling Mitch's mother her story. "I got pulled over by a policeman for speeding yesterday near Branch Avenue. The policeman got out of his car and walked over to me and said, 'Hello, young lady, do you know that you were driving fifty-five miles per hour? It's a forty-five-mile-per-hour speed zone.'"

"I said, 'Well … if you were following me, then you were driving just as fast as I was.' The policeman starting laughing and let me go with just a warning. It's funny, for some reason, I always get away with it."

After Mom finished her priceless story, I looked away and then eerily noticed that everyone around us, one by one, started to look up at the sky. Something spectacular had caught everyone's attention. A strange white oval object had been circling the neighborhood above our heads. The entire neighborhood watched in total amazement. Anyone who wasn't outside would soon be. Billy, Gerry, Mitch, Travis, and I started knocking on doors. "There's a UFO in the sky out in front of our building—come quick!" The UFO occurrence lasted for about twenty minutes and then just mysteriously disappeared. No one could explain the phenomena. Some of the neighborhood parents contacted Andrews Air Force base nearby for possible clues or answers, but Andrews acted like it was an isolated incident and offered no explanations whatsoever. I believe the Hickory Hills residents had shared a very special moment that evening. If it wasn't a real UFO, who cared, because we all bonded and got to know each other a little better that evening.

The following weekend after the Hickory Hills UFO incident, we packed up the Bonneville station wagon and headed for Bensonhurst. It'd been awhile since we had visited Grandma and all the rest of the family in New York. Normally we'd get to see them for weddings and bar mitzvahs, but Dad really wanted to see his mother. Mom had driven Abuela to Washington National Airport last Wednesday afternoon. Abuela wanted to spend some time with Aunt Terry and then visit with Gigi and Tony in Miami. I think it was the first time she wasn't around; Abuela usually went everywhere with us. When Abuela traveled anywhere in the car with us, she'd pass the time by twiddling her thumbs. When she caught me observing her thumb twiddling, she'd smile and say, "Look … I can go this way too." Then she'd start twiddling in the opposite direction.

While Dad drove the car onto the Baltimore Washington Parkway, I asked him, "Dad, what was it like growing up in Bensonhurst?"

He lit a cigarette and said, "Well, cookie, your Uncle Joey and me slept outside on the fire escape most of the time."

Then Howard jumped into the conversation and asked, "Why the fire escape?"

"Because we got tired of fighting with the cockroaches inside the house. Joey and I got to sleep out there because we were the oldest of all the boys. We were poor and had nothin'. We ate French fried potato sandwiches every day."

I asked, "So you never had any fun when you were a kid?"

"No we had fun, we just didn't have any money, that's all. We used to sneak into the movies or climb over the fence to ride on the subway. And we played with the other neighborhood kids."

I said, "Did you play baseball?"

"No, we played stickball! We also played punchball and handball. Your Uncle Moey was the handball champ of the neighborhood. Sometimes we went to Coney Island."

Mom asked, "Why did your mother and father leave Syria to come to the United States, Teddy?"

"To make a better life, I guess. Davey had a different story. You know my mother and father were from Halab (Aleppo) in Syria. Uncle Davey said that Grandpa left Syria because he was humiliated for being a Jew. He said he travelled to town one day and was told that Jews should only walk on the sand and were not allowed on the plank walkway. He said a policeman flagged down my father and told him to walk on the wooden planks. When my father asked why, the policeman said that he didn't want a Jew to contaminate the sand. My father was so angry after being humiliated that he asked his family to pack up their belongings to leave Syria and never return. I don't know if that's true or not. You know how Davey exaggerates sometimes."

Howard asked, "What did Grandpa do for a living when he came to New York?"

"He was a peddler. My father carried heavy rugs on his back while peddling them door to door. There were ten of us living altogether—that's a lot of mouths to feed."

"What do you remember the most about Grandpa?" I asked.

"I remember his fingers and teeth were stained yellow from constantly smoking cigarettes. He also made Syrian moonshine in our bathtub. It was called arak. Grandpa's father was a drunken bum who lived on the streets of the Bowery. He'd knock on our door sometimes when he knew I was home alone. He knew my father had the arak in the bathtub, so he'd beg me to get him a glass. Then when I wasn't paying any attention to him, he'd steal our food."

Howard asked, "Did anyone else try to make money besides Grandpa?"

"Me and your Uncle Joey shined shoes. I used to stash some of the change that I took from newsstands and hide it from my mother, so I could have some of my own money. I gave all the shoeshine money to her, to help everyone out. The newsstand customers would drop off their change and grab a newspaper, so I'd grab a newspaper in order to not look suspicious, along with all the change left for the paper guy. A nickel or a dime went a long way back in those days."

I noticed an upcoming sign through the windshield. One of the three landmarks I'd always search for on our New York trips was just ahead: driving through the Harbor Tunnel in Baltimore.

While waiting to go through the tunnel, I asked Dad, "Didn't you say that you never made it pass the sixth grade?"

"Yea, the sixth or seventh, something like that; I don't remember. I went to school at PS 205 and also at Seth Low Public School. Do you know, in my whole life, I read only one book all the way through?"

Mom asked, "Really, how come?"

"I didn't have the patience to sit there and finish a whole book. The only book I ever finished was called *Twisted Clay*. But you wouldn't like it."

I asked Dad, "Did Uncle Joey go to school with you?

"I don't know. The only time that I ever saw him was when we were hiding underneath the bed together."

We all looked at Dad kind of funny, and then Mom asked, "What do you mean, Teddy?"

"I'd run and hide from my father, and Joey would already be there hiding also, underneath the bed."

"Why were you hiding from your father?"

"Why, because he'd beat the crap out of us, that's why!"

I asked, "Why would he do that, Dad?"

"We hid from the truancy officer because we were skipping school. When the truancy officer found out that we weren't at school, he'd tell my father. My father would get really mad and hit both of us. So we hid from him."

"Why did you skip school?" Howard asked.

"I had to try and make money to help support the family. Then when I was seventeen years old, Joey and I gave fake birth certificates to the recruiter and joined the marine corps."

I asked, "What were you doing before you joined the marines?"

"Well, let's see … Joey worked in a butcher shop earning twenty-five dollars a week, and I earned thirty a week working in a tapestry factory."

Howard asked, "So you and Uncle Joey both joined the marines together?"

"We both had basic training on Parris Island in South Carolina, and we were later sent to Camp Lejeune in North Carolina. After that, I don't know what happened to him. I know he served in Japan somewhere. Anyway, I took a train to Camp Pendleton in San Diego, California. Then I was shipped overseas to Okinawa. I became a quartermaster. I was a corporal in the second marine division, second marine regiment, and I served on the Island of Saipan during the war."

"What did your parents think when you and Uncle Joey left home to be marines?" Howard said.

"I don't think they knew we were gone."

We had passed thru the harbor tunnel over an hour ago; I wouldn't see my next landmark until we were actually in New York. I said, "Howard, do you remember when Dad would tell us that he knocked out the gold teeth from the mouths of Japanese soldiers using the butt of his rifle?"

Howard added, "Yeah, and then he had a dentist put them back into his mouth, right? He does have gold teeth in his mouth, though. What about the bullet wound on his hip that he always shows to us?

"You remember that, huh?" Dad said.

I said, "Remember when Dad made us an Indian tent? We'd huddle underneath, and Dad would start talking like an Indian chief. But then he would end his stories on the Japanese Islands during World War II."

Howard said, "Yeah, that was a lot of fun."

An hour later, I saw my second landmark, the Verrazano-Narrows Bridge. We were in New York. I was excited to know that we were almost there. Asking Dad questions about his family really made the trip go by fast. I decided to ask him a few more before we got to my third landmark.

"Dad, what was Grandma like when she was younger?"

"She was like the queen of Bensonhurst. Everyone knew her, and everybody's lives seemed to revolve around hers. Did you know that she was a card shark? She spent many of her afternoons hustling the neighbors at the park."

"When did Grandpa die?"

"I don't know … I think he was in his late sixties or something like that. Grandpa was a respected member in the Jewish community and was even asked to become a rabbi. But he didn't think he had the know-how to do it. Your Uncle Ike said that when Grandpa suffered a heart attack, he was placed on an army cot and left in a hospital hallway to die. He pleaded with them to move him into a regular room with full medical care. Ike finally had him transported to another hospital and into a room with a bed and clean sheets. Ike said he died twenty minutes later."

We passed my third and final landmark, the "Welcome to Brooklyn" sign. Later we turned down Bay Parkway into Bensonhurst, and then we finally stopped in front of Grandma's apartment. We all got out of the car kind of slow; it'd been a long ride and we were all stiff. We walked up the cement stairs and noticed her front door was wide open, and so we all just went inside. Dad yelled out, "Ma!"

Grandma came walking out from the kitchen. In her heavy Syrian accent I heard, "Oh … hello, everybody is here? Abie, I did not think you were coming till much later." Grandma called Dad Abie because it was short for his real name, Abraham.

"We had no traffic, Ma," Dad said. She hugged and kissed him.

Mom walked over to kiss Grandma. "Hello darling, you stay so young and beautiful," Grandma said. Then she gazed over toward Howard and me. Okay, here it came, Grandma's traditional greeting for us kids. Howard wasn't exactly a kid anymore, but I'm sure he'd still get the same treatment. Anytime the kids would pay her a visit, she'd insist that we lined up in front of her, one by one, so she could pinch our cheeks really hard and recite, *"Abo tizo … Aboose abo."* It was Syrian slang that translated to "Kiss my ass" but in a nice and loving way. She sat down in her chair and then called Howard to give her a hug. "Howard, you are man now; come here to your Grandma." I started laughing because he still got his pinch on the cheek.

Then finally it was my turn. I slowly walked over to her and bent down to hug her. "Hi, Grandma, it's so good to see you." Here it came, the famous Grandma pinch.

Ouch! It felt like she grabbed the entire right side of my face. She twisted it around like it was rubber and then kept holding onto it. She looked so happy, though, and while she held on to my cheek, she screamed, *"Aboose!* You so handsome like your father."

Then I had an idea to distract her so she'd finally let go of me. As she held a huge chunk of my face in her tight Grandma grip, I could barely speak but managed to blurt out, "Grandma, I learned some new Syrian words for you."

"Oh really, how wonderful, tell me, tell me." Whew! She finally let go of my face.

I stood there in front of her and pronounced in my best Syrian accent, "*Mejnoon, fuluus,* and *khara.*" We used those words at Dad's store all the time.

She repeated the words back to me after I said them to her. Then she started laughing while nodding her head and clapping her hands. "You say *khara*? That means shit in Arabic ... very good!" She sat up from her chair and said, "Okay, now you all go eat!" She headed for the kitchen and then quickly walked back with an enormous tray furnished with all types of fruit. I could see the many gold bracelets that she wore around her wrists as she presented the tray. "Come, eat, eat!"

At that moment Uncle Maxie appeared from the back of Grandma's apartment and said, "Look who's all here; it's the Washington DC Shashows... I don't believe it!" His hair was all messed up like he had just woken up; he wore a white undershirt and no shoes, and he looked like he hadn't shaved for days. Uncle Maxie lived with Grandma and took care of her. After hugging and kissing everyone else, he finally looked over at me and said, "Come over here, Raymond, you little piece of *khara* you. Give your Uncle Maxie a big kiss." All the kids thought that Uncle Maxie was really cool. His trademark was his dark sunglasses. Ever since I was little, I rarely saw him without his sunglasses on. He usually wore them inside the house, so it was unusual for me to catch a glimpse of his eyes. Maxie was the youngest of my dad's brothers and sisters.

Only two events stood out in my mind about Uncle Maxie. Back in Baltimore, he once came to visit us and spent the night. We set up a basketball hoop in the basement. Uncle Maxie, Howard, and I played down there for hours. We must have had a lot of fun because we still talked about it. The other time was when we were on a family trip in Atlantic City. We visited Uncle Maxie on the boardwalk. He worked at a really cool store there and gave us a professional-looking bingo game as a gift. I usually only saw him at Bar mitzvahs and weddings.

Our family really looked forward to those huge family get-togethers. Dad said it was where the women came dressed to kill; everyone looked their sharpest at those big affairs. They all mingled and bragged about their accomplishments in life. There'd be Arabic music and a beautiful belly dancer too. Grandma always got up and danced to the Arabic music. She'd dance alone with her arms raised and hands waving in the air, and then all the other relatives would circle around her clapping their hands to the music. Then Uncle Ike's brother stole the show by dancing with a drink on top of his head. But at some point during the event, someone had made sure that a joyous rendition of "Hava Nagila" was played. And it was really something to see both of my grandmothers sitting side by side at the same table together; each were born in the late 1800s and came from two very different parts of the world. I could only imagine the history that may have been shared between them, if only they would have been able to communicate. They'd both sit at the table, proud and authentic, without uttering a word to one another. I think those were the moments we took for granted—spending more time with our elders and investigating their past. I think we can learn a lot from our grandparents, much more than any history book can tell us.

The ritual I always remembered at every huge affair was when my cousin Howard from Baltimore fooled around with Fat Bobby's daughter, Fawn. Uncle Joey's son kind of looked like Art Garfunkel because of his hair style. Fawn resembled the actress Susan Sarandon. What was so unusual about their bar mitzvah flings was that their personalities were complete opposites. My cousin Howard was really shy, quiet, and kind of awkward; Fawn was outgoing and flirtatious. I guess it's true that opposites do attract. I'd watch them slowly and inconspicuously inch their way toward each other at every big affair. Later, I'd see them smooching in a corner somewhere and then they'd just disappear. We had plenty of Howards in our family because of Grandpa. All of the firstborn sons were named after Grandpa Howard. Uncle Banjo's son was the first Howard, but he changed his name to Roy. If the first born was a female, then their name began with a C, after Grandma Cecelia.

All of Dad's brothers and sisters had Hebrew names, but they were all nicknamed like a who's who of 1930s mob bosses. My Uncle Isaac became "Banjo," Jack became "Jackie," Samuel became "Sammy," Moshe became "Moey," David became "Davey," Joseph became "Joey," Max became "Maxie," and my father Abraham became "Teddy." My Aunt Rachel became "Penny." Only my Aunt Esther used her given name. Almost everyone in my family owned a retail store.

Grandma's apartment didn't have any air-conditioning. But there were the sounds of electric fans running constantly, and we always seemed to visit during those hot and humid summer months. I'd usually sleep on a hard piece of furniture that appeared to be attached to the wall, but I think it was actually a couch. The room was like a separate den at the very front of her apartment; I looked out the window and saw the street. It was also the room where everyone watched television and socialized, even though it was small.

Grandma brought out some Syrian snacks like kibbeh, sambusak, baklava, and bags of ka'ak. Every time we visited Brooklyn, we'd bring back bags and bags of ka'ak. It was kind of a bread ring sprinkled with sesame seeds. Howard and I would keep eating them until our stomachs hurt. All day long more and more family dropped in to visit with us. I was always happy to see Debbie, Mona, and Cory, who were my older cousins and were very pretty girls. Debbie was probably the most energetic of the three; she always smiled, so it looked like she had permanent dimples. Mona and Cory were sisters. When Mona spoke, I could always hear the seriousness in her voice, so I always paid extra attention to what she had to say. I never called Cory by her real name; it was always "Twiggy." I guess to me, she always looked like that famous English model. And of course, all three girls had thick Brooklyn accents. I really liked that and thought they sounded cool.

Later, Uncle Jackie dropped in and took us all out to dinner at a Chinese restaurant down the street. In Bensonhurst, it seemed like everything you ever needed was within walking distance. I liked the people too. They were definitely different from the people in Washington, much louder and sorta rough. They were never afraid to tell you what they thought; they just came out and said it. I'm sure there were some people that were offended by that, but not me. I knew better; after all, my dad was one of them.

Uncle Jackie and Uncle Moey were built the same. Jackie worked as a salesman at my Uncle Sammy's store, Victoria Cameras, on Broadway. Uncle Sammy's store was open from nine to midnight and operated seven days a week. He had fifteen salesmen working there on commission. I visited the store once with Mom and Dad. Uncle Sammy's store looked a lot like Dad's store on F Street. Even all the signs looked the same. Dad always said that Syrians referred to their stores as a yo-yo store, because of the unusual mix of merchandise. Syrian Jews also had a natural technique for selling just about anything, and it apparently flowed through all of our veins. Our descendants probably peddled souvenirs after the Christ child was born or when Moses had parted the Red Sea.

Uncle Jackie never called me by my right name; he always called me "Rainbow." He knew I collected lots of baseball cards, but he always referred to them as baseball tickets. He was a huge Mets fan. Awhile back, he came to stay with Uncle Joey in Baltimore and then came to work at Dad's store for a day. I went to work on that day and got to watch him in action. He really enjoyed selling camera outfits. He'd offer the customer a 35mm SLR camera body at cost. Then he would "saff their brains out" on the camera lenses or any other accessories. It seemed like the New York salesmen always took it up a couple of notches more than we did; they were true hustlers. You could get away with sales tactics like that in New York City. Retail stores in Washington DC had a much different mind-set for conducting business with their customers, and so Uncle Jackie couldn't make the sale. But it was something watching one of the masters at work that day.

The next morning I woke up sweating and sore. Uncle Maxie, Dad, and Howard were chatting while watching television and eating fruit, just a few feet from my couch bed. After hanging out with them for awhile, we packed up and said our good-byes. Howard drove most of the way home, back to Maryland.

Chapter Eight

Psychedelic Days

By 1969, it was time to move again, and this time to a home in Camp Springs. We moved to a place called Westchester Estates, only ten minutes away from Andrew Air Force Base. Howard's bedroom was in the basement with Dad's built-in bar nearby. My bedroom was upstairs across the hall from Mom and Dad's room and next door to Abuela's. The back yard was huge with an upstairs sundeck. Mom and Dad threw several parties to flaunt their new home and Dad's success. And Howard threw a few psychedelic parties of his own.

Dad brought me down to work with him more and more, especially during the summer when I didn't have any school. Howard was dating girls at a Don Juan pace, and so he left most of his weekends freed up for dates. He'd break up with a girl and then they'd cry to Mom. I liked it when he brought his girlfriends home, though, because I'd be the cute little brother and usually got asked to sit on their laps. Mom needed a change and went to work for Woodward and Lothrop, a department store in Marlow Heights. She became the queen of the wig department and broke sales records selling wigs. It was usually just Dad and me going downtown to work together.

We left the house after bagels and coffee. Yup, I'd already started to drink coffee. Then we headed for F Street. Everyone at the store seemed to look hip, as if they blended in with the times or something. Longer sideburns were definitely the way to go for all generations. If you could grow mutton chops like Elvis Presley, then you were really something. All the men at the store grew long sideburns, and suddenly the wet head was dead, except for maybe Uncle Joey, who wasn't ready to conform yet. The men all grew their hair a bit longer too; Dad took it a step further and grew a mustache and goatee. Their baggy, high-waist pants were now replaced by flares or bell bottoms with big wide belts, and their skinny ties got fatter. Bernadette sported a huge afro.

Even the merchandise at the store got hipper. Besides selling electronics, Chin Lung Art Gallery now carried psychedelic black light posters, which were displayed on the walls where fine art once hung. The most popular posters were the black love and zodiac posters, especially the one that showed all the different love positions for screwing. We had black lights in all sizes and incense for sale. We sold items that displayed slogans from catchy TV shows like, "The devil made me do it," "Sock it to me," or "Here comes the judge." We sold lots of items that reflected the signs of the times, like a hand statue carved out of wood that resembled a peace sign and another that resembled a black power fist. There were peace rings, peace necklaces, and peace earrings, and we even tried selling paraphernalia used for smoking pot. After all, it was the Woodstock and soul power generations. Dad and Uncle Joey never discriminated; they carried the merchandise that the people wanted.

It was really hot, humid, and sticky outside. We sold table fans, so Uncle Joey asked me to set up a few on showcases all round the store. The front entrance double doors were wide open and allowed for the air-conditioning to escape. But if the doors were wide open that meant there'd be a better chance for Gs to walk inside the store. But it also let the flies in, which sometimes were unbearable. They were always buzzing around our heads. Dad used unconventional methods to battle the flying pests. He hung up Shell fly strips from the light fixtures on the ceiling. If you happened to look up at the ceiling as you entered the store, you'd see hundreds of dead flies sticking to the toxic strip; it was kind of offensive. Dad would hunt around the store with a fly swatter to try and exterminate any stragglers. But he didn't want to shut the doors, so I guess there wasn't any other way.

I stood behind the rings showcase with Bernadette. She was smoking a cigarette and drinking a cup of coffee. All of a sudden she looked up and said, "Uh oh, here come the hushos … They're early today." Four young, skinny black guys with sloppy T-shirts walked in and leaned over the watches showcase. All four of them leaned all the way over on the glass and started to feel for the sliding door behind the case. It was obvious that they were trying to get inside the case and steal something.

I looked over at Bernadette and said, "I got this!" I quickly walked over behind the watch showcase and said, "Please don't lean on the showcase." But they didn't budge, and they were practically laying down on the case. Since I was six years old, Dad and Uncle Joey had trained me to look out for hushos, which meant thieves in Syrian Jew lingo. They taught me to stare them down and never to take my eyes off them, not even for a second, until they were gone. And because they didn't listen to me nicely, I was taught to walk up almost in their face and say it forcefully … so I did. "Hey! I said don't lean on the showcase!" But the hushos still hadn't moved an inch; they just kept looking down into the showcase filled with watches.

Then one of them spoke, "Don't worry, slim, I'm not gonna steal nothing, we just checking out the watches."

Dad watched and saw they weren't listening, and he started to walk over toward them. "Hey, didn't he tell you to get off the glass?"

Finally they all stood up. Then I got into a staring contest with what appeared to be their leader. Ten seconds later, he said, "Come on, man, let's get out of here!" Bernadette and I followed them until they were completely out the front door. Sometimes gangs of hushos invaded and swarmed throughout the store, making it a lot more difficult to watch them. When that happened, everyone dropped what they were doing and followed them around the store until they finally left. In husho frustration, they'd usually knock over a display or steal a souvenir for spite before their departure.

About twenty minutes after the hushos left, I noticed a really tall black gentleman walking slowly toward me. He started to fumble around with the merchandise on the center aisle case and acted kind of suspicious. He finally stole something and hid it in his pocket. Then he continued to walk toward me and bent down to say something. I was ready to confront him about the stolen item in his pocket when he said, "Are you watching me, man? You'd better be watching me … because I'm a husho!" I was really confused, and I didn't know what to do after he said that. How did he know the Syrian secret language? Then he started laughing really hard, and he put his hand out to shake mine. "My man, I'm Davis, your dad's friend."

A few seconds later, Dad walked over puffing away on his cigar. He said, "You met Mr. Davis, huh, son." Then Dad jokingly remarked, "Watch him real good … he's a crook!" Mr. Davis was a real joker. He owned a store about four blocks away. It was pretty much a schlocky store that sold fireworks all year round. Dad said he once raced Mr. Davis on foot around the 1300 block and won.

I was feeling kind of good about my selling skills for the day. I sold five clock radios, a ton of posters, a couple of black lights, and some black power and peace sign statues. I also sold a pipe to a long-haired guy. Even Uncle Moey was impressed by my sales skills; he officially dubbed me "the clock radio king."

I started cleaning the showcases when I spotted Uncle Abe walking into the store, "Hello, everybody!" Everyone in the store stopped what they were doing, looked up, and said, "Hello, Uncle Abe!" He was my Aunt Sophia's uncle, but everyone always acted like he was their uncle. He was a really nice man, and his size and personality had always reminded me of that comedian Red Buttons. Uncle Abe always wore a shirt, a tie, a sports coat, and a hat. I noticed that his shirt and tie never seemed to match. He usually had the latest edition of the *Wall Street Journal* under one arm. Every time he walked into the store, he'd cheerfully announce the same greeting: "Hello, everybody!" Then he'd swiftly remove his handkerchief from his back pocket and pat his brow and then wipe his mouth. He did it every time; I guess it was his trademark. Dad said he never married because his one true love married someone else. Last month, Uncle Abe had set up a few racks of various types of nursing uniforms and outfits near the back of the store. It was all he had left from his uniform store after the riots. Uncle Abe wasn't one of the lucky ones; his store was burned out by the rioters. He was still wiping down his brow when he asked Dad, "Any action today?"

Dad nodded his head and said, "Yeah, not too bad."

Abe smiled and said, "The market is up sixty points; I made a few dollars today."

"That's very good Uncle Abe!" Dad said.

Uncle Joey was dusting the souvenirs with the feather duster when he yelled, "Raymond made all the sales today! How many clock radios did you sell today, son?"

I smiled and said, "Five! And I even sold a clock radio to Mayor Washington."

Uncle Abe smiled and said, "That's wonderful, Bubula, keep up the good work." Then he looked at Uncle Joey and said, "How about a drink, gentlemen?" I watched them crowd together behind a showcase, and then Dad poured from the stashed J&B bottle into three empty glasses. Uncle Abe picked up the glass to take a swig and noticed a fly floating in his glass. He reached into the glass, picked out the fly, and then said, "You had your turn; now it's mine."

***

After Howard graduated from high school in 1970, he went to work full time at Dad's store. Fat Bobby had already quit the store to pursue other interests somewhere in South America, and so Howard was the new 35mm SLR camera expert.

It was the Fourth of July at Chin Lung, usually a decent retail day but much better for the liquor stores. Bernadette was trying to stir up some business by hollering at all the customers in the lobby who were gazing at our show windows. "Come inside, we have some great Fourth of July specials, and it's nice and cool in there, too. If you see something you like in the window, let me know, and I'll give you a huge discount." She started laughing when she walked back inside. I think Bernadette cracked herself up.

I walked over toward Dad and told him about a huge event today at the National Mall. The event was called "Honor America Day." Bob Hope, Billy Graham, and a ton of performers including Ann Margaret were going to be there. Ann Margaret was actually the real reason why I wanted to go. I asked Dad, "So you want take a walk and check out the show for awhile?"

Dad always liked to investigate events around town, so without hesitating he said, "*Yallah* … let's go! Joey, I'm going to take a walk with Raymond; we'll see you later … Let's go, Bernadette, we need a few sales; it's payday."

Bernadette replied, "No problem, Mister S."

Dad and I walked all the way down to the National Mall. The mall is the area between the Lincoln Memorial and the Capitol; the Washington Monument provided a division. When we got there, thousands of people were already standing and waiting for the show to begin. We tried to get closer to the stage, but it was impossible. We were there for less than ten minutes when a cloud of smoke headed our way. Within seconds the toxic vapor slammed into us with vengeance; my eyes started burning, and I gagged and started coughing. The burning was so intense that we had to start running to avoid the torture. Dad and I ran as fast as we could alongside moms and dads with their small children, to escape the drifting mist of tear gas. Many of the sprinting families stopped at park water fountains to wash out the eyes of their children. Dad and I just kept running until we were completely out of harm's way. I found out later that the park police had tear gassed a bunch of protesting yippies (a radical group started by Abbie Hoffman and Jerry Rubin), who threw rocks at them after climbing up trees. The tear gas smoke had caught the wind and drifted our way. Anyway, we missed the show, and I didn't get to see Ann Margaret because of those yippie schmucks, so we headed back to Chin Lung. All was not lost, because I went home with a brand-new mini bike. Dad and Uncle Joey had bought a couple of them to see if they would sell, but it turned out to be more trouble just having them around, because of constant groups of hushos trying to steal them. I got the blue mini bike, and the brown one went with my cousin David. I inherited instant popularity and started a mini bike club back home with my friends.

In October, Uncle Joey had somehow got tickets to the 1970 World Series and invited me to go with them. This was one of the greatest moments in my life. Because the game was on a Wednesday afternoon, I told my teacher that I would need to miss class on that day. She was actually very happy for me that I got to go. She acted as if it was an historical event, and I guess it was. It was game four, my beloved Baltimore Orioles against the Big Red Machine, the Cincinnati Reds. If the Orioles won the game, they would be world champions—and I'd be there in person to see it unfold and be part of history.

Howard drove me downtown after school ended on Tuesday. I went home with Uncle Joey, Uncle Moey, and Bernadette that evening after the store had closed, and I spent the night at Joey's house in Randallstown. Bernadette caught a ride home with Joey anytime she stayed late at the store. I was going to watch the World Series the next day with my cousins David and Seth. We talked about the game till midnight and then had trouble sleeping; I was way too excited.

We got to Memorial Stadium on 33rd Street in downtown Baltimore early the next day. It was the first time that I saw an Orioles game at Memorial Stadium. Uncle Joey parked the car at the stadium parking lot, and we walked among thousands of Orioles fans to the front gate. As we approached the gate, Seth nudged me and shouted, "Hey, there's Casey Stengel!" I couldn't get a very good glimpse of his face. Seth pointed him out for me, and then I saw a man around eighty years old moving very slowly through the crowd of people.

It took us awhile to get through the front gate and get seated. Our group were split up in two different sections of the ballpark; I sat with Seth, and our seats were by the left field foul pole. If the ball was hit to us, it was a foul ball. The pregame festivities had ended, and I felt the energy building inside the stadium. It was the largest attendance of the series, as over fifty-three thousand awaited a sweep of the Reds and a second World Series championship for Baltimore.

It was a great game. My all-time hero, Brooks Robinson, hit a home run not far from where Seth and I had sat, and the Orioles were winning 4-2—until Pete Rose of the Reds hit a homer in the fifth inning. Then Brooks scored again in the sixth inning, making it a 5-3 ballgame. I just knew they were going to clinch the championship that day and that I'd witness the event in person. Even the crowd felt the anticipation building; the cheers were louder and longer. Then, Orioles manager Earl Weaver summoned Eddie Watt, his relief pitcher from the bullpen. It was the eighth inning, and Watt walked Tony Perez, and then Johnny Bench singled. I was never a big Eddie Watt fan, and so I was getting a little nervous. Then Lee May came up to the plate and hit a three-run home run off Watt. We lost the game, 6-5. I never forgave Eddie Watt for that game. I should have had my day in the sun, to be part of something great, and he blew it for me. The Orioles went on to beat the Reds in game five and still became world champions. It was great that they were champs; I had stewed the whole year prior when hit with a double whammy: the Orioles had lost to the Mets in the World Series, and then the Colts had lost to the Jets in the Super Bowl. That Super Bowl was fixed, I'm sure!

Mom was always my biggest fan when it came to watching me play baseball. She even fought with the umpires. I can recall a game against Oxon Hill when I slid into third base, and the umpire called me out. I never argued with the umpire before, but this time he was dead wrong; the third baseman clearly missed tagging me out. When I tried to explain to him that the tag never occurred, he warned that he was going to throw me out of the game. Immediately I heard Mom screaming from the bleachers at the top of her lungs, "You're wrong, umpire, you made the wrong call; you don't know what the hell you're doing!"

The umpire turned his head to look up at Mom in the stands and said, "If I'm doing such a lousy job, ma'am, then you do it!" He slammed his chest protector and mask down to the ground and stormed off the field. Everyone at the game was stunned. Howard happened to be watching the game that day with Mom and volunteered to call the rest of the ballgame. The Oxon Hill team got worried that he'd play favoritism, and so they replaced Howard after an inning with another umpire.

Sadly the summer of '71 was to be my final year of playing baseball. I was only used sparingly as a pinch hitter because my position was the same as the coach's son. My last at bat was a pinch hit triple that drove in a couple of runs. I had become a better hitter with each time that I had gotten up to the plate, and I always killed the ball during our practices. I considered myself a scrappy hitter who hardly ever struck out, and I was a lot better than the coach's kid ever was. When Mom and I arrived at the ball field, it started raining really hard, and everyone ran for cover. Mom and I sat in her station wagon and watched the rain turn the windshield into a big blur. Then she started to sing, "*San Isidro Labrador, quita el aqua y pon el sol.*" San Isidro Labrador was the patron saint of all the farmers in the world. Anytime we were some place and wanted the rain to stop, Mom would sing and ask San Isidro to remove the water and bring the sun. I think it was Cuban folklore. Mom sang for two minutes, and it stopped raining. I jumped out of the car to join my team in the dugout, and then the coach read the starting lineup. My name wasn't called ... again. A sudden anger started to build up inside me. I don't think I'd ever felt that mad before. When our team took the field, I started to get really pissed. I felt like I was getting screwed. I marched up into my coach's face, like a manger getting ready to feud with the umpire. "I should be playing more; why don't you ever start me?"

He said, "I don't know where else to put you, Ray."

I said, "How about right field, where your son plays?"

"No, I promised him that spot for the whole season."

"Okay ... then I quit, because this is a bunch of crap!" I walked over to Mom, who was sitting on a folding chair that she had brought from home, and I said, "Let's go home, Mom, I just quit the team!" After we got home, I threw out my entire collection of baseball cards, and I had some cards dating back to when Babe Ruth played.

Chapter Nine

The Basement

It was a typical Sunday afternoon at our home in Camp Springs. My Aunt Mattie had moved in with us for awhile until she could afford an apartment. She drove all the way up from Miami last week with her things packed in her car. We chipped in and fixed up the downstairs utility room to look like a bedroom. I walked downstairs into the basement and saw Dad drinking a Heineken while relaxing on his recliner and watching the pregame show for the football game, Redskins versus Cardinals. Our Collie named King was patiently waiting for Dad to throw him some more peanuts. Earlier in the day, Dad was listening to Arabic music on his eight-track stereo tape deck. He listened to his favorite singer, Om Kalsoum, for about an hour, and then he switched to the more contemporary Frank Sinatra. It was the first week of the football season; my friends would probably be knocking on my door soon to play street football. I sat down on the other recliner next to Dad and watched him light up a cigar. Our basement was a great place to seek refuge from the rest of the world. Dad asked, "Who's going to win the football game today?"

My alliance was still with the Baltimore Colts, but Dad liked to support the home team. "I don't know; I'm waiting for the Colts and

Jets game," I said. Dad had the fireplace going even though it was a long way from winter. "How come you started a fire, Dad?"

"There's a chill in the basement; can you feel it?"

"Yea, it is kind of cold in here."

All of a sudden I heard a strange noise coming from the fireplace. At first I ignored it, thinking it was just the logs breaking off from the fire. A minute later I heard the noise again. This time Dad looked at me and said, "What was that?"

"I don't know." I stood up to go see what the noise was, and a big black bird flew through the fireplace screen curtain. Dad jumped out of his chair and immediately called for Mom. "Jenny!" We both ran and hid, and then we just stood there and watched the poor bird fly recklessly around our basement.

Mom yelled from upstairs, "What's the matter, Teddy?"

"Come downstairs!"

Mom yelled again, "Why, what is it?"

"*Yallah* already, just come down!"

After she made her way into the basement, Dad said, "Look! A bird flew in through the fireplace."

Mom loved any kind of animal, so she immediately felt sorry for the bird. "*Ay pobrecito … Why* are you so scared of a bird? He was probably just cold and liked the heat from the fireplace."

Dad said, "It flew through the fireplace, and it looked like it was on fire; it scared the shit out of me."

Mom picked up the bird, cradled it, and then said, "*Mira,* there's ashes all over him … *Conjo,* you guys are a real bunch of cowards!" Mom carried the bird upstairs and out the front door to let it loose.

Our basement was very comfortable, but it looked a bit weird. Dad and Uncle Joey always tried selling new items at the store, and if the item hadn't sold, they'd sometimes bring it home. Dad ordered a bunch of stuffed mini alligators dressed in different costumes. There were alligators dressed in clown outfits, alligators dressed in baseball uniforms, alligators dressed in nursing uniforms, alligators dressed in cowboy outfits, and thirty other types of costumed reptiles. The alligators were never a big seller at the store, and so Dad brought them all home. He hung up wood shelves and proudly displayed the alligators on our basement wall. He said he liked talking to the alligators every night after a few scotches. The theme in the basement before the alligators arrived had been African ebony statues.

We had a pool table down there too, and it easily converted into a ping pong table. I walked around for a whole year in a cast and crutches because I tore a cartilage in my right knee playing baseball in the neighborhood, and then a few months after I got my cast off, I slipped playing ping pong in our basement and broke multiple bones in my right foot and leg. The only positive experience I got from walking around twice with a cast and crutches was that I got to leave classes earlier at my junior high school to avoid getting trampled in the hallways. I was also assigned a really cute girl to carry my books for me from class to class. She even offered to carry my books for the rest of the school year, but I told her that I'd be able to handle it alone. Stupid, stupid, stupid!

King stayed in the basement because we didn't have a fenced in yard. During rainstorms, Mom always carried her groceries through the downstairs garage and into the basement. A few months before she gave King away, she bent down to put one of her grocery bags down on Dad's recliner, and *wham!* From out of nowhere, King leaped up at Mom, striking her directly in the right eye with his big long nose. Mom was all right but received quite a black eye. When she went back to work at Woodward and Lothrup the next day, everyone was convinced that my dad had hit her. The more she tried to explain that it was the dog, the less everybody believed her.

One day Mom, Mattie, and Abuela slowly walked downstairs and headed for the utility room. I knew exactly what they were up to; it was their normal ritual. First they'd turn on their Cuban music, usually Celia Cruz, and played it really loud. It's funny that sometimes Arabic music played downstairs, while mom's Cuban music played upstairs. And then I'd be in my bedroom listening to rock music.

The second stage of their ritual was Mom giving Abuela and Mattie a permanent. Afterward they'd take turns under the old stand-up hair dryer that Mom had since her beautician days. The third stage was manicuring each other's nails. After the women painted their nails, the fourth stage was Abuela presenting their future with her tarot cards. The fifth and final stage was sipping on a Cuban espresso and reminiscing about their days in Cuba.

Dad was watching the first quarter of the Redskins games. I ran upstairs through my beaded curtain and flopped on my bed. I liked to lay on my bed wearing headphones while listening to WPGC, and I'd stare at the walls, which were completely filled with black light posters. You couldn't see any part of the wall, only posters. Some of them came from Dad's store, but I bought most with my friends from Spencer's and at record stores downtown. I think my favorites were the big green rat fink with the flies swarming around him, the Easy Rider guys on their motorcycles flipping the bird, and a Grand Funk Railroad poster. If I got in the mood, I'd turn on my black light and psychedelic light that moved in and out like a spider. This past summer, Mom and Dad took me to my first concert at the Merriweather Post in Columbia. We were outside but under a tentlike roof, and it poured down rain during the entire show. We watched Jose Feliciano and Curtis Mayfield. It was a great show, and Mom especially loved Feliciano because he sang so many of his songs in Spanish.

It was kind of nice having Aunt Mattie staying with us. She was a redhead like her baby sister. Aunt Mattie was stout and stood at around five foot two, but she had huge breasts and big full lips. Mattie was married four times. She once dated Pedro Ramos, a right handed Cuban pitcher who began his career with the Washington Senators. In her fantasy world, she was in love with actor George Kennedy. She had a beautiful operatic voice but never sang professionally. I always thought she lacked confidence in herself. Aunt Mattie occasionally exposed a certain amount of negativity and stubbornness, and I was told she was not the easiest person with which to live. Nevertheless, everyone still loved her. I never met any of her former husbands; she was always single when I was around. I felt sorry for her for being alone.

I decided to walk back downstairs into the utility room and talk with her for awhile. When I walked in, they were all looking scary serious. No one said a word when I came in. I sat quietly watching as Abuela turned up a card from the tarot deck and explained their destinies in Spanish. She clapped her hands, and just like that, their serious trance was broken. Mattie was the first one to say something to me. "Hello, *Ramonsito!*"

"So *Tia* Mattie … how do you like the room we fixed up for you?"

Mom got up and said, "Ray-Ray, I'm going to get everyone *cafesitos, quiere uno?*" She always called Cuban espresso a *cafecito.*

I said, "Yeah, I'll take one."

Mattie said, "To answer your question, *Ramonsito,* before I was rudely interrupted …" Mom stuck her tongue out at Mattie and left to get everyone the espressos. Mattie continued, "You all did a very nice job on the room. If I get bored all by myself here in the utility room, I can always go to your father's bar and get drunk … Ha ha, how about that? I remember drinking with your father when he lived in Miami. We go way back."

"Dad lived in Miami? I didn't know that."

"Of course; he met your mother there. They never told you the story?"

"I don't think so. Didn't you and Mom live in New York together?"

Mattie said, "Yes, that was during the war, though. We worked at a candy factory together near 42nd Street."

I said, "So you guys were the real Lucy Ricardo and Ethel Mertz?"

Mattie laughed. "I guess so." Mom walked in with the espressos and sat them down on a foldable TV tray. Mattie said, "Jenny what's the matter with you, you never told your son how you and Teddy met?"

Mom said, "I thought I did … maybe no?"

Mattie said, "Anyway, your mother and I lived in New York City during the war. Abuela sent us there to learn English and get an education. For a long time we didn't speak any English at all. When your mother and I went out to eat, we always ordered bacon and eggs because it was the only thing that we knew how to say."

Mom took a sip from her espresso cup and said, "I was riding the subway one day when a strong, good-looking army soldier gave up his seat for me. It turned out to be Joe Louis, the boxer. He was such a nice man. Anyway, Mattie and I then moved to Miami together. And later we shared an apartment with Abuela after she left Cuba."

Abuela just sat there quietly, sipping her espresso, listening, and smiling.

I said, "So when did you meet Dad?"

Mom said, "*Tia* Terry was already living in Miami with your Uncle Aaron. Mattie and I got a job together working at a toy shop in Miami Beach. Your father worked for Jack Sultan on 76th East Flagler Street. Uncle Davey and Banjo worked there too. The store sold expensive linens, table clothes, and all kinds of gifts. *Tia* Terry liked to shop at Jack's store, and she loved to buy expensive tablecloths."

Mattie added, "In those days, fancy embroidered linen tablecloths were very popular."

Mom said, "May I continue, Mattie?" Mattie stuck her tongue out at mom. Mom continued, "Your Uncle Aaron was a distributer for Schenley Whiskey, so Mattie would trade Aaron's Whiskey for the tablecloths. My sister Terry had a special business relationship with your father; eventually she told your father about me. Mattie and I needed help decorating our windows at the toy shop. Your father was an excellent window dresser, and he volunteered to do our windows. Then one day he asked me out. Our first date was at the Clover Club in Miami. After we went out a couple of times, he told me that I wasn't going out with anyone else anymore."

I said, "What did you think about that?"

"I thought what an arrogant remark, who does this guy think he was. And I had a lot of boyfriends back in those days, too. But then we got married on July 14, 1951."

Mattie said, "And the rest is history!"

I always liked hearing about the past. It didn't matter who I was talking with, either. Everyone enjoyed telling me their stories. I guess it helped that I was a good listener. Because I had Mom, Mattie, and Abuela all in the same room together, I decided to ask them about Cuba.

"Mom, what was Cuba like?"

"It was so beautiful; the beaches had white sand, and the water was so clear and blue. All the famous people used to come to Cuba. We had so much fun in those days. I was a model before I met your father, you know, and I was good friends with the owner of Cuba's largest perfume factory. We'd sit together at the best table in the house at the Tropicana Club in Havana. One night we shared a table with Robert Taylor and Barbara Stanwyck. Robert was so handsome!"

Mattie said, "Robert Taylor, really? I don't think I remember that … What were they like?"

"Mr. Taylor was very charming. Mrs. Stanwyck seemed annoyed; she may have been a little jealous over a younger and prettier girl sitting at her table."

Mattie said, "You think she was jealous of you?"

"I think so, Mattie; she'd give me a dirty look every time I tried to talk with him. You know everyone used to tell me that I looked like Rita Hayworth in those days. I also met Nat King Cole at the Tropicana; he was such a sweet and gentle man.

Then Mom said to me, "You know Ray-Ray, your Abuelo was an engineer with the Standard Oil Company in Cuba. Papa was actually born in Catalonia, Spain. He was always so full of life. *Pobresito* Papa, he died of bone cancer. And Abuela had a beautiful penthouse apartment in Vedado. Abuelita's father, Augustine Cruz, was a congressman in Santa Clara."

They all started talking to each other in Spanish for about a minute or so, and then Mom said, "*Oye ye,* Mattie, do you remember when Ozzie came home with that baby pig for *Nochebuena?*"

Mattie said, "Yes, all the girls didn't want Papa to kill it."

I asked, "So what happened to the pig?"

Mom said, "Our brother Osvaldo brought home a baby pig to … you know, butcher. And we all felt sorry for it because it was so little. So we begged Papa to let us keep it. The pig became our pet, and then he grew tremendous."

"Was I ever in Cuba, Mom?"

"I flew alone and pregnant to Cuba in 1952, so Abuelita could deliver Howard. Then when Howard was little, I'd fly back and forth with him. My sister Terry use to bring your cousin Blaine. Howard always had Blaine to play with there, and Mattie would usually fly down with Terry. Your brother still remembers Cuba like it was yesterday. After I gave birth to you in 1959, I brought you with me to Cuba."

Aunt Mattie added, "I remember when my nephew Alberto Osvaldo locked the door to the master bedroom in Mama's apartment because he didn't want Howard to play with his toy train. You were sound asleep in your crib inside the locked bedroom. Tony couldn't break down the door and rescue you, so he raised Howard up on the balcony and then practically threw him through an opened window in the master bedroom where you were sleeping. And you never woke up during all the commotion."

I said, "Yeah, I think I remember Tony telling me that story a long time ago. But I didn't know that was in Cuba."

Mom added, "While I was at the airport in Cuba, my arms were full when I approached the customs gate. I carried you in my arms along with a suitcase and my passport information. That *mierda* Castro had already taken power. A guard with a rifle offered to hold you while I presented my information to the customs official. I was very nervous, but I let the guard hold you in his arms."

"I'm glad he gave me back to you."

Mattie said, "You were such a fat baby. And I was very surprised too because you were premature."

Mom added, "Yes, that's right, you were almost three months premature. You had to stay in an incubator for awhile, you were so tiny. When you got heavier you were so adorable. As a matter of fact, someone approached me and wanted you to model as the Gerber baby. Your father didn't want me to let you do it, though. He thought it would be a jinx."

I said, "Man, he blew it; we could have had millions by now."

Mom sarcastically remarked, "You know how your father is; what can I tell you?" I heard the doorbell ringing, and everyone stood up. The ritual was over, and so they started to clean up. I ran upstairs to answer the door. Just as I predicted earlier, it was my friend Fisk, looking to play street football. I looked out beyond Fisk toward the street in front of my house and saw the other guys throwing passes to each other and warming up. There were six other guys out there that I knew from the neighborhood. I was kind of excited because we could have four guys to a side, which was a lot for us. Usually we'd get only two guys to a side. I yelled downstairs, "Mom, I'm going out to play football, bye!"

Chapter Ten

The Newport-Miami Beach

Dad, Howard, and I went to work downtown together on the following Saturday. I got to ride downtown in Howard's Oldsmobile 442. It was a really cool sports car; the exterior was painted gold with black racing stripes. When the three of us walked inside Chin Lung, my cousins Howard, David, Seth, and Caren were all there. I always felt like I was in competition when I was working at the store, to see who could make the most sales for the day. But not against my cousins—just against the sales pros like Uncle Moey, my brother, Bernadette, Uncle Joey, and Dad. I wanted to be better than all of them. My cousins weren't as serious about selling at the store as I was.

We had way too much help at the store, and so it became a goof-around day with my cousins. Of course we all took our turns cleaning the showcases and straightening the merchandise, and we managed to make a few sales here and there. But our refuge became the carpeted stairs that led to the second floor. When business was really slow, David, Seth, Caren, and I chose our favorite step to reflect on our young lives. I was really fortunate to be able to bond with them. After all, they were family around my own age, and we were all brought up around the crazy family lingo. But I always felt a little different. They had always talked about going to shul since we were little kids. And except for Caren, they were all bar mitzvahed. My only Jewish ties were Dad, of course, and being circumcised by a rabbi when I was a baby. Sometimes I felt somewhat discombobulated. One minute I'd be wearing a yamaka on my head while I watched an Arabic belly dancer performing at a bar mitzvah, stuffing my face with Syrian cuisine. Then in another instance, I'd be getting splashed with holy water while celebrating Easter mass inside the Catholic church, later getting fed a huge Cuban dinner. Was it possible to be a Cuban Catholic Syrian Jew? I could even use a clever acronym and call myself a "Cubyrian Cathojew."

Seth chose the highest step; he was almost sitting at the second floor. David sat one above Caren, and I sat one step below her. Caren and David started talking about the trouble he got into at his high school. He and some of his friends got caught breaking into the school late at night. I think some of his friends may have got caught stealing school equipment. Then David asked laughingly, "Does anybody really know how my dad and Uncle Teddy came up with the name Chin Lung Art Gallery for the store?"

Caren said, "I thought it was the name of the store before they opened up this one. Maybe it was a Chinese Art Gallery before, and they didn't want to spend the money to change the sign."

Seth added, "I know Dad and Uncle Teddy were interrogated twice by the FBI after they opened this store. I think the FBI thought the store was a front or something, like for some big-time Chinese money laundering operation."

Then I added, "Dad told me that Uncle Davey actually named the store. You know, he was one of the partners when they first opened the store."

Caren said, "I guess it'll always remain a mystery."

Caren was short and stout and liked to highlight her hair with blonde streaks. She and her younger sisters, Elana and Linda, had spent many happy summers at our home in Camp Springs. We played badminton and pickle in the backyard, went bowling and to the movies, and still continued to play childish games like hide and seek. Caren and I use to hide from her sisters in the storage closet underneath the stairs in my house. I remember an amusing moment when both of us stood quietly and uncomfortably in the dark closet waiting to be found. All of a sudden I heard a thud followed by a confused "Ouch!" I reached around in the darkness, and Caren was gone. I hurried to pull the light chain to see what had happened, and I saw Caren laying there on the floor, perfectly flat on her back and laughing hysterically. Then with tears rolling down her cheeks and uncontrollable laughter, she finally spoke, "I went to lean back on the wall, and there was no wall there to lean my head on." She fell to the ground like a tree in the forest. The only thing that was missing was me calling out, "Timber!" As I helped her back up on her feet, she seemed a bit punch drunk. But if backward falls in the closet had been an Olympic sport, Caren would have definitely captured a gold medal.

While we sat there on the steps, two songs played back to back through the outdoor lobby speaker. We were kind of far away to hear the music, but David had turned on one of the Panasonic home stereo systems located near the back of the store. He had the volume turned up really loud too. He set the station on WPGC to match the radio that played out to the lobby. It sounded really cool, like the music was resonating throughout the whole store. Those two songs, Carole Kings, "It's Too Late" and the lyrics of Marvin Gaye's "What's Going On," will always take me back to the images, sounds, and smells of inside the store and working in the city. We got up and headed downstairs to the sales floor, but not before we all engraved our initials into the old, dust-covered hanging lamp.

***

By 1972, my brother Howard had enlisted in the United States Air Force. He was going to be drafted into the army but decided that the Air Force would be a better fit for him. Mom was really upset because the Vietnam War was still going on strong. He packed up one day and flew out to Lackland AFB in Texas for basic training. He mailed a lot of pictures back to us; I especially liked the ones that showed his newly shaved head. It was the first time that mom was separated from any one of her kids.

Howard got his first military leave after completing basic training. Our traditional summer vacation to Miami Florida was already planned during the same time of his leave, and we decided to rendezvous at the Newport Beachside Hotel Resort on Collins Avenue. Abuela had decided to stay home with Aunt Mattie. I drove down with Mom and Dad in their station wagon; Howard flew into Miami International airport. Monica, one of Howard's girlfriends from high school, was flying in from Washington National. We got the car all packed up and headed south. Our traditional halfway mark was to stop at South of the Border in Dillon, South Carolina. I counted 120 Pedro (the restaurant mascot) billboards advertising the South of the Border on the way down. We ate lunch and had ice cream, Dad and I bought some firecrackers, and then we continued our journey to Miami. About 680 miles later, we arrived on Collins Avenue and pulled into the Newport Beachside Hotel Resort. The Newport was our regular stay of choice; it had a beautiful beach, a huge fishing pier, restaurants, and live entertainment. We took our time settling down inside our room. Aunt Terry called to let us know she was leaving to pick up Howard at the airport. When Howard finally knocked on our hotel room door, Mom answered it and broke down crying. We hadn't seen him since he'd left for basic training, and I had never seen him so thin before. Howard was always a husky kid, but now he looked like a completely different person. He even had a mustache. We spent some quality time talking with Howard, and then he left with Aunt Terry to go pick up Monica from the airport.

Mom, Dad, and I decided to walk around the hotel while we waited for them to come back. The lobby was huge and was full of gift shops and restaurants. It had an arcade room, and there was an artist painting portraits using pastels. Last year, Howard and I sat for the artist and got our portraits done, but we didn't like them very much. Mine wasn't that bad, but Howard's didn't even look like him. Mom still has both of them hung up on the basement wall. The hotel lobby even had a showroom with live entertainment. I stared at the marquee that announced the coming attractions for the Ike and Tina Turner Revue, Little Richard, Frankie Avalon, and The Coasters. The live show that night was Fats Domino.

We walked outside to see the swimming pool. Beautiful girls in bikinis were serving cocktails around the pool to all the hotel guests, and there were signs everywhere announcing a big pool party for tomorrow night with a live band. We walked out to the long fishing pier on the beach; the pier entrance had a bait shop. We stared at all the pictures showing the giant fish that were caught up on that pier. After walking through the bait shop, we saw about a hundred people with their fishing rods in the water; the rest of the people were chopping up their bait. The aroma from their bait was all around us; I think it was mostly shrimp. When we finally got to the end of the pier, there was a loud commotion and finally the sounds of clapping hands. A small crowd had formed and was staring at something on the wooden floor. I finally got close enough to see that it was a hammerhead shark. It was still bouncing up and down on the pier floor, gasping for air. I thought to myself, "Wow, this is going to be a cool vacation!"

We walked back to the lobby and sat on the couch that faced the entrance to the hotel. Ten minutes later, I saw Aunt Terry walking through the front entrance. Howard and Monica were right behind her, laughing and holding hands. Monica was dressed in her hot pants and sported a Connie Stevens hairdo. I always liked Monica; she was certainly the best choice Howard had ever made, and I really hoped they'd stay together. Monica use to dress like a strict Catholic girl back in high school. Ever since she had started wearing clothes that were a lot more revealing, Howard paid a lot more attention to her. Mom liked Monica too, especially because her parents were from Spain and she spoke fluent Spanish.

We had a great week at the Newport, lying by the pool, catching rays, and frolicking in the waves on beautiful Miami Beach. We all went to that big pool party together, and I danced around a group of really cute girls in bikinis while the deejay played Wilson Pickett's "Land of a Thousand Dances." I was a really good dancer, so girls liked dancing with me. I guess I learned from watching Tom Jones on TV. Howard and Monica went to see Little Richard at the club inside the hotel. We ate great food at restaurants like, Wolfie's, Nathan's, Pumpernick's, and the Rascal House. Tony, Gigi, and the kids came to visit us at our hotel, and we walked down the street to a huge outside arcade area and played games for hours. Then we all walked out to the pier and night fished. Mom used her hand line, and instead of catching a fish, she lassoed eels and stingray. Anytime we'd go fishing, Mom caught everything but a fish.

A third reason for our Miami trip was to attend my cousin Brice's wedding; it would be his second marriage. Brice was my Aunt Terry's son and Gigi's half brother. He was a couple of years older than Howard, but they frequently hung out together ever since they were kids visiting Cuba. When they were teenagers, they'd sneak out of Aunt Terry's home at night on San Marino Island and then raise hell up and down Collins Avenue with Uncle Aaron's credit card. Of course picking up girls was their number one priority. I have a lot of great childhood memories of visiting Aunt Terry and Uncle Aaron's home on San Marino Island; it was a really cool house. I recall splashing in their pool with all of my cousins. When I broke my finger playing baseball, Mom wrapped a plastic baggy around it so I could still swim. Uncle Aaron taught Howard how to swim in that pool—by simply throwing him in the deep end.

Uncle Aaron's family was very wealthy. He was a Russian Jew born in Philadelphia. He loved to play the game of golf. He had really thick glasses, big ears, and eyebrows that always looked like they were pointed upward. He spoke slowly, but his voice resonated throughout the whole house. He always had a cigarette in his hand. He'd show me how to bend down for a golf shot by saying, "Bend your knees like you're going to make kaka and … swing!"

I remember walking onto a small wooden pier at the end of their backyard that overlooked Biscayne Bay. If we stared at the water long enough, we'd see schools of sergeant major fish, or if we were really lucky a dolphin fish. One morning, my cousin Bebe and I spotted a dazzling, multicolored dolphin fish lingering by the pier; it glanced at us and then swam off. We ran into the house to tell someone, but Brice was the only one at home. Brice was somewhat of an instigator growing up, and he really enjoyed teasing Bebe. When she told Brice about spotting the dolphin fish, he grabbed his guitar and started to sing, "Liar, liar, pants on fire, your nose is longer than a telephone wire." Bebe tried to stop Brice from singing those lyrics by a band called The Castaways, but every time she tried to explain our fish story, Brice played his song louder.

Brice paid us a visit once when we use to live at Hickory Hills. It was around Christmastime, and there was a lot of snow on the ground. There was an abandoned house with an elevated colonial porch, and for some odd reason it sat directly in front of our apartment building. Eventually the house was used to gain access to the swimming pool. Howard, Brice, and I were hanging out on that porch. I had just finished making a snowball and pretended like I was going to throw it at Brice. I looked back at Howard, and he gave me the nod to go ahead and fire away, but Brice sneered at me and warned, "I dare you to throw that snowball at me."

I looked back at Howard a second time, and laughingly he mimicked the words, "Go ahead, do it." I cocked my arm back and flung the snowball at Brice's face. It was a bull's-eye. My snowball wasn't very big, but it almost knocked the glasses off of his face. Brice instantly picked me up over his head and threw me off the porch. I dropped about fifteen feet before crashing into the snow. Brice was always a bit extreme like that.

At their house on San Marino Island, my Aunt Terry kept a pet spider monkey named Cappy. Cappy was only friendly to my Aunt; he'd try and bite everyone else. One of the funniest moments I can remember about that monkey was when Aunt Terry had to apply an ointment on his ass. The ointment was burning him, so Cappy started to blow into his hand and then swiftly moved his open palm to his ass, hoping his breath was still on his hand to cool his burning ass. It was both brilliant and hysterical. She also tried to get Cappy to go into the swimming pool at times, but he hated the water and threw a fit. He'd scamper away from my aunt and then climb to the top of one of her coconut palm trees in the backyard. Sometimes it would take hours to get him down.

We all drove Howard back to Miami International airport, where there was a tearful good-bye with Mom. His next stop was Keesler AFB in Biloxi, Mississippi. Monica already felt like part of the family. We all gathered behind the hotel to take a final glace at the sandy beach and rolling waves before taking Monica to the airport.

There were two men sitting alone on the beach, an older man wearing a captain's hat and a guy in his late twenties. We stared at them for awhile, and all of a sudden Monica screamed, "Frankie!" The younger of the two men turned around and waved at us. It was Frankie Avalon. Seeing him there, sitting on the beach, took me back to all those beach movies that he made with Annette Funicello. My favorite character in those movies was motorcycle gang leader Eric Von Zipper. His gang was called The Ratz and Mice, and they were the archenemies of the surfer kids. Monica ran down to the beach and took a quick photo of him. She got the snapshot with her old Kodak Brownie 127 camera. Throughout the whole trip we'd have to explore countless retail establishments to find the rare 127 type roll film.

We drove Monica to the airport, and she flew back to Washington National Airport and then had a thirty-minute drive to her parents' home in Suitland, Maryland. Later that day it was our turn, and we checked out of the Newport hotel and then jumped onto I-95 North. Later, I started seeing Pedro signs again, all the way through the South of the Border sombrero tower. Six hours later, we were back home in Camp Springs.

Chapter Eleven

Long Live the King of the Jungle!

I still had some of the summer left before I had to go back to school, but I chose to make money and spend the time I had left working at the store. A man drove up and parked in front of the store once a week and opened his car trunk filled with hundreds of eight-track tapes. Dad and Uncle Joey found another hot item to sell in '72: bootleg eight-track tapes. The quality of the tapes actually sounded kind of decent; they just had weird labels on the outside. David, Seth, and I were the aficionados of the new eight-track tape section at the store. We knew the popular music and what tapes to buy from the guy. We couldn't just pick out what we liked; this took a little research, and we needed to know what would sell. We bought *Billboard* and *Rolling Stone* and scanned for the hottest hundred albums before picking out a fantastic selection of tapes. Our best sellers were the soundtracks from *Superfly* and *Shaft*, "Let's Stay Together" by Al Green, "Brother, Brother, Brother" by the Isley Brothers, and anything by Marvin Gaye or James Brown. We sold a lot of eight-track tapes; the average G bought three and four tapes at a time for $3.99 per tape. We only paid about $1.25 per tape wholesale, so the PR was pretty good.

My sales skills were as good as anyone else's. I wasn't looked upon as just a kid cleaning the showcases anymore. I was an equal to the sales veterans, and Dad and Uncle Joey counted on me to make sales with good PR. I was selling everything and anything inside the store. When I was selling to the Gs at the store, I felt like an adult trapped in a thirteen-year-old's body. It was too bad I hadn't figured out how to get girls yet, or I could have been way ahead of my time.

Dad and Uncle Joey had a great pricing system in place. I learned that their pricing system was actually in every SY store. An SY (esswhy) is a clever slang for a Syrian Jew. Most of the SY's abandoned Syria and settled in Bensonhurst. My uncles in New York used the same pricing system in their stores. Say I brought out a Lloyds model J627G-203A clock radio from out of the wall case. Both the actual merchandise on display and the box were marked with a small white sticker. Pay attention, because here comes the huge family secret—the SY *Top secret lot code system.* Here's how it worked all through those years, and the Gs never ever figured it out. We'd mark the clock radio with a sticker and a code—for example the code lot 9409—and then we'd attach a price tag on it of $49.95. Pay attention to the numbers between the lot 9s. Half of forty would be our wholesale cost, so the clock radio cost Chin Lung Art Gallery twenty dollars from the wholesaler; anything above the twenty was profit (PR). We'd refer to the wholesale number as C-Line. If I wanted to try and saff their brains out, I'd try and sell the clock radio for the price tag, marked $49.95. If we carried a blind item or merchandise that no one else carried or even heard about, we'd mark the item up even higher. If we doubled the PR, we'd call it making yuk-yuk. This system applied to every single item in the store. It was a simple but brilliant system.

Our communication around a customer was a mix of pig Latin, SY lingo, Arabic, or just plain gibberish. A gay person was secretly labeled as a lot 6. Why? Half of lot 969 is 3—Get it? Remember the saying, "Queer as a three-dollar bill?" Also, the number three represented a third sex. We had absolutely nothing against gays; we had friends and colleagues that were gay. Dad and Uncle Joey just had a thing for labeling everyone and everything with their own secret code.

We had some new faces at Chin Lung. First there was Seymour, who moved his engraving and watch repair shop from Becker's down the street to the back of the store. Seymour had a lot of loyal and faithful customers; for Dad and Uncle Joey it was a great way to bring in new business. Seymour was heavyset and jolly. He had a personality similar to comedian Steve Allen, and he acted much like a stand-up comedian performing his act, but in Seymour's case I'd say he was more of a sit-down comedian, because he sat most of the time. He was quick with his jokes, very funny, and loaded with wisecracks. He engraved anything and everything. Seymour fixed and designed jewelry, repaired watches and lighters.

Seymour's son Evan worked with him most of the time; Evan was an expert ring designer. He was a burly, laid-back guy with a big black bushy mustache and curly hair. He was molded out of the hippie generation and witnessed some great rock concerts in his time. He was in the audience for the Beatles first concert in America at the Washington Coliseum, and he attended the Woodstock festival in '69. When business was slow, one would usually find David, Seth, and me hanging out at the back of the store, bullshitting and screwing around with Seymour and Evan.

Then there was Roland, who was a master sign maker and a window dresser; he also repaired electronics and was a salesman. Roland was a really cool guy who resembled an old-time sailor, and that made perfect sense because he was a navy veteran during the Korean War. Roland had a strong attraction for the opposite sex. When, as Roland put it, "a hot piece of ass" walked into the store, he would say, "I need to put my glasses on for this one," and he'd immediately pull them out of his shirt pocket to check her out. He'd rush over to be the first one to wait on her. His first objective was to get her to bend down or lean on the showcase so he could check out her boobs. You could see him staring at them really hard through his thick glasses, hoping that he'd get a complete glimpse of the entire boob and wishing that one of them would eventually fall out. He'd still try and make the sale, but his mind was definitely fixated on her boobs.

When anyone waited on a hot G, it was usually an embarrassing moment for me. After spending a few moments waiting on a good-looking woman, we'd hear a loud and direct voice from afar that asked, "Do you want to take her upstairs and give her a fast one?" It was usually Dad that asked the burning question. Joey would collaborate by announcing, "Ask her if she wants to take you home with her." I was really embarrassed when it was directed at me, because I knew the hot G had heard Dad's and Joey's flippant comments—the whole damn store heard their comments, for that matter. But when the question was directed at Roland, he'd seem to revel in it. As a matter of fact his answer was usually, "Yes, sir, Mister S. … I'm ready if she is." And everyone knew when Roland was thinking about something pornographic because his face instantly turned bright red. When he went out for lunch, he'd come back with a red face too, but that was from drinking whiskey sours. One day Roland was sitting at the lunch counter of the Blue Mirror and sipping a cocktail when Mom walked in to pick up Dad's takeout order. A strange man approached my mom and offered his best pick-up line. Roland overheard the man trying to make his move on Mom and immediately jumped off his stool, angrily interrupting. "The lady is with me!" he said. Roland was very protective and jealous that way.

One week a cute young white girl walked into the store. This was a first; we never had young white girls in the store before. Roland decided that he was going to fix me up with her; I was way too shy to do it on my own. She was a waitress from Reeves Restaurant down the block. I was thirteen years old and she was sixteen. With Roland's help, I set up my very first date with an older woman. Mom drove me to her apartment, and I walked upstairs to meet her. I wasn't sure if I could pull it off, but I did know that I was scared shitless. Then Mom drove us to Andrews Manor Shopping Center and dropped us off. My plans were an early dinner at Bambinos Pizza Parlor and then a funny movie, *What's Up, Doc?* starring Barbara Streisand and

Ryan O'Neal. The cozy pizza sit-down went well with not too many quiet or awkward moments. It was kind of hard to screw up when you were eating pizza. Then it was time for the movie portion of the date. Twenty minutes after the movie started, I made the boldest move of my thirteen years of life: I put my arm around her. She didn't resist, either. Then came the biggest mistake of my thirteen years of life. I never took my arm off her shoulder until the movie was over. My arm was stiff and sweaty, and I'm sure her shoulder was too. She didn't look very happy when we left the theater, and it didn't seem like she wanted to talk anymore either. Mom picked us up, and I walked her back upstairs to her door. I never saw her again after that. I think the age difference was just way too much for me to handle. Hey, at least I broke the ice and went out on my first date—and with an older woman no less. I think she expected a lot more out of me, but my inexperience and naïve nature couldn't handle her. I couldn't figure it out, I wasn't naïve or timid when it came to waiting on the Gs at the store; I even copped an attitude and became shrewd like the rest of them.

My cousin David was working with me. I thought he was the coolest of all my cousins; he was two years older than me. David had curly hair, so he fondly named himself "curly shithead." He was always full of nervous energy and could never sit still; he'd shake his legs or bang out a beat on a showcase with his fingers or twirl his hair— sometimes all three things at the same time. While waiting for a customer to walk into the store, he'd straddle his legs between two showcases as if he were suspended in mid air. David ate his lunch while sitting on the drawers that connected to each wall case. He always acted like he knew what you were going to say before you said it, and he seemed to be one step ahead of everyone else. I never saw him mad or upset; he always smiled and laughed a lot. And unlike me, he wasn't shy around girls. When he was fourteen, he'd steal his brother Howard's car to spend the night at his girlfriend's house. Howard always wondered why he never had gas in his car, especially after filling it up that day. David's midnight rendezvous ended after his girlfriend's father caught them in bed together, and David had a shotgun shoved in his face.

It was already late in the day. Seymour and Evan had already closed up their engraving shop at the back of the store and gone home. David had a few items piled up on the register counter for his customer, a pretty white woman in her early thirties who appeared to have just gotten off work. They were both looking inside the new Speidel ID bracelet revolving display case. She pointed to one of the bracelets inside the case. David flicked the switch to stop it from turning, unlocked the case, reached inside, and pulled out a sharp-looking gold ID bracelet with a black nameplate. It was the most expensive bracelet in the case. The lady wanted to buy it for her husband as a birthday present, but she also wanted it engraved with his name on it. David said that the engraver left for the day but that he would be able to do it. His customer was ecstatic because she really wanted to give the bracelet to her husband that evening. David always enjoyed working with his hands and was always fascinated watching Seymour and Evan's artistry up close.

Uncle Joey warned him not to do it, but David was always way too convincing. "I can do it, no problem," he said. I watched David sweating bullets that day. He gave it a good effort but destroyed the bracelet. His dad walked back to the engraving booth to check out his progress. David looked up at his father laughing, and Uncle Joey looked back at David with his notorious sneer and muttered, "You fucked it up, didn't you, son?"

David just shrugged his shoulders and said, "It looked a lot easier when Evan did it … I guess I need a little more practice." David had to give his G another bracelet. He looked embarrassed when he handed it to her and had to come clean about what happened. After Uncle Joey checked line and she left the store, I started laughing when David walked over. He looked over at me and said, "What are you laughing at? I really thought I could do it."

In September I reluctantly hopped on a school bus and journeyed into an unfamiliar neighborhood for the first day of school. It was the first year of mandatory busing-desegregation for Prince Georges County schools. Everybody protested the decision but to no avail.

I was transported from Taney Junior High, which was about ten minutes from my house, to Walker Mill, forty-five minutes away. Rumors spread while we were on the bus that a white student had been intentionally hit over the head with a lead pipe, as a warning to us not to come to their school. Everyone on the bus was unusually quiet that morning. We arrived at the school without a hint of expectation from Taney's administration. When the buses unloaded, I expected to see an old, depressed building, but that wasn't the case at all. The school building actually looked brand-new. When I finally made it inside, the hallways were carpeted. I never knew school hallways could be carpeted.

The attitude of the students who lived in that neighborhood was unaccommodating. I had an advantage over most students in dealing with all the shit, because we were white and different. I dealt with that kind of stuff all the time working at the store, so dealing with a little racist attitude wasn't going to bother me. I was already immune to it. Their unwillingness to accept us made me think about baseball. I remember listening to legends like Hank Aaron, Roberto Clemente, and Willie Mays talking about their experiences on the road—how crappy they were treated because of the color of their skin. Being bused to a black neighborhood doesn't come close to what those ballplayers experienced, but I could definitely relate.

While I was in shop class, the black students introduced me to a card game called Tonk. They were real friendly about teaching me how to play the game, and they wanted to make the game a little more interesting, so they suggested that I bet my lunch money. Their rules were very clear: if I won a hand, they got to keep their money; if they won a hand, they got to keep my money. Hey, it was their school and neighborhood—I just wanted to survive the year. I did get excellent grades though, although it seemed that the education standards were lowered just a bit.

Mom picked up the phone late one evening, and it was Howard calling from Korat, Thailand. We usually communicated with him through letters, and sometimes we included a cassette tape with all of our voices recorded on it. It was a rare treat to actually get to talk with him. He was very difficult to hear or understand through a constant echoing effect after every word. We'd also have to end each spoken sentence with the word "Over." Howard was part of the 552nd, AEW&C Wing and College Eye Task Force. He was a radar operator on an EC-121 Constellation. His plane was an airborne early warning surveillance aircraft, and he flew combat missions that included stops at Da Nang Air base in Vietnam. I could tell from Mom's voice that she was both happy and nervous to hear from him—and especially nervous after Howard told her about diving into a bunker with a colonel because of artillery fire. I asked Howard if he got the cassette tape that I had recorded for him. It was a very special mix of songs I recorded on a ninety-minute tape; I even included excerpts from Harv Moore's show on WPGC, which was Howard's favorite. Howard was gone so long that I started feeling like an only child. Anyway, the phone conversation only lasted for a few minutes, and Mom cried after she hung up the phone.

Even though he still smoked his cigars inside the car with the windows up, I still really enjoyed riding to work downtown with Dad every Saturday; it had become our ritual. Mom had quit working at Woodward and Lothrop because the excessive hours were just too much for her. Her colleagues gave her a parakeet as a going-away present. Mom named it Woody.

It was a chilly November morning when Dad and I walked through the doors of Chin Lung. Though it was cold outside, the double doors were still wide open for business as usual. The Billy Paul song "Me and Mrs. Jones" was playing through the outside lobby speaker. I passed by Uncle Moey's favorite spot, between the first and second showcases. I could almost see him there leaning on the case, ready to pounce on his G like a lion on its prey. But Uncle Moey was in the hospital after suffering a heart attack. Mom was at the store the day before he got sick. She said he seemed to be very tired. She noticed him occasionally sitting on the steps that led to the second floor, and that was extremely uncharacteristic for my uncle. His wife had left him for another man, and he was taking care of his three daughters alone. He worked hard and needed someone to take care of him, because he never took care of himself.

The store was busy, and it was getting closer to Black Friday, one of the busiest shopping days of the year. But everyone that Saturday was in a somber mood; we worked through the day quietly and mechanically. It was around three o'clock that afternoon when the phone rang. Uncle Joey answered, "Chin Lung?" Then there was a long pause. Everyone stopped what they were doing and watched for Joey's next move. You could almost hear a pin drop at that moment, if it weren't for the music that played outside in the lobby. Uncle Joey hung the phone up and glanced at everyone with a dispiriting look, and then he announced, "He's in bad shape ... get the gates!"

Uncle Moey died that evening. Chin Lung lost a legendary salesman, I lost my mentor and favorite uncle, but much worse than that, my cousins Caren, Elana, and Linda lost their beloved father.

Chapter Twelve

Who's Going to Make the Next Ale-say?

After Howard completed his stint in Thailand, he served in Sacramento, California; Keflavic, Iceland; and Murphy Dome Air Force Station near Fairbanks, Alaska. Howard and Monica's long-distant relationship apparently worked because they got engaged. Mom created a scheme to get closer with her future daughter-in-law—she entered Monica in the Miss District of Columbia beauty pageant. I was positive that mom bulldozed a reluctant Monica into entering the contest, but it built up her confidence, and she really looked great. Mom was really proud of her future daughter-in-law. Monica was a beautiful girl and really had a shot at winning it all. They worked diligently, preparing for the pageant, and she finished among the top ten finalists, but I think Monica was relieved when it was finally over. Of course, Mom believed that Monica should have been crowned.

Mom never liked the idea of forced busing to and from schools. The bus driver brought us home really late, usually around five o'clock every day from Walker Mill. She and Dad decided to enroll me at Bishop McNamara's all-boy Catholic high school for my ninth grade year. I went from a school that lowered their academic standards to a school that was hard as could be. I flunked biology. No matter how hard I tried, I still continued to get bad grades. I had never flunked anything before in my whole life. Mom even had to get me a tutor for Spanish class. Can you believe that? I had a hard time learning Spanish from an American teacher. The pronunciation and meaning of certain words were different than I was accustomed to. He didn't even have an accent. I was really worried about getting a few bad grades. I believed that those teachers who were flunking me thought of me as a piece of crap or something, because I wasn't meeting their academic standards. Then I tried out for the varsity and JV basketball teams. During tryouts, I made a great half-court shot. The coach said, "Who made that shot?"

I raised my hand and said, "I did it, coach!"

He laughed and said, "What a lucky bullshit shot that was." I knew I'd never make the team after that. I probably would have made the freshman team, but I was too mad.

There was a very strict dress code at the school. No jeans, T-shirts, sneakers, or any kind of statements made what so ever. I started getting frustrated over their socialist rules. It sure didn't feel like I was living in the land of the free. I couldn't take it anymore and received over twenty detentions that school year. All of them were for wearing Chuck Taylor sneakers. I ignored all the warnings that teachers gave me and continued to wear my Chucks for most of the school year. I guess it was my way of protesting. I started wearing my hair really long too but there wasn't any school code for that. To serve a detention, I usually had to stay after school for an hour. Everyone sat in a room together and couldn't talk or make any noise. One day I fell asleep. Mr. Era, the gym teacher, was in charge of detention on that day. When the bell rang for the end of detention, he never woke me up and left me there sound asleep. I woke up after everyone else had already left the building. I didn't get home till seven o'clock that evening.

Bishop McNamara won the city football championship that year. I sat in the stands for the big game. It was the Bishop McNamara

Mustangs versus the predominantly black Anacostia Indians, at RFK stadium in DC. After the Mustangs won the game, the Anacostia students pelted our buses with rocks, breaking windows. I don't think it was a race thing, though, because McNamara was about 50 percent black. But then again, you never know; maybe they didn't like Catholics.

I attended my first real rock concert in 73. I didn't consider the Jose Feliciano event, which I had witnessed a few years earlier, to be a true rock concert. Mom and Dad took me to see Santana at the Merriweather Post Pavilion. A band called Tower of Power was the opening act. Mom wanted to go to the concert because she always loved the Latin influence and salsa rhythms of Carlos Santana's big hit, "Oye Como Va." It was a full-blown '70s rock show experience. While we sat and watched the concert, Dad helped the partiers that surrounded us in lighting up their marijuana pipes and joints with his cigar lighter. I was pretty sure that the secondhand smoke had given all three of us a decent buzz that night.

A week after the Santana concert, I bought my first electric guitar. Mom's best friend's son, Don, drove me to Chuck Levin's music center in Wheaton. Don played bass guitar for a rock band and knew all about buying music equipment. I left the music store with a brand-new maroon Fender Telecaster, a Vox amplifier, and a fuzz box to add distortion to the sound. Keith Richards, the guitarist for the Rolling Stones, usually played a Fender Telecaster, and the Beatles used Vox Amps. Ever since I was very young, I had always been a dreamer. I'd imagine that I was one of my Oriole heroes, hitting a home run over the fence in my backyard on Johnnycake Road, and I duplicated their unique playing styles on the baseball diamond when I played in uniform with the Boys' Club. And now I was going to be my favorite rock star playing to a sold-out arena. Don got me started by teaching me a few barre chords, and then he showed me how to play "Money" by Pink Floyd.

Some old friends were back in the area. Gerry and Billy moved to Camp Springs a few miles from our home. I still wasn't quite old enough to get my driver's license, so I'd ride my bike over to Billy's house. I grew my hair past my shoulders and wore a headband, tight blue jeans, and T-shirts with rock band logos on them. Oh yeah, and of course my Chuck Taylor sneakers. Even though my hair was really long, I kept it perfect—not a hair out of place. I'd blow dry it every morning after my shower. If I was somewhere near a mirror, you could bet money that I'd be in front of it primping. I did have really cool hair, though. It was dark brown and really thick. Girls were always telling me that they liked my hair. They'd act like they wanted to run their fingers through it, but I'd never let them. Man, if they did that, I'd have to find a mirror quick and comb it all over again. Once I blow dried and combed it in the morning, I didn't want to have to worry about it for the rest of the day. I know it sounds kind of weird, but I was somewhat of a neat freak anyway; I usually took two showers every day, and if I had a date or something, sometimes three. I ironed my jeans and T-shirts every morning before school and on weekends. I had to look perfect. I also kept my bedroom immaculate. But that may be just a habit from cleaning the showcases and straightening all the merchandise at the store for all those years.

Billy's hair was greased; he wore banlon or fishnet shirts, loose fitted Mac pants, and Chuck Taylor high-top sneakers. You'd think by looking at the both of us that we were the worst of enemies, but we had so many great childhood memories that had kept us as friends. Billy and Gerry were constant smokers. I'd watch them both smoke cigarettes so much that I too started to smoke. I was never a smoker but did it to be cool like they were.

Then Travis, my old buddy from Hickory Hills, came to see me for a short visit. He dressed a lot like me, and his red hair was actually longer than mine. He brought into my bedroom the latest Allman Brothers album and a roomful of smoke. Like Billy and Gerry, he was a chain smoker. My room reeked like a wartime bar, but I never said anything to him about it; I was just happy to see him again. While Travis visited me in Camp Springs, we met up with Billy and then hitched a ride to Iverson Mall. Travis was a natural hitchhiker;

it was my second and final experience for sticking out my thumb. Billy also hadn't seen Travis since our Hickory Hills days. When we got to the mall, we looked like we were up to no good, but we were completely innocent. We mainly hung around and didn't do much of anything until the mall cop decided to give us a hard time. The mall cop stopped us as we walked off the elevator. He said that we were loitering and had to leave immediately. I'm sure he felt threatened by our appearance because we weren't doing anything. Billy had a field day with the mall cop's name—Officer Doodles. He started to snicker and sarcastically remarked, "Okay, Doodles, we'll leave."

For the next thirty minutes we played "Come and get us, Doodles." We'd duck into the elevator and then popped out and waited for Doodles to see us, and then we ran back into the elevator and jumped out on another floor. He'd spot us on the first floor walking around and started to run after us as if we were escaped fugitives. When we spotted him running down the escalator after us, we'd run back into the elevator and climbed back to a different floor. The three of us laughed uncontrollably during the thirty-minute pursuit. We could have kept the cat-and-mouse game up all day, because we were at least thirty years younger than Officer Doodles.

I continued to keep Travis amused during his brief stay with me. Aunt Mattie had left our home and moved into an apartment building in Suitland. She introduced me to her neighbor's daughter, Val. She was a really cute blonde and spoke Spanish fluently; I think her mother was from Venezuela. I set up a double date for Travis and myself. While Travis got ready for our big night out, I watched him standing in front of the mirror in my room. It took him twenty-five minutes to blow dry and comb his hair—and his long red hair was straight and thin. I didn't feel so weird anymore. The four of us walked to the movies and watched *American Graffiti*. We had a good time. There were no fireworks or even sparks around those two girls; it was more like just hanging out with friends. The next evening, Monica drove us to the Guess Who concert. I had asked Monica if she'd take us, and I knew she would. She really liked the lead singer of the band, Burton Cummings. We had a great time at the concert.

I really liked the song "Cardboard Empire," from their new album called *#10*. Pot smoke drifted through the outdoor pavilion for the entire show. Driving home from Columbia, Monica's brown Chevy Nova overheated somewhere off the highway. She popped the hood while smoke poured out, and then Travis twisted off the burning hot radiator cap with his T-shirt. After the smoke cleared, we took turns staring at the engine. We weren't mechanics, but it didn't take a rocket scientist to figure out that the radiator needed water. We were parked a long way from civilization and didn't know where to find engine coolant or even water. Jokingly Travis said, "I could pee in the radiator"—and that's exactly what he did. Travis had to pee real bad anyway. Travis's urine got us to a gas station and then home that night.

After Travis left, I did ask Val out for a second date. I double dated again, this time with James Scalia and his girlfriend. He was a few years older than me. Our families were really good friends. His girlfriend was handicapped, but she very pretty and really sweet. We all went to see the rock group Chicago at Cole Field House on the University of Maryland campus. I didn't know why, but for some reason I stopped calling her after that.

It was another typical Saturday at Chin Lung. Bernadette and Roland were joking back and forth with each other, and he teased her with sexual innuendos. With the loss of Uncle Moey, the store was shorthanded in good and aggressive sales talent. Uncle Joey recruited Nate, his oldest daughter Carly's new husband. He was tall and thin and always seemed to display his big white teeth. Nate was a nice guy and always funny. I thought it was kind of cool that Pimlico Race Track stood right behind his parents' house. My cousins David and Seth were at the store too. Seth was a few years older than David. He had a lot of David's energy but didn't have a problem trying to relax or sitting still. Seth stored all of his nervous energy into his laugh; he liked to laugh, sometimes uncontrollably and for no apparent reasons. He had the darkest complexion of anyone in the family, and his hair style mimicked David's. Seth had a sharp mind for business and an unbelievable memory. He always looked unshaven, his fingernails were always long, and his shoelaces were usually untied. He dressed alright, though; he even kept up with the latest styles. But for some reason, simple, everyday grooming chores were an inconvenience or bother to him.

Uncle Joey also brought in a temporary salesman, a guy in his early sixties named Irving. He seemed oddly out of place at Chin Lung. He was a short man with big thick glasses, and the few hairs that remained on his head were slicked back. Irving was an old-school salesman. If there was a piece of crap laying on the floor, he'd try and sell it to you. But he had a speech impediment, and he talked through the side of his mouth, making it even more difficult for the customer to understand what he was talking about. I watched him trying to sell these sketch jewelry sets that sat on the display bin at the center of the store. The jewelry set included a rhinestone necklace, bracelet, and a pair of earrings, but they were packaged inside a really flashy display case. I think the Gs knew they weren't real, but the hushos tried to steal them anyway. Any customer who walked inside the store was immediately assaulted by Irvin's sales pitch. Irving always carried a jewelry set around with him, and when the customer walked inside, he'd fling open the fancy box and lifted the jewelry set toward their face as he started his sales spiel. Irving was a nice guy but a pain in the ass. For some reason, all my Gs that day wanted to buy batteries. Of course Irving noticed, so he'd been calling me "the battery man," and he was announcing to everyone. "Hey look, the battery man is going to sell another battery!" I kind of felt sorry for him, so I didn't get mad or anything. I let him have his moment.

Uncle Joey looked a bit anxious behind the register counter. He eyeballed all three of us kids goofing around and amusing ourselves. It was a really slow Saturday, and I could tell that Dad and Joey were getting nervous. It was also payday, so we needed a good sales day. Uncle Joey seemed bothered by our clowning around. He sneered at the three of us and then suggested, "Why don't you three yo-yos take a walk and find out what the other stores are doing." The rest of the day at Chin Lung would've been pure torture, if we hadn't taken

Uncle Joey's suggestion and leave immediately. It was definitely not an enjoyable work day when Dad or Joey lost their temper. David, Seth, and I strutted out the front door and headed down F Street to check out the competition. We walked a few blocks down to Douglas Stereo; they were one of our biggest competitors, and the owner of the store happened to be an SY. We walked inside to loud soul music blaring out of huge speakers. The three of us split up and scattered throughout the store, checking for new merchandise and comparing their prices with Chin Lung's. They sold similar goods that we handled, but they mainly carried high-end stereo components and speakers. Their entire downstairs area was devoted to selling record albums. We obviously acted like rookie spies from down the street, and it made matters worse when Seth agitated the owner with fabricated accusations about their expensive prices. Seth just wanted to piss him off because he was our competitor. The boss man from Douglas Stereo was so peeved that he chased us completely out of his store. For Seth, it was mission accomplished; David and I thought it was comical, and we couldn't stop laughing.

We continued our fact-finding mission and walked toward Uncle Davey's store on Ninth Street. While our posse walked down F Street, I continued to listen to Seth's excessive laughter, still keyed up over the Douglas Stereo fiasco. We passed by all the traditional F Street beggars. First I spotted "the man with no legs." He was an old black man that rang his bell while propped up on a small wooden cart on wheels, and he waited for people to drop money into his hat. Seth claimed he saw a large black limousine picking him up at the end of his shift each day. A block further down we passed by "the singing blind man." He was an old black gentleman with a resonant voice so strong that it carried for several blocks. He held his hat out for money as he sang. Both of these old-timers were permanent fixtures on F Street for years. Unfortunately there were *mejnoons* on the street too, like the time Dad and I saw a guy walking around the streets of DC completely naked. But Mom had a worse experience when she walked by a tall, well-dressed black man that held a derbylike hat by his genital area. When Mom walked by him, he slowly moved his hat and showed his exposed *je-je*.

We three so-called yo-yos walked into Federal Discounts, Uncle Davey's store. Uncle Davey had the perfect gangster face. He was actually inside the store to welcome us; usually he'd be out hanging out with his F Street cronies. Uncle Davey's only son, Howard, was busy selling an African G some suitcases. Seth hollered at him, "Saff his brains out, Howard!" Howard exhibited a smug look and said, "I already did." Uncle Davey had a huge store that included a fantastic selection of suitcases and travel items, but he'd make most of his money during the CB radio boom; he had the biggest selection of CB's in all of Washington DC, and he always believed in carrying an abundance of inventory. Uncle Davey glared at the three of us with his gangster mug and said, "So, did your father send you guys out to spy on me?"

My cousin David laughed and replied, "Of course, you know the drill."

Uncle Davey asked us, "Are you guys making any PR off the Gs? You three learned to sell from your father; I learned as a clip man on Fifth Avenue, selling diamonds, ivory, and art, in New York City."

I asked him, "What's a clip man, Uncle Davey?"

He said, "We developed certain sales techniques for overcharging the customer, mainly so we could collect heftier commissions. We were the clip men, and I'd saff everybody's brains out in those days. You know, when I was a kid, I worked as a bookie's runner. And I learned to jump out of my boss's car while it was still moving. He never wanted me to get caught inside his car when he thought we were being tailed by cops."

Then I asked Uncle Davey, "You also worked with my father in the early days, right?"

He said, "Are you kidding, your father and me go way back. We worked on 76th East Flagler Street in Miami together. That's where your father and mother met. He was the manager of that store. Did he ever tell you how he traveled back and forth to Cuba during Batista's dictatorship?"

"No, he didn't."

"One of your father's duties as the manager of that store was to collect from customers who bounced checks. Many of our customers in Miami were Cubans, so your father flew to Cuba regularly to recover the stores losses. He trekked door to door and usually collected around 80 percent of the debt."

David asked, "Didn't you and Uncle Teddy work together in Ohio, too?"

"That would be correct."

David added, "I just can't picture you and Uncle Teddy working together in Ohio. What kind of store did you have?"

Uncle Davey replied, "We had a baby store, you know—infant clothing, gifts, toys, bedding. We named the store Park Lane. It was in Akron, "The Rubber Capital of the World." While we were there, one by one, the factories started shutting down, and then the whole town went on strike. We had nobody to sell to, and the frigid cold and snowy weather didn't help business, either. It was horrible! You know, Alcoholics Anonymous was founded in Akron, and maybe there was a reason for that. Do you remember Tony Bennett's song, "I Left My Heart in San Francisco"? Well, I; my wife, Jeanie; Teddy; and his wife, Jenny lost our asses in Akron, Ohio. We went broke!"

Uncle Davey had a different attitude about protecting his store during the '68 riots. He was out eating dinner in Baltimore with his wife while we were busy emptying our windows at Chin Lung. When they got home from the restaurant, he received a phone call from his alarm company advising him to go downtown and check out his store because the alarm had gone off. Uncle Davey told the alarm guy, "Are you crazy? I have insurance; let them take what they want."

Uncle Davey gave David, Seth, and I the nickel tour of his retail acropolis. We checked out everything that we needed to see and said good-bye.

On the way back to Chin Lung, we stopped at a Waxy Maxy Record Store. Earlier in the day, we had all talked about the latest Jethro Tull album, *A Passion Play*. We spent about twenty minutes browsing through the rock section, and then I headed for the cashier to pay for the new Tull LP. Seth already had the album, and while I was in line waiting for the cashier, Seth said, "It's a good album, but it's kind of different, don't expect the same Tull sound; open your mind to something new. I think you'll like it." David had bought us all tickets to see Jethro Tull in concert at the Civic Center in Baltimore, and there was a good chance that they were going to play *A Passion Play*. I wanted to get familiarized with the album before the show.

When we returned to Chin Lung, I witnessed Nate sitting on the floor with twenty peeing-man liquor dispensers surrounding him. We had included novelty items in the long inventory list of goods sold at the store. The men on the dispensers were not peeing straight, so Nate altered the *je-je* of each man with a pair of pliers. We circled around Nate, laughing at him. He actually looked perverted sitting there on the floor with all the naked men dispensers surrounding him; it was funny as shit. Bernadette and Roland were giggling like they were up to something. I learned earlier in the day that Roland had bet Bernadette on a dare that he'd pull out his *je-je* in one of the showcases at the back of the store. I had a feeling it was going to be a crazy Saturday.

A sharp, good-looking black gentleman walked in and asked to see a pair of binoculars. We had a fantastic selection of Selsi binoculars, and I unlocked the showcase and pulled out a basic pair of 7×35s and also the next size pair up, 8×40s. He looked through both pair and then asked to see a stronger one. I had a feeling that my customer had a lot of *fuluus* (which is the Syrian word for money) so I brought out the top-of-the-line pair of 12×50s. I start out with those smaller magnification binoculars so that he would really see the difference.

I opened the box that the binoculars came in and showed him that it came with a case and strap. He walked the binoculars outside by the sidewalk and focused down F Street. Then from out of nowhere, three pretty young black girls with big smiles ran over to talk with him. Shyly they asked, "Are you Mr. Luther Ingram?"

My customer lowered the binoculars, smiled, and replied in a very smooth voice, "Yes, I am, beautiful ladies." He shook their delicate hands ever so gently and signed an autograph for one of the girls. Then they slowly walked away, still smiling and giggling. He walked back into the store and said to me, "I'll take them." I asked him if he wanted me to attach the strap to the binoculars and he said, "Yes, that will be fine, and I don't need the box."

I said, "It's very nice to meet you, Mr. Ingram … Are you performing somewhere in town?"

He laughed and replied, "As a matter of fact, I'll be at the club right next door tonight." The Champagne room, once known for their famous strippers, was now a soul club starring famous R&B entertainers. Mr. David had invited Dad and Uncle Joey to the new club when it first opened, and they had a few drinks with Al Green in his dressing room. The Lowes Palace Movie Theater, on the other side of the Blue Mirror Grill, was also showcasing live entertainment. Cardboard signs were plastered all over the city advertising concerts by James Brown, the Chi-Lites, the Dells, the Delphonics, the Whispers, the Blue Notes, the Stylistics, and the Ohio Players, to name just a few.

I said to Mr. Ingram, "Thank you very much, and have a great show." Then Uncle Joey checked the line. I always thought Luther Ingram's tune "If Loving You Is Wrong, I Don't Want to Be Right" was one of the greatest soul ballads of all time.

David, Seth, and I huddled around Roland and studied him for awhile. He had an earphone in one ear and listened for clues as he attempted to repair a radio. All three of us rocked in a side to side motion as we watched. Everyone on Dad's side of the family was notorious for using their nervous energy to rock side to side. At weddings and bar mitzvahs, you'd see the uncles and cousins chatting with one another while they exhibited "the Shashow rock." It made normal people seasick. All of us naturally rocked side to side; it was in our genes and part of who we were.

I turned my head to look outside and witnessed Officer Raymond Terzak walking in through the front door; he flashed a big smirk on his face when he saw me staring back at him. Terzak was a cool DC motor scooter cop who stopped by the store from time to time. The first thing he'd do when he walked in was to slowly take off his helmet and gloves and then lay them down on top of the show case. David, Seth, or I would then sneak over behind him, and when he wasn't looking, we'd steal the bullets from his belt, one by one; this was our routine every time he'd walk into the store. We'd always give Terzak a free earphone for his walkie-talkie when his broke, and he was extremely appreciative. He'd shoot the breeze with us for about ten minutes or so and then slowly put his helmet and sunglasses back on, slipped on his gloves, and unexcitedly announced, "See you guys later." Then he strutted out the front door and climbed back on his motor scooter and zoomed away.

Right after Terzak left, a couple of Gs from India walked into the store. Dad was straightening the cameras in the wall case when he noticed the approaching Hindus. Dad looked up and shouted in his best Hindu accent, "Very, very costly ... but also very, very dear." It was another one of Dad's infamous catchphrases. Indian customers were usually cheap, and it would be a miracle if they bought anything at all. The catchphrase was Dad's way of alerting everyone not to waste their time. Bernadette started to laugh after Dad's impersonation, and she remarked, "You know one thing, Mister S., I never know what's going to come out of your mouth. You got a saying for everybody." She laughed even harder, and I could see her eyes filling up with water. "You are really something else, you know that?"

Dad was laughing really hard too. Then he said, "You like that one, huh?"

Bernadette said, "You know, it's a wonder that I'm not a *mejnoon* after all the years of working with you."

She was right; Dad routinely came up with countless catchphrases, and no one ever knew what would come out of his mouth next. My Uncle Ike in New York liked to use Dad's "true or false" catchphrase after ending every sentence. For example, dad would say, "It's going to rain today; true or false?"Or "Roland's going to make all the sales today; true or false?" Another catchphrase of Dad's was admired by his friend Jimmy Scalia. Jimmy's son, James, was someone with whom I double dated. The Scalias were a lot of fun and very Italian. Instead of saying leave, get out, or take a walk, Dad would say, "Ball four!" Anytime Jimmy heard Dad say "Ball four," he'd start laughing and shaking his head in disbelief. Then he'd repeat Dad's catchphrase to himself, "Ball four … Ball four," over and over again, like he was trying to solve a riddle or something. I guessed Dad was sort of an enigma. He made a lot of people laugh, but I didn't think *he* thought he was very funny. Another one of Dad's expressions was demonstrated when the store was unusually quiet. A loud holler of, "Give me strength to go on and continue!" echoed throughout Chin Lung and would scare the crap out of everyone in the store. Bernadette used Dad's adage too, but in a much softer tone. I got to witness that expression hundreds of times at home too, especially when Dad woke up from a nap or sat up out of his chair.

It was 5:15 in the evening, and Bernadette waited on her favorite type of G, an African. Africans usually needed to purchase multiple items to bring back to their country. This lone African gentleman was from the Ivory Coast. Bernadette had already sold him 50- and 100-watt, 220-volt transformers, so he'd be able to use the things he had already bought overseas. Not all the Africans bought with ease like the Nigerians had in the past. Bernadette and her G stood at the very first showcase on the right side of the store, where we kept the packed display of the latest and greatest calculators. The

African pulled out a shopping list from his top shirt pocket and asked Bernadette, "Do you have HP 45 calculator?"

Bernadette scrambled to unlock the showcase and then sat the calculator on its box on top of the glass showcase. She excitedly asked, "How many calculators do you need?"

The African responded, "I need to buy two HP 45s."

Bernadette took out her red pen and a small brown paper bag and wrote down a figure. "I give you both calculators for this price." She flipped the paper bag around so her customer could read what she wrote. Then she pointed to her circled asking price of seven hundred dollars.

I could see the disappointment in the Africans face when she revealed her asking price. He remarked, "Oh, they are too expensive; my nephew did not tell me how much they would cost." He really wanted to buy two Hewlett Packard HP 45 scientific calculators but didn't have enough money. The calculators were priced at $399.95 each. Bernadette questioned the African, "What's wrong? Take the both of them … I gave you a very good deal."

"I don't think I have enough money," replied the African.

Bernadette said, "Okay … Take out your wallet and let me see how much money you have." This was a sales ploy Bernadette and Dad used over the years, and for some reason it had always worked. You would have thought a customer would have felt threatened or insulted by it, but the African took out his wallet without hesitation and showed Bernadette all of his money, mostly in traveler's checks. Bernadette then grabbed his empty wallet and shook it. She started eyeballing him up and down and then looked over at Dad and started to laugh, but she controlled her composure and stopped. Bernadette asked, "Are you sure you don't have money hiding anywhere else? Pull out your pockets … let me see."

The African cooperated and pulled out the lining from inside all of his pants pockets and exposed only lint. He demonstrated a serious demeanor and said, "See, no more money … I am broke."

Bernadette counted out the African Gs money and asked, "Why don't you buy just one calculator for now? Look, looky here …" She scratched out the original asking price for the two calculators and wrote down a new price. "You buy one calculator now for this price." Bernadette quickly boxed up the calculator and headed for the register counter; the African was still standing by the showcase with his wallet out and looked somewhat surprised. She shook her big *abo* (SY slang for ass) on the way to the counter, perhaps thinking that it may help to seal the deal. Bernadette gazed back at the G from the Ivory Coast and motioned for him to join her at the register counter, "Sir … come on over here! Let's go, Joey, quick check line … chop-chop! I want to make an ale-say before I go home." The African walked over to the register counter, signed over all of his traveler's checks, and bought one HP 45 calculator and the two transformers. The HP was lot 94209; Bernadette sold it for $350.00. She thanked the African, patted him on the back, and said, "You come back and see me again, all right? You're a good man." Bernadette moved like the speed of lightning, and I don't think the African fully perceived what had just happened. But then, reality caught up to him, and so he nodded, smiled, and said, "Okay … thank you very much," Then he headed for the exit carrying one of Dad's trademark brown paper and twine packages.

It was already after 6:30, and Uncle Joey yelled out, "Get the gates!" David and I jumped up off the drawers we sat on, and David grabbed the long metal hook used to reach up and pull down each of the four security gates. He ran outside and pulled down the gates while Seth and I grabbed the heavy gold locks, and then we lined up the metal loops on the gates and snapped each lock closed. I never did find out whether Roland won the bet and took out his *je-je* in one of the show cases. After Uncle Joey set the alarm code, Dad locked the front door and shook it, David pulled down the last gate behind us, and Seth and I snapped shut the final two pad locks. We all walked down the street toward the parking garage on Twelfth Street. Seth's new yellow Mercury Capri was the first car to drive down the ramp. The parking attendants had seen us walking down the street and ran to get our cars. It was the first time that Dad and I had seen Seth's new car. We gawked at the shiny yellow automobile for several minutes and then wished Seth, "*Mazel tov!*" Seth and David jumped into the Capri and drove off. The rest of us waited for our cars, said goodnight, and then drove home.

Chapter Thirteen

"Rock" Raymond

Howard and Monica were married in a small church wedding. The wedding party consisted of Monica's parents, her sisters, and us. Mom was never happy with a meager gathering; she'd always envision a huge affair. Howard flew in from Alaska to get married and then flew back to Murphy Dome Air Force Station near Fairbanks after a weeklong honeymoon in Atlantic City. Monica went back to work at PEPCO in DC after the honeymoon was over, and then she hung out with her new in-laws and me. Every time Monica left our home at night, she'd turn on the interior light to her Chevy Nova and wave good-bye to Mom and me, followed by several short beeps of her car horn.

Monica and I did a lot of cool stuff together while Howard was in the service. We'd drive downtown together around Christmastime to see the live Santa reindeer display, and for some reason we always got lost driving home. She'd pass the time talking about her conspiracy theories regarding the Kennedys and the time when she and her friends held a séance at her parents' beach house and talked with Marilyn Monroe. Then she'd gossip about a guy she dated before Howard, who happened to drive an Opel GT. She didn't care much for the guy but loved his car. Monica was captivated by her favorite cousin, Mateo, who was a bass player in a Latin R&B group called Villa (as in Poncho Villa), so she drove me to GWU's Lisner Auditorium in DC, and we watched him play; they were the opening act for a band called Gil Scott Heron. She even drove her youngest sister Lynn and I to Landover Mall to watch all the latest blockbuster flicks. Landover Mall had one of the first multiscreen movie theaters in the area. We'd watch one show for awhile and then sneak out to start watching another. Afterward, Monica led us into deep discussion as she drove us home. She was funny; when she didn't want to finish her sentence when talking to someone, she'd conclude by saying, "This, that, or the other." When Monica wasn't trying hard to show me a good time, she'd attend her tae kwon do classes. Once she demonstrated one of her new moves to me and accidently flipped herself over. When I walked over to check on her, she was only semiconscious.

I remember one evening when Howard had a chance to fly into Washington National on a two-day pass. Monica and I waited for him at the airport, but he never showed up, and so we decided to have dinner together there. While we ate, I witnessed three college-aged kids dressed in weird costumes. One of them carried a gigantic powder puff. Then she started to smack the other two weirdos with it, and powder flew everywhere. It was a really bizarre scene. Howard not showing up that evening was strange enough.

The Capital Centre in Largo opened in 1973, and it was only a twenty-minute drive from my house in Camp Springs. The new concert and sports arena was near Landover Mall, right off of Interstate 495. It was the home of the NBA Washington Bullets and the NHL Washington Capitals. It was the first arena to have a four-sided video screen called a telescreen that hung down in the center of the arena. But more important, it became my personal haven to see rock concerts. And on February 19 of 1974, on a Tuesday evening, I saw my first rock concert there. Billy's brother Gerry picked me up at my house at 6:00 that evening. I was really excited to see the new arena; everyone had been talking about it. The

concert was general admission, meaning no assigned seating. When
we arrived at the arena, all the gates to get inside were still closed,
which was somewhat unusual so close to show time. We stood in
line waiting while thirty minutes passed by. There was still no sign
of people inside the arena to let us all in. Then the crowd outside of
the new arena started to get ugly. Everyone was restless and began
yelling and banging on the glass doors and windows. I thought it
was really cool to be part of that rowdy crowd, so I started banging
on the glass with Billy and Gerry. The banging got really intense,
and if it wasn't for the extra thick glass on the windows, we'd all
be inside sitting at our seats. Then finally—perhaps from sheer
fear—the doors flung opened. Thousands of Black Sabbath fans ran
through the gates looking for the best view of the stage. We were
among the first wave of concertgoers to enter the arena and sat at
the lower mezzanine in section 119. While waiting for the show to
begin, we listened to the large speakers on the stage blasting various
selections of rock and roll and watched the long-haired disciples
bounce beach balls off each other. I was proud to be one of them.
As I listened at my seat to the repetitive lyrics of "No Doubt about
It," a great song by the J. Geils Band, the arena lights went dark,
and the crowd roared. The first band to grace the stage was Cozy
Powell. Powell was a prestigious drummer who had played with the
Jeff Beck Group. After their set was over, the lights came on again.
More flying beach balls, and then twenty minutes of "Check-check,
test-test" from the stagehands, and the arena darkened once again.
This time, the crowd roared louder, and the flicker of lighters lit up
the arena. The band climbed the stairs that led to the stage, and
then we heard the warming up of electric and bass guitars, then
drums. Suddenly I heard the PA announcer's introduction, "From
Birmingham, England, would you welcome please, Black Sabbath."
The music started in unison with the stage lights. A large, lit-up cross
hung over the band members, and they opened the concert with a
song called "Tomorrow's Dream." At around the middle of their set,
confetti rained down upon the stage. Lead singer Ozzy Osbourne
shouted out, "I … am … Iron Man" in his leather outfit and lifted
his tasseled arms above his head, flashing peace signs to the beat of

Bill Ward's steady drumming and Toni Iommi's monstrous guitar rift. At that time Billy started acting a little freaked out over the music and asked us to walk around with him. We all got up from our seats and headed up the arena stairs to near one of the concession stands. While we stood there waiting, Billy dropped to the floor and began doing push-ups at a record pace. Gerry and I stared at each other with confused looks on our faces. Billy wouldn't stop, and so Gerry grabbed him and broke him out of his apparent trance. Gerry asked him, "Billy, are you all right?" But Billy just acted like he was trying to catch his breath. His eyes even looked weird. I never saw Billy ever lose his cool before. After a few minutes, he looked normal again. When we got back in our seats, Billy asked me, "Did you see them all around the stage?"

I said, "See what, Billy?"

"The red devils; they were floating all around the band. I see them every time I hear Black Sabbath." I wasn't sure what to say after he said that, but I was sure glad that he recovered quickly. After the concert ended, Gerry drove me home.

I became so obsessed with going to rock concerts that I would call a taxi cab from my high school payphone, leave the premises, and cab ride to the Ticketron outlet inside the Montgomery Ward department store, where I'd purchase concert tickets immediately after the show dates were announced on the radio. I flunked my sophomore year of high school because of my addiction to rock concerts. I'd buy tickets to shows without even knowing whether I had a ride or not, and so there'd be a bunch of shows that I never made it to. In high school, I became somewhat of an introvert and believed that listening to rock music and attending concerts were good for my psyche.

I hated my sophomore year at Crossland. First of all, I didn't like being treated as a newbie; I thought I was more mature than most of the seniors. I also didn't like how everyone classified each other in particular social cliques. Remember when my friend Billy said that there were three types of social groups in society, Mods, blocks, or the collegians, and I'd have to decide which one I fit into? Some of those principles could be applied to my early years of high school. The blocks were still around but thinning out fast. They always wanted to pick fights. Mods were now called freaks. And I guess if I had to be classified, than I was a freak. For some strange reason, I felt more comfortable with them. The freaks knew all the best rock and roll music and went to all the rock concerts. They were easygoing and would never hassle anyone. The collegians were usually the jocks. Most of the black students were in their own clique. And let's not forget about the nerdy kids who usually went on to schools like MIT and then earned millions of dollars. Each social group stuck together like glue and rarely communicated outside their realm. With the exception of the freaks or the nerdy kids, other groups would identify you as an intruder and would even try to cause you harm. It was more apparent to me when I was a sophomore. I didn't notice those kinds of cliques in my freshman year, everyone seemed more mature, were willing to communicate, and offered a helping hand. Maybe it was because we had a dress code and we all looked alike anyway. We weren't permitted to express our individuality. I had worked at Chin Lung since I was six years old and had waited on Gs with diverse cultures from all over the world. At the store, although we looked and sounded very different to each other, we somehow communicated and tried to work together and always parted as friends. The kids at my high school wouldn't try to relate with anyone different than themselves. I dealt with the real world at Chin Lung, unlike the superficial world inside of my school. That's why I felt those first few years of high school were senseless, and I had to escape.

Skipping school had become an art form. I never thought about the consequences; all I knew was that I wanted to get as far away from the school as possible. I'd rebel against the system and then pay for it later. After I finally got my driver's license, Dad helped with the purchase of a 1975 maroon Pontiac Astre, which was Pontiac's answer to the Chevy Vega. I immediately installed a Sanyo stereo cassette player with an auto reverse feature and four Jensen speakers. Then I recorded countless rock and roll mix tapes for my listening pleasure while I cruised around. At school, I'd never park my car where I was supposed to. Instead of obtaining a simple student parking permit and using the student lot, I continually parked my car in the teacher's parking lot and in front of neighborhood homes in the area. I turned into a regular nonconformist, refusing to follow any rules. The results of my stubbornness were being towed seven times, and then getting my car windows busted out with a brick when my new car stereo was stolen.

You'd think I'd learn my lesson after that, but I rebelled yet again by skipping school and getting into a car accident. I convinced a fellow freak friend, Keith, to skip a few classes with me one morning. He'd skip classes every once in awhile, but he maintained a decent enough grade point average, so he didn't have to worry about the consequences. I on the other hand just didn't give a shit! Skipping at my high school was relatively easy. Most of the time, I'd sidle through the school's front entrance without anybody noticing me. Keith and I walked out to my car parked in front of one of the neighborhood homes and then climbed in. We decided to buy a six pack of beer from this little country store that had no problem selling to minors. We drove around for awhile drinking a beer, and then we decided to kill some extra time parked on a deserted country road. It had been drizzling earlier that morning. I turned my steering wheel to pull over onto the side of the road to park, and I completely lost control of the car. The card skidded, and I applied the brakes and tried turning the steering wheel in the opposite direction, but it seemed to be locked in a certain position. It was like we were being controlled by a powerful magnetic field, and the telephone pole up ahead was a giant magnet. Then time moved in slow motion, and *crash!* We hit the telephone pole head-on. Keith and I stared at each other in disbelief. He remarked, "Holy shit!" Then I noticed that he had a scratch on his forehead. He said he hit the windshield on impact. He noticed that my lip was bleeding; I must have hit the steering wheel with my face. I wore braces on my teeth, making the blow a bit more intense. Keith and I were lucky in that accident; we only sustained small cuts and bruises, but the front end of my Pontiac Astre was completely demolished. Smoke poured out of the hood, and the entire front end of the car was all scrunched in and twisted. I couldn't understand why the car was in such horrendous condition; we were driving no faster than thirty miles per hour. The car had reacted like a beer can crushed by someone smashing his foot on top of the can.

After we got over the shock, we knew we had to get rid of the beer, so we catapulted the rest of the six-pack into the woods. The accident wasn't caused by drinking; we had drank only half of a beer each at that point. We skid due to the mud created from the early morning rain. A car stopped to see if we were okay and assured us he'd call 911. Within minutes Keith and I heard the distant sounds of sirens. I think hearing those sirens coming toward us was scarier than the accident. Two large fire engines, an ambulance, and a police car arrived at the scene. The paramedics took a fast look at Keith and me but didn't think we needed further treatment. The policeman saw the skid in the mud and wrote that in his report. He didn't write me a ticket; I guessed he thought I'd suffered enough. A tow truck picked up my car and drove it away. I should have asked the cop to take out his revolver and put my poor car out of its misery. The policeman drove Keith and I back to my house. My car ended up in the shop for several months. Mom was angry with the fact that I was skipping school, not because I wrecked my car.

It was actually the second time that she was aware of my adventures away from school. On the first occasion, I had left school and decided I'd go get my car washed, oblivious to my mom driving her car in the adjacent lane on Allentown Road. Of course she spotted me. She started pointing her finger at me, and I could see her mouthing the words, "Why aren't you in school?"

Howard's last tour of duty in the air force was at Homestead AFB in Florida; Monica decided to move in with him, and so they moved into a trailer park near the base. It was the first time they had lived together in a home as husband and wife. Later, Howard was honorably discharged from the air force. The newlyweds moved back to Maryland and into an apartment complex on Allentown Road near Andrews AFB. After four years of military service, Howard went back to work at Chin Lung.

To escape the stress that I endured in high school, I turned my bedroom into a wondrous and serene hideout. I was living downstairs in the basement in Howard's old room; I had moved down there immediately after Howard joined the air force. I started to create my sanctuary by painting all the walls and the ceiling of my bedroom a deep purple. Then I created a solar system in my room using Styrofoam balls and black light fluorescent paints. My cousin Sonia came to visit us from Miami one week, and she pitched in with painting the balls to resemble planets. After the paint dried, I positioned all the planets around my room and started to hang them one by one from my ceiling. I centered a beautiful yellow sun at the middle of the room. I even attached moons to each of the planets, implying the illusion of orbit. Then I drove to Spencer's and bought these fluorescent objects that resembled three-dimensional atoms and hung them up on each of my walls. It gave an effect of objects floating in space. I hung three very large black lights around my room and turned them on. When I turned the room lights out, the room looked surreal, and it felt like you were actually floating in space. To complete the celestial space experience, I played *The Dark Side of the Moon* by Pink Floyd. Dad was so impressed by my cosmic creation that he told everyone at Chin Lung about my planets.

One evening during the week, Uncle Joey and my cousin Seth came home with Dad after work. We all relaxed in the basement watching TV. Dad and Joey started drinking J&B scotch on the rocks, while Seth and I guzzled Dad's Heineken beer. I could tell that the twin brothers were getting a bit sloshed, and I brought the party into my newly created universe. I ran into my room to turn the black lights on and then flicked off the normal lights. Then I quickly threaded the Pink Floyd album *Wish You Were Here* onto my turntable. Seth had already seen my spaced-out adventure earlier. He stood up from the couch and said, "Dad, you've got to see Raymond's room,"

Uncle Joey said, "All right, let's go check it out." Everyone was buzzed. When they entered my room, I watched their astonished looks. Uncle Joey glanced around the room holding the glass of scotch in his hand and nodding his head with approval; he smiled and said, "Wow, Rock, your room looks fantastic!" At Chin Lung, my cousin David had dubbed me Rock. Dad and Uncle Joey also started referring to me as that. I lived the rock and roll lifestyle as a follower, not a groupie—I was too cool for that. I'd buy everyone's concert tickets and kept everyone informed about all the latest tours. I even slept overnight at the Capital Centre on a cold, wet cement floor in freezing rain, while waiting for the box office to open the next morning to purchase Led Zeppelin tickets. I was a fanatic! And my cousins David, Seth, and Caren were occasionally right there with me. I even went to a concert with Evan the engraver. Evan and I saw the Grateful Dead. It was comical when someone passed him a humongous Cheech and Chong–sized joint. Evan was the only one that I ever knew who went to more rock concerts than me. But anyway, my room did look really cool—and it looked even more spectacular when one was plastered. We all sat on the couch in my bedroom and drank for the next hour or so before going to bed.

Near the end of the school year, I decided that I wanted to try and work somewhere different. I had never worked anywhere besides at Dad's. I tried working at Burger Chef making French fries, but that only lasted a few weeks. My Hindu manager wanted me to help him break down and clean the kitchen equipment every night until very late. I still had school the next morning and was earning minimum wage, so I said screw this and quit. Then I thought to myself, "What do I like to do more than anything else in the whole world? Rock concerts! I'll get a job at the Capital Centre." I tried to get a job selling tickets at the box office, but apparently it was the hottest job to get among high school kids. Then I applied with a maintenance company that held the contract for cleaning the Cap Centre. My job was simply explained to me. Myself and six other crew members were to mop every aisle and under every seat of the 18,756 capacity arena. We were called in after every event, usually at five o'clock in the morning and right after the graveyard shift crew picked up all the trash. The pay was a few dollars more an hour than minimum wage, but it wasn't the money that appealed to me; it was getting to be part of the rock concert experience. I had first crack at concert tickets, and we had full access to roam free around the arena, which included backstage and the dressing rooms.

I wasted no time; on my second day of work, I visited the box office window from the inside of the arena as an employee. With my mop and silver bucket at my side, I bought a front-row center seat for the Rolling Stones concert. Apparently they held the good seats back for the employees. The ticket price was $9.50. I thought I'd get the best seat possible if I bought only one ticket, so I decided to attend the concert alone. I don't think I could have gotten a better view. It was the "Tour of the Americas '75" concert, and the Stones' first tour featuring their new guitarist, Ronnie Wood. Keyboardist Billy Preston was also on stage with the band. The first group on stage that evening was a gospel band called the Mighty Clouds of Joy, surely out of place for a rock and roll show, but they performed admirably. The Stones were late as usual coming out of their dressing rooms, and they opened the show with "Honky Tonk Woman." It didn't seem like the band was really in sync that night, and the crowd hadn't responded with much exuberance. I didn't care; I had great seats, and so I'd cheer and support them anyway. Jagger even tried riding on a giant inflatable penis, a stage prop used during their performance of "Star, Star." I tried to incite the lifeless crowd by standing up at my seat and waiving my arms around, but I got Mick Jagger's attention instead. He suddenly stood still, put one hand on his hip, and stared me down with one of his famous flirty effeminate looks. I was handpicked from the audience by the Stones frontman, and it was awesome.

On my second week of working at the Cap Center, the southern rock band Lynyrd Skynyrd arrived early while we were busy cleaning up the arena. The roadies and techs had set up their equipment for an early rehearsal and sound check. We stopped working and took a break with some of their crew members. The band was extremely polite; you'd never know that they were big rock stars until they played. The band casually walked up on the stage, picked up their instruments, and jumped right into their debut song, "Saturday Night Special." The six of us had our own private concert with Lynyrd Skynyrd. Man, how cool was that? I had tickets for the show that night, but the other guys didn't, and so they hid in the mop closet till it was safe to come out. When my shift was over, I left the arena through the back entrance ramp to go home and change my clothes for the concert that evening. On the way out, I accidently walked into Ronnie Van Zant, the lead singer of the band.

At the concert, one senseless act kept me agitated throughout the remainder of the show. It appeared as though too many tickets were sold for the event. People were lined up crowding the stairwells and had nowhere to sit. All of a sudden, a simpleminded goon wearing a security shirt shoved everyone down the stairs as if they were a stack of lined up dominos. Bodies flew everywhere, and many of the innocent and unaware concertgoers were injured. There was absolutely no reason to this guard's madness.

Chicago and the Beach Boys marched in next for several shows. I watched the systematic backstage turmoil as the equipment arrived for both groups. Right before our shift ended, we stood on stage and drank beer with the stage hand, whose job was to sit, drink beer, and watch the instruments that were already set up on stage. Of course, I ended up going to the concert that night. I can remember thousands of beautiful young girls dancing at their seats to every Beach Boys tune.

Dad and Howard surprised me with a visit to the Cap Centre while I was busy mopping floors. They were worried when they tried to get in touch with me and I hadn't returned their call. I think they were looking for an excuse to come see me—and to get me to go back to work at Chin Lung. It worked; a few days later I quit and went back to work at the store. I was fed up with mopping floors anyway. I had quenched my thirst for the behind-the-scenes concert phenomena; now I needed to get my dignity back.

Chapter Fourteen

That's My Cousin, You Asshole!

Shortly after I went back to work at Chin Lung, I waited on comedian Lily Tomlin. She walked in, and I sold her a Polaroid camera with several packs of film. Before she left, I asked if I could take her picture, and she reluctantly said yes. She was actually very bashful for the photo op, but she also had a very sweet personality. It's funny; you'd never think that someone famous could be so modest when it came to getting their picture taken. But I'd seen this happen with many celebrities I'd waited on. It proves that they're just people like we are.

We had another new addition at Chin Lung. Seymour and Evan inherited a young man a few years older than me; he was inspired to learn from them as an apprentice and later to become a jeweler. He was a fellow Cuban named Ignacio, but he preferred for everyone to call him Iggy. He and his family had escaped Cuba and began a new life in Tampa, Florida, when he was just a young boy. Iggy was tall like me and had long, black, curly hair. When I first met him, I instantly liked him. He had that certain charm and a charismatic personality that made everyone smile and laugh. His brother-in-law had opened a jewelry store on 17th and G Street, and he'd work at both locations to accelerate his experience. He had a genuine passion in learning to become a master jeweler. Iggy and I hit it off from the first time we met. We were both heavily into rock music and shared very similar tastes. Iggy idolized the immortal Jim Hendrix, Santana, and contemporary electric guitar virtuoso Robin Trower.

My cousin David was at the store. He and I were going to Paul McCartney's "Wings over America" concert together at the Capital Centre after work ended. I cut my hair and had a completely new look. My long-haired days were over, but I still attended concerts at a record pace. But first, I was going to take a walk down to Ninth Street; I needed to get a fake ID. I wanted to get inside clubs, but I wasn't old enough to drink yet. David told me to ask Uncle Davey about getting one, and so I did. Uncle Davey revealed to me a top secret, hush-hush address to visit by his store on Ninth Street.

When I got to the building, it looked abandoned. The address was on the second floor, and so I had to take the elevator. The elevator was an antique, a cage with see-through metal bars holding you in. My first thought was that if I got stuck in this piece of shit elevator, no one would ever find me. I was a little scared but stepped in anyway and rode the elevator to the second floor. When I stepped off the elevator, there was a man sitting behind the only desk, completely alone. There were no other offices, and the walls were bare except for a lone calendar. The entire second floor was completely silent. I looked over at the man's desk and noticed hundreds of IDs scattered everywhere. I'd come to the right place. He sized me up; perhaps to see what age he thought we could get away with. He had to make it look somewhat legit, right? Several minutes later, I left with a pass to buy alcohol and headed back to Chin Lung. When I got back to the store, I showed David and Iggy my fake ID. Iggy looked at it and said, "All right, man, now that you're legal, let's go out next weekend and try it out."

I said, "Cool, let's do it!" Then we shook hands the cool black man's way.

Business was slow that Saturday, and believe it or not, Uncle Joey let us leave the store a little bit early. He knew David and I had tickets for the concert, but he had never let us leave early before. We were really glad too, because we had general admission seats, and there would be bumper-to-bumper beltway traffic heading into the parking lot of the crowded arena. I noticed David was more hyper that day than usual. And he was sweating a lot too. I thought he was on something. Before we left the store, I watched actress Lynn Redgrave walking quickly toward Seymour and Evan's engraving shop. Two celebrities in one day was definitely a rare occurrence. It was kind of funny though—Dad and Uncle Joey didn't know who either one of them was.

After David and I arrived at the arena, we stood in line and waited to get through the gate. David stood next to me in line. He walked away from the line for a split second while I continued to stand in place. From out of nowhere, a fat security schmuck grabbed him and threw him into a bush by the arena entrance. It was almost like David's presence had intimidated him for some twisted reason. David just laid there in the bush, powerless; he was totally stunned. I had to help him get back on his feet as if he were a feeble old man or something. I always hated the security goons at the Capital Centre, especially after the Lynyrd Skynyrd incident, and so I lost it! I ran over and quickly rummaged through the nearest trash container, looking for a weapon. I pulled out a soda bottle from out of the trash and broke off the top. Then I ran after the fat bastard and held the sharp glass object to his throat. I screamed in his face, "That was my cousin, you asshole!" My adrenaline was out of control. A crowd of people assembled around me and watched in horror. After reading his cowardly reaction, I removed the jagged object from his throat and hurled it into the parking lot, just missing two teenage girls sitting on the curb. I felt really bad after watching the girls' petrified reaction. The security goon walked away, and we entered the arena to watch the concert in peace. David seemed weak and shaken. He never took shit from anybody, and I was surprised he didn't fight back. There was definitely something wrong with him.

The following week, Dad had asked me to bring my newly formed rock band down to the store and play in the lobby. It had all started when my friend Mark had asked me to jam with him at his house. I was really impressed by the setup he had in his basement; it resembled a mini recording studio. His friend Allen was also invited over to play the drums. Our sound immediately blended well together, and we mostly jammed to our own creations. We had only played together for a couple weeks when Dad asked us to play at Chin Lung. It was way too soon for playing our first gig. We knew we weren't good enough to play anywhere yet, but we were given an opportunity to be rock stars for a day, and so we went for it. We also knew that it would take huge *cojones* to play in front of a crowd on F Street in downtown DC.

Our three-man rock band parked in front of Chin Lung and set up our instruments. Mark and I weren't even sure who the rhythm guitar player was and who was going to play lead. All we knew for sure is that we had a steady drummer. All of us hesitated to set up the equipment—we were scared. Man, here we were in busy downtown DC and about to play some newly created rock fusion shit in a predominantly soul music city. We were screwed! We fit Allen's seven-piece drum set and two guitar amplifiers inside Chin Lung's lobby. The whole objective of this gig was to create a commotion so that the Gs would notice Chin Lung and walk inside the store, a clear-cut Mister S. marketing ploy.

Our first tune was a long, repetitive jam session that attracted a small crowd. David and Seth watched and pretended to rock out by the double door front entrance. In the middle of our second song attempt, a DC cop walked over and told us to stop the music. He asked me whether we had a permit to play on the streets of the city. Of course we didn't have a permit—Dad never mentioned that we needed a permit! The cop told us to call it a day until we had a permit in hand, and we knew that was never going to happen. I think we were actually relieved when he came by and halted the music, because we were just improvising anyway. We loaded up the car with our equipment and headed back to Maryland. The band broke up shortly after our infamous F Street gig.

Howard and Monica moved into their first house way out in southern Maryland. Their new home was twenty-five minutes away from Mom and Dad's home. The residential community of Saint Charles was brand-new but had little commercial growth. The town of Waldorf was once known as a gambling destination and was actually called "Little Vegas" when slot machines were legalized in Charles County. When we used to live in Silver Hill, Dad drove all of us down to Waldorf on mini outings. We'd arrive at the Stardust Inn, bowled a few games, ate lunch, and then watched Abuela play the slots.

Monica gave birth to her first child, Sean Michael, and for the first time Ted and Jenny were grandparents. The tradition of naming every firstborn male Howard was finally over.

When Jimmy Carter was inaugurated the thirty-ninth president of the United States in '77, Dad and Uncle Joey were ready to capitalize on it. Carter was known as a wealthy peanut farmer, so for inauguration week, Dad and Joey made Roland spray paint the shells of real peanuts in gold. Roland spray painted thousands of peanut shells; he even added a chain to them so you could wear them around your neck. They were very inexpensive to produce, and so the PR was fantastic. Some of the gold nuts were displayed with the souvenirs along with a sign that read, "Buy Jimmy Carter Peanuts," but most of them were proudly displayed all over the store. It was a great idea and we sold plenty of them. Dad and Joey were always into gimmicks and fads to make money. The income Chin Lung made from the inauguration helped to make up for the horrible losses from the bicentennial celebration a year earlier. Everyone thought that Washington DC would be loaded with tourists spending their money during the bicentennial festivities in '76, but it turned out to be a total bust. I think all the Gs went to New York City and Philadelphia instead.

It was Memorial Day weekend in '77. David, Seth, and I always drove to Ocean City on that day, or on Labor Day. I got on the road at ten o'clock that evening and headed for Randallstown, a suburb of Baltimore. David and Seth always wanted to leave around three in the morning to avoid the traffic. I didn't mind and thought it was kind of fun. I arrived in front of their home on Coronado Road at 11:20. I knocked softly on their front door because I knew Uncle Joey and Aunt Sophia were probably asleep. Seth opened the door. When I walked inside, my cousin Renee raced down the stairs to greet me. I never got to hang around her because she was the youngest, but we were actually only a few years apart. Renee liked rock concerts as much as we did, but no one ever invited her to come with us. Seth told me to come downstairs into their basement, where he and David both slept. Renee wanted me to go upstairs to see her room, so I told Seth that I'd be down in a minute. When I walked inside her bedroom, it was plastered with rock posters. She had Chicago and Led Zeppelin posters on her ceiling. She didn't look very happy, though, and I asked her if there was anything wrong. She was kind of crying and said, "Cousin Raymond, my father took my beautiful cat that I had for almost five years and threw him out on the freeway."

"You're kidding, right? Why would he do that?"

"I guess he just got tired of him ... But can you believe he would do something like that?"

"I'm sorry, Renee, that's horrible."

"You guys are going to Ocean City, huh? Well you be careful!"

"We will. I like your room, it's really cool." Then I hugged her and headed downstairs for the basement. Seth was in David's room. David's room looked like a small apartment; it was actually the garage, but they'd converted it into a room. Seth just slept in the basement on a couch that converted into a bed. They both had great stereo equipment. We sat in David's room, drank a few beers, and listened to Barclay James Harvest. Then we tried to get a couple hours of sleep before we left for Ocean City.

It was really hard getting up after just a few hours of sleep, and we were exhausted and cranky after we woke up. When we walked outside, it was so quiet that it hurt my ears. We discreetly piled into David's light blue Chevy Camaro. He started his engine, and I immediately squinted when I saw the extremely bright digital clock displayed on his dashboard: 3:15 AM. It took David about two and a half hours to get to Ocean City. He pulled into a parking space on the beach. It was still way too early to check into a motel. I had brought a portable eight track player with me, so I slipped in the Relayer tape by, "Yes". It was one of our favorite albums to listen to. We sat on a bench facing the ocean, and the three of us spaced out while watching the waves rolling in.

After the sun came up, we checked into Mike and Mary's Motel. We stayed there every time we visited Ocean City. It wasn't located directly on the beach; we'd have to cross a few streets first. It was probably why the rooms were so reasonable. We'd spend the whole day at the beach listening to music, checking out the girls, and soaking up rays. All three of us loved the sun, the hotter the better. It must have been our Syrian genes. We were partying in the motel room before we hit the beach, and so we were all a bit buzzed, but I started noticing that David was always more incoherent than the rest of us.

It was late in the afternoon, and we went back to the room and took our showers. We decided to ride the go carts that we rode last time we were here. Only one driver was permitted to race at a time. A huge digital timer stood on an island at the middle of the speedway. The motive for the lone driver was to beat the fastest recorded time. The go cart looked more like an Indy race car and was extremely fast; the car made you feel like you were a professional driver. We even had to sign a waiver before taking the wheel. Seth and I had just finished our run and actually got close to beating the record time. Then David climbed into his car slowly and awkwardly. About halfway through his run, we saw a huge cloud of dirt and smoke. Dave drove clear off the race track, spun hard, and capsized. Seth and I didn't think it was possible; the cars were extremely safe, and one would almost have to make a calculated effort to crash the way he had. The track supervisor immediately ran out from inside the glass booth after David. When Dave climbed out from underneath his car and stood up, it was obvious that he was stoned. The track supervisor was infuriated. He told David to get the hell out and banned him from the track. I was a bit concerned, but we were young, and so I just laughed about it with Seth and David.

I had already attended two years of summer school and made up the credits that I needed for the time I missed as a sophomore. I still missed out on graduating with my own class in '77. A couple of things got me back on track in finishing high school. First, I was fortunate to be able to attend a new class that was being offered on TV production. That class kept me interested in school. The classroom was actually a TV studio with removable lighting, cameras and monitors, and a production switching console. We created our own sets. For two whole periods during the school day, I was fascinated and had fun. I even got permission to leave the building on special assignments. I produced a Star Trek parody that had the landing party from the USS *Enterprise* materializing on a planet made entirely of marijuana. The crew copped an instant buzz once they landed on the planet's surface. I played Mr. Spock. I even created the glow on Spock's face when he stared into the device used on the bridge for studying planetary conditions. And we had the special effects down pat for beaming down to the planet and back. I was also involved in a parody of Starsky and Hutch that we called, "Kowalski and Hernandez." Guess who Hernandez was? We did some really cool stunts for the show with my partner's Plymouth Road Runner on the school's parking lot.

The other factor that changed my way of thinking about high school was when I finally noticed how a lot of the guys in my social group (freaks) were either deteriorating from drugs or became freeloaders. I think the freeloader thing really pissed me off, especially when they tried doing it off me. For some reason it made me think about those bums that used to hang out near Dad's store a long time ago. I was always a sharp guy and a hard worker. It was like I had been asleep for the last two years of high school, and then I finally woke up.

In my senior year, I decided to take a black history class. The teacher and I appreciated one another. She looked very African. She kept her hair very short and wore authentic African attire every day at school. When I first got to chat with her, I mentioned how I worked with Africans from many different countries, like Nigeria, Ivory Coast, Kenya, and Togo. She was very impressed with my knowledge and association of the different African cultures, so she decided to give me a special assignment for the rest of my school year. I was to read *Roots* by Alex Haley and then get quizzed on each chapter. A final exam would be administered at the end of my school year, which was in January. The rest of the class had to learn the basics about the continent, including where to find it on a map. While I was reading *Roots* in class, I could hear the rest of the students taking a simple geography test. One of the black sophomore students turned around and looked at me while he was taking his test. He whispered, "Psst … Hey, Shashow! Show me where Africa's at, man." I knew I had an advantage over the rest of the students in my class, but come on … he didn't know where Africa was on a map? Of course I told him where it was; I didn't want anybody to look that stupid.

I got to leave school at noon each day when I agreed to a work-release program. I landed a job working in the men's work clothes department at Montgomery Ward for the duration of my senior year. There was plenty of friction going on at Chin Lung. My cousins Seth and Howard were working more hours there. Then they found out that my brother Howard was making more money than they were. Howard was the 35mm camera expert, and he spoke Spanish fluently, so Dad and Uncle Joey thought that he deserved more money for having the additional skills. I think the sons eventually convinced Joey to do something about it. Overnight, Seth and Uncle Joey's attitude toward me changed. They started to hassle me for no apparent reason; Uncle Joey started calling me a "stupid kid." I didn't do anything to deserve that, and I was definitely a better salesman than any one of his kids. I really felt that they wanted me out to free up payroll money for Joey's sons. Of course they'd never hassle my brother Howard; he was the oldest and I was the youngest. I thought back to when we were kids, to our sunflower contest on Johnnycake Road. His flower got to stay and mine got chopped down. Well, Uncle Joey and Seth pissed me off to the point where I didn't want to have to deal with it anymore. Seth got me so angry one day that I ran up in Uncle Joey's face and yelled, "You'd better keep your kid away from me, or I'm going to kick his ass!" No one uttered a word to me after I erupted. I quit that day. It just didn't make any sense to me—why would they let a good salesman like me leave? And I wasn't happy that Dad didn't say or do anything about it. He could have defended me. But Howard was bringing in the Spanish Gs and making the store money. I guess he didn't want to screw that up. He'd just let me get screwed instead.

I worked full time at Montgomery Ward and finished high school. I sold work shirts, pants, coveralls, jeans, down jackets, and leather coats. I had to learn how to use a very complicated cash register, and I also broadcasted the store's public address announcements regarding the latest and greatest sales. It took me back to when I used to read the sports scores over the PA system in elementary school after the principal read the morning announcements. Montgomery Ward had their share of hushos too; they'd hide inside the rack of leather coats and, when no one was looking, grab almost half the rack of expensive leather goods and run for the exit. About half of the time, the store's undercover security guards would catch them. I hoped to eventually transfer over to the commissioned camera sales department because of my experience at Chin Lung, but an opening never arrived.

An Asian guy around my age worked in the department right next to mine. He always bragged about knowing George Takei, the actor who played Helmsman Sulu on *Star Trek*. I wanted to believe him, but it sounded a bit farfetched at the time—until the day he brought pictures of the actor in his pajamas at his home. A picture is worth a thousand words … and he was right. It was a good experience working at Montgomery Ward. I made a lot of friends, and everyone seemed to like me. During the Christmas season, I worked several days till midnight, but the holidays were a blast! We worked hard and played hard. Every department had ongoing parties in their stock rooms. Everyone got drunk and then continued to work on the sales floor. And management was there, right along with us. I never saw anything like it. I continued to work at Montgomery Ward until a few weeks before my high school graduation in June.

Chapter Fifteen

Brown Institute of Broadcasting

I partied heavily on weekends and alternated between disco outings with Iggy and my old buddy Hassan. Iggy and I were devoted to rock and roll but admittedly had succumbed to disco. Our regular weekend hangout was at a nightclub called Gus and John's in Camp Springs, but we'd sometimes end our evenings at the Crazy Horse or Pall Mall in Georgetown. Why did rock and roll music lovers go to a disco? Maybe it was our Latin roots that gave us the urge to "shake our groove thing," or maybe it was the suaveness of strutting through a nightclub dressed in polyester pants and satin shirts, with our top two buttons undone and gold chains that dangled down upon our exposed chest. Maybe it was the coolness of holding a cocktail in one hand while a cigarette dangled out of the corner of our mouth. Nah ... who am I kidding, it was being surrounded by all the hot women.

Hassan's dad, Chafic, had introduced me to him when I was twelve years old at a family picnic. Chafic had worked behind the lunch counter for Mr. David at the Blue Mirror Grill since I could remember. I'd walk in for lunch and see him wiping down the counter with a big smile on his face; he'd look up at me and say in his thick Lebanese accent, "Hello, Raymon', tuna on rye with French fry today?" One day while he worked behind the sandwich counter, a huge Washington DC rat flew up his pants leg and bit him near his crotch. He ended up getting a series of rabies shots.

Hassan and his family had recently moved to Camp Springs, only a few streets away from our home. When we were kids, we were both about the same height and weight, but after not seeing him for several years, I was surprised to find he'd turn into the Incredible Hulk. Hassan had gotten huge from bodybuilding, and I was really shocked when I saw him again. We attended our senior year together at Crossland. He played punter and linebacker on our high school football team and was featured on the front page of the sports section for reintroducing the drop kick. I was the PA announcer for the homecoming game. At lunchtime during school hours, we'd routinely drive to my house and eat Abuela's delicious BLT sandwiches. Abuela knew what time we were coming home for lunch every day, and she'd have them ready for us. One cool thing about hanging out with Hassan and Iggy was that I could swear in Arabic and Spanish around them. Hassan and I swore at each other in friendship, calling one another a *khara* or remarked *kess emmak,* which is probably one of the worst Arabic curse words of all-time. Then Iggy and I would fondly refer to one another as a *cabron* and *maricon,* or direct one another to *comemierda* (eat shit). We'd dish it out and take it, without ever really getting mad at one another. It was all in good fun.

Our parents threw us a joint graduation party at my house. It was mainly a gathering of the local neighbors and a big chocolate cake. Mom was happier than I was after graduation. I did put her through a lot in those first few years of high school, skipping school and all. I even told her that I wasn't going to attend the ceremonies because it wasn't my true graduating class. Man, she flipped out when I told her that. She said, "You're not going to deny me the satisfaction of watching you walk up on that stage and accept your diploma. I earned that right to see it!" I guessed she made a good point. After the party, we coordinated our efforts and toilet papered the entire school. I relinquished all my high school frustrations in a single night with hundreds of rolls of toilet paper. After we turned the school into a winter wonderland, we drove back to my house. Hassan and I both sat on the curb by the street in front of my house. It was already after one o'clock in the morning. Both of us had already made choices about our future; we felt our lives were about to change dramatically. We sat and reflected—chances were that we wouldn't see each other again for a very long time. Hassan had joined the air force, and I was moving to Fort Lauderdale to attend broadcasting school. I'd be the first to leave in just a few days.

Later that week, I said my good-byes to Abuela, Howard, Monica, and Mattie. It was finally my turn to fly the coop. I was nineteen years old and more than ready to be out on my own. I had my car repainted dark blue a few weeks back; I felt it would present the illusion of driving a brand-new car. Then on a bright sunshine morning, I drove out of Camp Springs with Mom and Dad in my illegally packed, dark blue Pontiac Astre. The three of us sat uncomfortably until we arrived at the Amtrak Auto Train Station in Lorton, Virginia. When we got there, the Amtrak crew loaded up my car, we found our coach seats aboard the train, and then it was a noisy and bumpy ride all the way to Sanford, Florida. When we got there, we waited for Amtrak to unload my car, and then Mom, Dad, and I climbed back in for the long haul south to Fort Lauderdale. I couldn't see anything out the rear view mirror for the entire trip.

Once we arrived in Fort Lauderdale, we checked into the Oakland Park Motel. The motel was right next door to my new home, the Oakland Park Apartments. I had to stay at the motel for a few weeks while I waited for the previous tenant to move out. Mom helped me to pick out all the essentials I needed to live alone. She didn't get to help organize the apartment with me, though, because Dad had to get back to work at Chin Lung.

While Mom and Dad were in Fort Lauderdale, we hung out with Tony and Gigi and then visited Aunt Terry and Uncle Aaron at their condo in Pembroke Pines. Tony and Gigi were back together again after a brief marriage separation. On the evening before they flew back to DC, we made dinner reservations at this really cool Polynesian restaurant on Commercial Boulevard. After we were all seated at the restaurant, a very attractive waitress walked over to our table and greeted us with a beautiful smile and menus. I watched Tony staring at her every move. While she took our drink orders, Tony whispered something into Gigi's ear. Each of us gave the waitress our orders, but Tony continued to badger his wife about something, I heard him say, "Ask her, *cielo,*" Tony always called his wife *cielo*, which meant "heaven" in Spanish. The alluring hostess retreated to get our drinks. A few moments later she returned, and Tony was at it again, "*Cielo?*" Gigi exhibited a look of total frustration and then looked up at the voluptuous waitress and asked, "Excuse me, miss, my husband wants to know if you're wearing any underwear." Everyone at the table started to laugh but curiously awaited her response. She smiled and kept her composure, and then she answered, "Yes, I am … sorry."

Gigi stared hard at Tony and asked him, "Are you happy now?"

Tony cleverly responded, "Not really; she's wearing underwear."

I drove Mom and Dad to Fort Lauderdale-Hollywood International airport the next morning, and just like that I was alone. The next day Tony and I went to a strip club. I guess he felt sorry for me because I was still stuck in the motel. Actually, I was kind of honored that he asked me to go. Tony was a pro; he and Dad spent many evenings together at the Champagne room, downstairs in the Blue Mirror Grill. We were sitting there at a table together when Tony and I spotted a completely nude woman. It's always a surprise to see a naked woman, even in a strip club, and especially for me. The nude woman was standing with her big ass toward Tony, only a few feet away. After he was finished eyeballing her ass, Tony turned around to look at me wearing a goofy look on his face and said, "She has a very nice smile, doesn't she?" That comment made me stare at her ass even harder. Yup, Tony was definitely a man's man.

I finally moved into my apartment a week later and then started my first day of broadcasting school at Brown Institute. I first learned about Brown through my cousin Gigi; she worked in the office for WINZ in the Miami-Fort Lauderdale radio market. Before I made the decision to attend Brown, Gigi invited me to take a tour of their station and talk with the deejays and general manager. On the day I came out to visit, the station had a special guest: actor Peter Graves was in the studio to help promote a new smoke alarm product. Mom kiddingly said that she came all the way from Washington DC to see him. The *Mission Impossible* star smiled and said, "Now, I don't believe that one bit little lady." While Mr. Graves was on the air, a *mejnoon* called in and mimicked the sound of the smoke alarm; all you heard from the caller was, "Beeeeeeeeeeeeeep!" Of course they eventually hung up on him and took the next caller. Everyone had a good laugh about it, though.

Brown Institute looked really small from the outside and was positioned at the end of a shopping plaza. At the other end of the plaza stood a drug store, where our class frequently ate our lunches— sometimes with the occasional biker gang member. Located at the middle of the plaza stood an oddly out of place strip club. Inside the school, there was a large classroom used exclusively for the three-month FCC training and testing courses. There were also three radio broadcasting studios, each with their own separate call letters and music format; a news booth that broadcasted throughout the entire building; several auditioning booths for creating air checks; and a television broadcasting studio. On the hallway wall hung the inspiration and hope for all of us future broadcasters, a huge map of the United States with pins that represented each graduate from Brown Institute and the station locations where they were currently working. The real reason I chose Brown Institute over a college was because of its success rate in placing students into their first radio job, and it was an accelerated way to start a career in broadcasting. I wanted school to be all about my career choice and didn't want to be tormented into taking other subjects just to rack up credits. Even though I rallied in my last two years of high school with good grades, my grade point average and SAT scores were just not good enough to enter a major university in my first year. Before learning about Brown, I was accepted to Scottsdale Community College in Arizona. Either way, I was determined to leave Maryland for a needed change in my life.

The faculty at Brown was awesome. All of the teachers were either currently on the air as radio personalities or retired after an illustrious career in broadcasting. Brown had always boasted about one of their famous graduates, Jim Lange, the host of *The Dating Game*. We were told Lange had graduated from Brown's other campus in Minneapolis, Minnesota. The faculty always had great stories about radio's past and even talked about the infamous disc jockeys who had taken payola. Payola was when a disc jockey took money from someone to play their record on the air. All the teachers at Brown had big-league radio voices. Our first teacher at the WBIB studio was my favorite. Mr. Hirsch was the epitome of a radio broadcaster and a wonderful teacher. When he first introduced himself to the class, he told us the story of how he and his wife survived a horrific car accident with a speeding train. His wife ended up a paraplegic, and he had lost about a hundred pounds after the accident. Mr. Hirsch was both nerdy and cool. He was very skinny, and his pants were always baggy. His wavy gray hair and thick black glasses were reminiscent of the 1950s. He would have made the perfect TV game show host. We all loved Mr. Hirsch; he made a lasting impression on all of us. The one lesson that stuck in my mind was the first one, when he taught us the correct way for pronouncing "W." It was extremely important for a disc jockey to pronounce "W" correctly when repeating the radio station call letters. While we were in the studio, Mr. Hirsch would always emphasize the letter "W." He'd say, "Okay, Ray, it's your turn behind the microphone on station Double-U BIB." He'd accentuate the "double-U" as if he were singing it. I think most of us had ignorantly pronounced it as "Dubba-Ya" before we had met Mr. Hirsch.

My class had twelve students, but there were two guys in class to whom I immediately took. Reed was white, thin, and tall, and his appearance was a cross between John Travolta and Dr. Frank-N-

Furter from *The Rocky Horror Picture Show.* I mentioned that he was white because he lived in Miami all of his life and never exhibited a tan. Reed always displayed a smirk on his face, but he enjoyed laughing. His laugh sounded like a car trying to start on a freezing cold winter day, and there would always be a flood of tears dripping from his eyes. Reed was a terrific writer and had his own music column in several of the Miami papers. He interviewed many new and upcoming rock bands like Cheap Trick and AC/DC. He even rode with them in their limousine while conducting the interview for his column. And he still carried his Screen Actors Guild card, from when he appeared as "the kid playing with a ball," in a background scene of the 1968 movie *Lady in Cement,* which starred Frank Sinatra and Raquel Welch. Reed drove to school every day in his green AMC Gremlin from his parents' house in Miami.

Eric was short; he had a big forehead, long hair, and a beard; and he was loaded with sarcasm. He was from Springfield, Virginia, and so instantly we had a lot in common. Eric drove an aqua colored 1966 Volkswagen Bug. His dad was a retired lieutenant Colonel in the marine corps. The colonel spent twenty-six years of active duty, including seventeen months in the Pacific during World War II, on the islands of Peleliu and Guam. Eric and I both lived on Andrews Avenue. He lived in a small, rented bungalow past the railroad tracks, about ten minutes away from my neighborhood. We spent the most time together because Reed lived so far away in South Miami. Just about every day after school, we'd play racquetball on the outdoor courts at Holiday Park. Eric and I competed in fierce matches against each other and then teamed up for doubles matches against some very tough opponents. He played up front and looked for the short shots off the corner walls, while I had the long reach and covered the rear for all the shots that got passed him. He and I won about 90 percent of all our matches played. Eric and Reed met at my apartment every morning before we all left for school.

On the first Friday night of the school year, Eric and I decided to check out the local club scene. We heard that Fort Lauderdale was a party town; after all, the city was referred to as "Fort Liquordale" because of its beaches, bars, nightclubs, and a history for attracting tens of thousands of college student spring breakers. We drove to a popular night spot on South Fort Lauderdale Beach. Our intention was to visit several bars that evening, and after thirty minutes we decided to leave. We carried our beers outside to his parked VW Beetle. I took a swig from out of my beer bottle and noticed a flashlight shining in on me through the passenger side window. I turned around and it was a cop. He ordered the two of us to get out of the car. The two policemen immediately started searching Eric's car and appeared to be irritated when they didn't find anything. We weren't sure what they were looking for, and we began to worry that they would intentionally plant drugs in the car just for spite. They proceeded to search the both of us but thoroughly manhandled Eric, tossing him around like a rag doll. I guessed they were intimidated by his long hair and beard. We stood around in the dark after being searched. Eric looked ruffled and nervous. I couldn't believe what was happening. Were we going to jail for drinking a beer by the beach in Fort Liquordale? This was insane! Then one of the cops looked at me and asked, "So, what is your driving ambition?" I didn't know what the hell he was talking about. The words that spurted out of my mouth were, "I drive a car." Eric stared down at the ground and shook his head in disbelief, and I immediately knew what Eric was thinking. He thought if we weren't already going to jail, we were definitely going to jail now. My response angered the cop even more so, but then I explained to him that we were broadcasting students and recently moved to the area. Then I heard a dog barking and noticed a ferocious German shepherd pacing side to side in the back of their squad car. One of the policemen smiled and said, "I tell you what, guys, if you can outrun our police dog, we'll let you go."

I thought to myself, "Man, what the hell is happening here?" Eric and I looked at each other with horrified expressions on our faces, and I knew we both thought the exact same thing: "This was going to really suck!" If they released that German shepherd on us, it would probably end our stay in Florida—and maybe even our lives. We told the cops, "No thank you, sir, we don't want to run; we'll stay right here sir." Then the same cop who did most of the talking said, "All right, you two, get out of here, and we never want to see you on our beat again." We scampered over to Eric's VW and quickly jumped in, and then we took off and drove straight home. Man, what a hassle! We never went near that place again, in fear of bumping into those same cops. But it didn't stop us from going out to more clubs other weekends, and those times, nobody got hassled.

Reed introduced us to his favorite rock and roll hangouts around Miami. We enjoyed watching a band called Zed Cars. Their lead singer was an Englishman named Peter Patrick. The band played original tunes and covers from the Who, the Kinks, and the Yardbirds. One of their most popular original song was called "I'm Your Bobby Dazzler." We'd watch Zed Cars play on stage whenever they were in town. Another reason we liked the band so much was because they liked to smash their equipment on stage. We liked anything that was rebellious. When we went out to rock clubs and liked the band, we'd demonstrate our approval by throwing beers into each other's faces. If we hated the band, we'd start kicking over chairs and tables. One night before Zed Cars had taken the stage, Reed was talking with Peter Patrick. He told him that we were all in a punk rock band called The Drugs. During the show, Patrick ordered his light man to move the spot light toward our table, and he introduced us to their audience. "I'd like to welcome tonight an exciting new punk rock band, and they're sitting in our audience tonight, ladies and gentlemen … The Drugs!" Of course we didn't have a punk rock band called The Drugs, but it was really cool pretending that we did.

For some reason, I drove over to Eric's place a lot more than he drove over to mine. He lived in a secluded bungalow, and so he got to play his stereo really loud. He had most of his music recorded on reel to reel; the quality was remarkable. And the acoustics inside of his bungalow weren't so shabby, either. I guessed it made more sense to hang out at his place, because I was over there almost every night.

It was a Saturday night. I brought over a few six packs of Michelob beer. The drinking age was eighteen in Florida, and so I could enter any liquor store and get anything I wanted. I didn't need my fake ID anymore; liquor was sold just about everywhere in Florida. Eric always kept a big bottle of Canadian Club Whiskey on his coffee table, and he would take huge swigs from it throughout the night. Earlier, when I arrived at his bungalow, the front door was left wide open. He always kept his door shut because he was somewhat paranoid. I walked inside and called, "Eric, where are you, man?" I walked all around looking for him and couldn't find him. Then I walked back inside the kitchen to take a second look, when all of a sudden he erupted from out of the pantry screaming, "*Wow!*" He scared the living shit out of me. We spent most of the evening drinking and laughing while listening to Iggy and the Stooges on his reel to reel. We were laughing over last weekend's events. We got a bit rowdy and kicked over a few trash cans in another neighborhood. After we watched *Saturday Night Live* on TV, we drove out to an all-night sub shop and stuffed our faces. When we got back, it was already two o'clock in the morning, so I decided to leave.

After arriving home, I stepped out of my car onto the parking lot that sat directly in front of my apartment complex. While walking on the parking lot, I heard a telephone ringing loudly. All the lights were out at the complex, and it was very quiet and still, except for the piercing ringing of an isolated telephone. I walked toward the stairs that led to my second floor apartment I started to wonder if the ringing was coming from my place. I walked faster and finally reached my front door. I quickly unlocked the door and entered the earsplitting room. I became distraught thinking that the call may be bad news from home, and I nervously reached for the phone and answered, "Hello?"

The voice on the other end responded, "Fuck You!" and then hung up abruptly. It was Eric.

On rare occasions, Reed would hang out at my place after school. While he was there we'd write music together. I'd hook up my Fender Telecaster to a stereo system that Dad gave to me from the store before I left, and I played through its speakers. I banged out the barre chords on my guitar, mimicking the sounds of the latest punk rockers, and Reed sang his ingenious lyrics. We were drunk and loud, and surprisingly no one ever complained. Reed was definitely a natural songwriter, and when he obtained that certain euphoric buzz, his voice had mirrored Led Zeppelin's Robert Plant. We came up with several hardcore but clever tunes and recorded them on cassette. One memorable but alarming tune that we wrote together was called "Abortion Baby," which hinted some of Reed's brilliant lyrics. The song was composed as a parody for the Sex Pistols hardcore reverberation, but it may have been seriously used as a deterrent to abortion—I think the song would have scared the crap out of any woman that even considered getting an abortion.

Reed had always used the slang "scoop" for trying to pick up girls, so he incorporated his clever catchphrase into a song and called it "Scoop, Scoop." I thought some of our songs were good enough to record in a professional studio, but Reed wasn't convinced. I really felt that he had a boatload of talent but was too modest to do anything about it. Eric, Reed, and I were rock and roll music aficionados. The music knowledge between the three of us was uncanny. Our expertise was never of the same musicians; we contributed differently, and that's why we meshed so well together. We were all true music lovers and felt that we could make a huge contribution to the music world as deejays with our own radio shows. All three of us were clearly passionate about attending Brown Institute.

However, the three of us were also the class clowns. When one of us was on the air broadcasting in one of the school radio studios, you'd usually find the other two holding up signs with disgusting cartoon images on them and trying desperately to make the on-air student crack up. When we were in a classroom setting, you'd find the three of us in the very back of the room mocking everybody else. We were sarcastic and cynical. I think our attitude was what we thought separated us from Joe Schmo and kept us cool. That attitude became our mainstay, and it became extremely hard to shake loose.

When we weren't in school, we were usually at a record store hunting for the latest releases and discovering new artists. We'd ride or sometimes walk to the huge Peaches record store, where we spent countless hours researching each rock, new wave, and punk rock record aisle. Visiting Peaches was like visiting a cathedral to all of us. Before entering the doors of Peaches, we'd stop to stare at the many cement imprints of all the famous bands to have made an appearance at the store. Eric and I were fortunate to be there when the band Genesis came in for a special autograph session, and I got the whole band to sign the *A Trick of the Tale* album." The three of us also enjoyed driving to the water park right after school was over and sliding down the flume fully clothed. It was especially refreshing after those long and grueling classes that had prepared us for the FCC licensing exams in Miami.

Eric and I got to watch Jerry Lewis direct a scene for a movie called *Hardly Working.* He and his film crew were shooting right down the street from my apartment complex, as well as at the shopping center where I bought by groceries. Jerry Lewis was dressed in a clown costume while sitting behind the camera and being lifted up by a crane. The scene involved releasing hundreds of rabbits onto the blacktop of the shopping center parking lot. Actors Harold Stone and Steve Franken were also on location. I could have been an extra in the movie, but I didn't feel like hanging around all day.

Abuela flew down to visit her daughter in Pembroke Pines. She asked Aunt Terry to drive her to my apartment so she could visit with me before flying back to DC. Abuela spent most of the day with me in my apartment, and she cooked a delicious spaghetti dinner for us both. I really missed Abuela and her cooking, but we did share a very special day together. Then Howard, Monica, my nephew Sean, and Monica's sister Lynn all came to visit me. It was a quick visit; they were making the rounds visiting all the family and then drove to Disney World. Lynn taught me how to dive into the swimming pool. I was almost twenty years old and had never learned to dive. She was around fifteen but a great teacher, because I was diving into the pool within minutes after my first lesson. Then Howard got violently ill while visiting with me inside my apartment, and we had to call 911 for an ambulance. While he was being carried down the stairs on the stretcher and carted away from my apartment building, Aunt Terry disclosed to all the concerned onlookers, "He's not on drugs, everyone!" Howard was released from the emergency room later that afternoon with a diagnosis of … "It's probably the Florida water."

Eric, Reed, and I made it through the toughest part of the nine-month program at Brown Institute, achieving a third-class, second-class, and then finally the prestigious first-class FCC license. A first-class license meant you were authorized to fix the transmitter as an engineer. We were book smart on how to do it, but Brown hadn't taught us how to actually perform the task. We didn't want to be engineers anyway—we wanted to be deejays and shake up the music world. Even other deejays we had spoken to, who were already working, had confirmed to us that obtaining a first-class FCC license was the ticket we needed to work at the large-market radio stations. Our class passed its last radio studio broadcasting course, and the teacher gathered us all together for one of our final meetings. He was very blunt in his announcement to all of us. First he said, "You will not succeed in radio if you get married anytime soon."

I thought, "Okay, I don't even have a girlfriend yet."

Then he unloaded a bombshell on all of us and said, "Most of you will drop out of radio in less than a year."

I thought, "Wow, great timing, man; we're graduating soon, and you already have our tuition money in cash." Eric, Reed, and I looked at each other liked frightened mice. We wondered why the hell he was saying that, especially when the class was already psyched.

We had a month left until graduation when Reed decided to opt out of TV broadcasting training and accept a job at a radio station in Punta Gorda, Florida. In my mind I thought, "Man, if Reed's ready then I'm ready." I didn't want a job in television, so I didn't care about missing that portion of the course either. And besides, I took TV broadcasting for two years in high school. I asked for a meeting with the school director and asked him to start looking for a radio station that would hire me. I already had my air check ready to be sent for a general manager or program director to hear. The first job that was offered to me was in Meridian, Mississippi, and for some reason images of the Ku Klux Klan kept popping into my head. I wasn't too familiar with the state anyway and thought perhaps I'd land a job closer to home. A week went by, and I was called into the director's office for a second offer that came up in Sebring, Florida. By that time I was extremely anxious, and so I took the job.

Chapter Sixteen

"This Is Ray Richards on 1340 WSEB"

I said my good-byes to all the teachers and the rest of my class at Brown. Then I said good-bye to Eric. Eric didn't seem like he was in any hurry to leave like Reed and I were. He completed the TV broadcasting course and then graduated with the rest of my class. Eric spent most his days without Reed and me, hanging out with his girlfriend, who had flown down to stay with him, and he worked at a gas station to make ends meet. He eventually landed a job in his home state of Virginia, inside of Luray Caverns.

I started my first day on the air at 1340 AM WSEB in Sebring, Florida. It was a small, five-thousand-watt radio station that was separated by a window and its sister, a ten-thousand-watt Christian format station. My radio air name was Ray Richards. I selected the last name from the Rolling Stones guitarist Keith Richards. My deejay show was the six o'clock to midnight shift, and I signed off every night with the Mason Williams tune "Classical Gas" followed by our "national anthem." The station was an MOR (middle of the road) format. After awhile, I grew tired of the music library that the station had kept, and so I bought my own records to play. It was obvious that the station didn't have much money to spend;

there wasn't a program director around to run things. I played the current hits on the charts, like Anita Ward's "Ring My Bell" and Peaches and Herb's "Reunited," and I then mixed in the songs that I had brought in, from artists like Lou Rawls, Barry Manilow, Tom Jones, and Johnny Mathis. The general manager of the station, Mr. Manchester liked my show so much that he'd call into the station every night with his own personal requests.

The only place that I could find to live in Sebring was in an old trailer park, which was furnished with worn-out furniture. It took me a good week to find that place. I had been sleeping on the floor at Rick's apartment, another deejay from the station. I admit it was a bit spooky moving in there. Outside of the trailer, there was a huge orange grove that had stretched for miles. If you crossed the fence and tried to pick an orange you'd definitely hear shotgun fire. Inside of the mobile home, it was inhabited by several gigantic wolf spiders, and there were spider and mouse droppings everywhere. The place sucked, but I didn't have any choice.

On some weeks, I'd work sixty hours at the radio station, but it didn't matter because I still earned only ninety-nine dollars a week. The worst thing was when our paychecks hadn't arrived on time. I remember being flat broke, and I had to borrow money from Mr. Manchester. Every night after I closed down the station at one o' clock in the morning, I'd drive on Highway 27 North to Denny's and eat a huge breakfast. I was a regular, so the waitress would have my food waiting for me before I got there. If I was going to make it in broadcasting, I'd have to learn everything that I could and take the good with the bad. WSEB was going to be a temporary gig anyway, just to get the experience that I needed to move up to a larger market station.

I was ecstatic the day I landed a roommate with which to share my misery. The station needed another deejay, so our station GM called Brown Institute for help. His name was Jack, and he was going to be the new morning man. Jack graduated from Brown right after my class did; his hometown was New York City. He was big and awkward and wore big thick glasses, but he was my companion. I didn't like Sebring much until Jack arrived. When Jack moved in, he was pretty freaked out over the mouse droppings in his chest of drawers, and he definitely hated the big wolf spiders. While he took naps, I'd throw pennies on his chest. He'd wake up screaming, thinking they were rats. Ed, the deejay from WSEB's sister Christian station, and I would also tap on Jack's bedroom window while he slept, and we wore paper bags over our heads. He'd wake up and look out the window and then start screaming. Yeah, it was great to have a roommate. We finally got an exterminator and kept the place in somewhat order. But what kept Jack and I from going completely insane was our huge collection of smut. Our daily outing after he got off the air was to drive to the local convenient store together and buy a *Playboy* or *Hustler* magazine. You could build a house with our amassed collection of smut.

The both of us were ready to turn WSEB into a fierce competitor— but Rick, the only other deejay at the station, wouldn't let that happen. He had been working at the station for quite a while and thought he was the one that should be calling the shots. Now he was surrounded by Brown grads that were ready to turn things around, with or without his help, and so naturally he felt threatened. When we asked for his help, he continued to do things the old way. But according to the GM, we were hired to make the station better. The on-air deejay should always have his carts and records put away before the next deejay started his shift; it was supposed to be a smooth transition, and it was not difficult to achieve. Rick would continue to check each of the carts that he had played during his shift, to make sure they were all cued up correctly. Rick was obsessive-compulsive about checking the carts, and he did it during my shift. I asked him nicely several times to be completely done and out of the deejay chair when my shift began, but he purposely ignored me. Well, I had just about enough of that! I confronted him in a not so nice way, and we started pushing each other around in the studio while we were on the air. This guy didn't earn anyone's respect. He was a lousy deejay and really should have been replaced. I might have been a little cocky because earlier in the day, our sales manager said that he heard I was going to be selected as program director for the radio station. But after my altercation with that mental defective, Jack got the job. It ended up being a lot of work for the same amount of money, but it looked really good on your resume. I felt like I was being screwed once again. It took me back to when I was thrown off the student council in first grade for talking. I was starting to think that there was someone or something preventing me from getting a break in life.

Once Jack took over as program director, he gave me the afternoon drive time slot and put Rick on nights. Jack asked me to join him during his morning show sometimes. We talked about current events in the news and celebrities in Hollywood. We also made a big deal about trying to call Liberace on his birthday. We felt comfortable working together, and the show was funny. The owner of the station was visiting from Tennessee, and he called Jack and I to the side after Jack's morning show was over. He told us that adding a second deejay to Jack's morning show was unprofessional, and we needed to stop immediately.

Jack and I worked really late sometimes at the radio station on production work. We were cutting a spot together for a local restaurant called Bucky's Snack Shop. We acted out the parts of a game show host and a contestant. Every time we tried to run through the commercial, we'd start to laugh. After countless retakes we finally recorded a decent take onto a cart. Then I erased one of the used carts with the bulk eraser, a device used to erase magnetic tape without having to record over it. We finished up and decided to eat breakfast at Denny's.

After finishing breakfast, I remembered that I may have left the bulk eraser plugged in. We returned to the radio station, and I immediately smelled smoke. We ran back to the production room, and the desk that the bulk eraser had sat on was smoldering, practically on fire. I pulled the plug out that was attached to the bulk eraser, and Jack soaked the desk with water. A large burn mark was evident on the desk's surface. Those bulk erasers got really hot and were kind of dangerous if not used correctly. If we hadn't gone back to the radio station, the whole place may have gone up in flames. It could have been a devastating inception to my rookie year in broadcasting. It definitely wouldn't have looked good on my resume.

After a few months of my living like shit in Sebring, Howard came down to visit me. He had gotten free tickets to Walt Disney World because Chin Lung had sold Disney super eight movies. The WSEB radio station building was extremely small but was located right on the main highway. The station also had a small antenna; sometimes a big bird sat on it and dimmed everyone's radio reception. During my shift, I'd have to run outside and scare the bird away so that our listeners could continue to tune in and hear us.

When Howard told me he was coming, I told him that I'd literally leave all the station lights on for him so he could find it, and he thought I was kidding. He only passed it by twice; on the third try, I ran outside and finally flagged him down. I gave him a tour of the radio station while I was still on the air. After my shift was over, he followed me over to Denny's. I called Jack to meet us there, and we all ate a huge breakfast together. For some reason breakfast always tasted better in the wee small hours. We left Denny's and headed for our trailer. When Howard stepped inside, he looked kind of shocked over the poor living conditions. The following morning he bought us a shower curtain. I'm really not sure why we never bought one; I guess we were just plain lazy. He was impressed with our smut collection, though. After Howard hung up the shower curtain, we drove out of Sebring and into civilization. Seeing Mickey Mouse was like visiting a psychiatrist. My life had consisted of working really long hours at the radio station and then going home to a spooky old trailer late at night. Every night when I arrived home from the radio station, I'd see multiple sets of eyes staring back at me from the orange groves. I think I was starting to go crazy, but I didn't realize it until I finally left Sebring. Howard and I rode a new roller coaster at Disney called Space Mountain, and it was probably the highlight of the trip. Our entire Disney adventure was free, thanks to Chin Lung. We spent the entire day there. The following morning Howard flew back to DC.

The faculty at Brown Institute had always said to stay no longer than six months at your first radio gig and then move on. Stay just long enough to gain the experience. After four months of torment, I broke down and called Mom for a ticket home on the auto train. This time it was easy to say my good-byes because I wasn't really going to miss anyone—well, maybe Jack a little. I threw out everything that I had accumulated since Fort Lauderdale or gave it to Jack. Very early next morning, I woke up and then drove out of Sebring forever. Two hours later, I arrived in Sanford. I remembered how happy I was after arriving there with Mom and Dad from DC just a year ago. After boarding the auto train, I immediately headed for the nearest bar. I sat at the table in the dimly lit Amtrak nightclub car finishing up my second glass of Seagrams Seven and Seven. I reflected on all the good times I had in Fort Lauderdale, and all the miserable times I endured in Sebring. The night club car was empty that evening except for a lot six (gay guy) around my age, who tried to pick me up. Once he found out that I was straight, he resorted to sharing a few moments of intelligent conversation and then said goodnight.

I moved back home for awhile and immediately started looking for another radio job. I sent air checks out to stations all over the country. Of course Mom and Dad were really happy that I was back home, but for me it just wasn't the same. Once I'd been out there on my own, it was difficult to live at home again. One day I got a call from a well-known progressive rock station in Bethesda, Maryland, called WHFS. Man, I couldn't believe it; this was the perfect gig. It was Eric's favorite radio station, and I called him up and let him know about my upcoming interview with the station general manager, Jacob Einstein.

I arrived at the station and waited in the reception area for my name to be called. As I sat there, all kinds of fantastic thoughts raced through my mind, mostly about me and radio stardom. After fifteen minutes, the general manager called me into his office. I sat in the chair in front of his huge desk. I noticed a signed picture of Frank Sinatra hanging on the wall behind him. He started the conversation by saying, "I see you have a first-class FCC license; can you fix transmitters?"

I thought to myself, "Damn it, why would he be asking me that?" I nervously cleared my throat and waited a few seconds before I responded. In those endless seconds, I watched him staring at me and waiting for my answer. One simple answer would decide if I'd get one of the best radio gigs in the Washington metropolitan area. Finally I reluctantly replied, "No, sir, I can't; I was taught the theory but cannot actually perform the task."

Mr. Einstein looked at me like I was crazy. He said, "So what the hell good is having a first-class license then? I'm looking for a deejay that can also fix transmitters. I'm sorry if we hadn't made that clear to you when we called you. Thanks for coming in anyway." The meeting only lasted about thirty seconds. I was pretty crushed over the meeting from hell, but then a few weeks later I got another call from the program director of WNAV radio in Annapolis. They needed a weekend and fill-in deejay for their top-forty format radio station. The station reminded me a lot of WPGC; it even broadcasted with that echo sound effect. I drove out to Annapolis in my new 1979 black Pontiac Trans Am and met with the program director. He gave me a live audition and a sixty-second spot to read, and he must have liked it because I got the job. It seemed as though my new career was back on track again.

Then Dad asked me to come back to work at Chin Lung. It made sense; my new radio gig was limited to only the weekends anyway. On my first day back, I chatted with Iggy at the engraving counter in back of the store, and he mentioned to me that he needed to find a new place to live. I told Iggy that I wanted to move out of my parents' house. I'd been staying out really late and sometimes never came home at all. Even though I was almost twenty-one, Mom still worried about me. Plus, I just started seeing this girl named Lacy. She lived in the same apartment complex as Iggy. She'd gone out with him a few times, and then they became really good friends. We first met when she came to visit Iggy, and I was there hanging out with him. She walked into his apartment wearing just a bikini. She hadn't been to the pool or anything, so I thought it was kind of strange that she walked around like that ... but she did have a smoking hot body. She assumed I was one of Iggy's non-English-speaking buddies, because I didn't talk much after saying hello to her. Once I did start talking with her, I was like Rodney Dangerfield doing his stand-up comedy act, rattling off one liners. I was in an unstoppable groove, and she ate it up. She loved to laugh. I really didn't want to have to tell her that I was living with my parents, though. After I told Iggy that I was ready to move out, a devilish smile appeared on both of our faces. Iggy was the first one to say it: "Hey, man, let's be roomies!"

A week later, we moved into a somewhat affordable townhome complex in Alexandria, Virginia, called Orleans Village. Let the partying begin! We set up what we thought was the ultimate bachelor pad. We had a tiki bar stocked with booze, positioned two stools in front, and draped the bar in fishnets. Two fish tanks sat in between the living and dining room area. A forty-gallon tank stood with a huge Oscar and a Jack Dempsey fish swimming inside. A smaller thirty-gallon tank was filled for the five piranha fish inside. My Fender Telecaster with a newly acquired Peavey amplifier was displayed in one corner of the home, and Iggy's conga drums stood at the other corner. After we were totally and completely inebriated, we'd jam out together till the wee hours of the night. We had lots of houseplants scattered everywhere. Our furniture consisted of a large couch and a huge square glass coffee table that sat in front of it. Of course music wise we were golden. I had my Sansui four-channel stereo receiver and a Pioneer turntable hooked to six large speakers positioned throughout the living room, we had hundreds of record albums that stood ready for play in their wooden crates.

Both of our bedrooms were pretty desolate, though. I had a queen-size bed in my room, a throw rug, and a ten-gallon fish tank. But my fish always died. I'd spend hours fixing up the tank with colored gravel, plastic plants, and really cool ornaments. Then I'd mix into the tank a variety of fish to appear as though it were the ocean depths, only to wake up the following morning and find all of them lying dead at the top of the gravel. It looked as though the fish had fought in an epic battle, and everyone lost. I never had much luck keeping fish. Iggy only had a twin-size mattress lying on the floor in his bedroom, with a revolver stuffed somewhere underneath it. He liked weapons and started collecting guns. He bought a German Model 24 hand stick grenade from somebody and kept it inside his bedroom. I had many sleepless nights wondering if the grenade was still live.

Iggy and I partied a lot; the weekends were ours, and actually the weekdays were ours too. Friends were always stopping by for a visit, and they usually stayed until really late. We were still going out to clubs together, although he started to hang out more with his new girlfriend, Allison. Iggy was always a womanizer; he had a knack for conversation and for picking up women. I remember one night in particular. I had just finished dancing with some girl at Gus and John's, and when I walked back to the table, there was Iggy with his arms around a whole table full of beautiful girls. There must have been eight girls with him that night. He looked up at me smiling with a big ol' cigar in his mouth and said, "Look what I got, man… Ha ha ha … You want one?"

Dad had been secretly talking with a real estate attorney about a retail space. One day I got a call from Howard. "Raymond, we're going to open a new store down the block from Chin Lung. Can we count on you to work there?"

"Whose store is it going to be?"

"Dad and I will be partners, and we'll cut you in for a piece. We already signed the lease."

"All right, but I can't work Saturdays because of my radio gig."

"We'll really need you on Saturdays; you know that's a big day, and you'll be making a lot more money than you will in radio."

"No, I really want to try and make it in radio; after all, I went to school for that."

"Okay, I guess I'll try to find someone else to work Saturdays for now."

"What's going to happen to Chin Lung?"

"Dad and Uncle Joey are splitting up. They're going to let the lease run out and go their separate ways."

"How come no one told me about this earlier? I feel like I'm being left out or something. I was a big part of the store too, you know. As a matter of fact, when you were in the air force for four years, I worked with Dad every Saturday and all summer long."

"We didn't want to tell you anything till the deal was finalized. You know, we didn't want to jinx it. So … can I count on you to work at the new store?"

"Yeah, I guess I'm in."

Chapter Seventeen

Worldwide Electronics

After eighteen years in business, Chin Lung Art Gallery was closing its doors. Dad and Uncle Joey's lease was running out, and a new planned city project for the 1300 block would prohibit them from renewing it. Soon their partnership would be dissolved. It was hard to believe, but I supposed life goes on. All the merchandise, showcases, and wall cases were to be split up between them. Joey and Roland were planning to open a store selling household goods in downtown Baltimore. Seymour decided to retire, and his son Evan began looking for retail space for another engraving and jewelry repair shop in DC. Iggy got a job as a carpenter with the government and continued to work at his brother-in-law's jewelry store on weekends. The government paid well, and he needed the cash; after all, we were splitting the rent on our townhome in Alexandria. My cousin David's drug problem had surfaced, creating new concerns for the family. David worked for Uncle Davey on Ninth Street. Uncle Davey started selling beepers, and David had the idea of selling them in downtown Baltimore. Seth opened a retail electronics store on Howard Street in Baltimore. The store's longtime neighbor to the left, the Blue Mirror Grill, soon closed down and reopened under new management on 15th and E Street. I imagine that Mr. David was ready to retire; a year earlier he had been tied up, gagged, and then robbed in his own home. The Lowes Palace movie theater closed down for good. As for Dad, Mom, Howard, and me, our adventure on F Street continued.

Howard and I walked down F Street to 1341 the next day and checked out the new store. To the right of the store was Radio Shack, and Yummy Yogurt stood next door to the left. The face of the building looked as if it belonged in a small town in Switzerland; the last tenant was an expensive men's haberdashery. Howard had the key, and we walked inside the vacant building. The sales floor was much narrower than Chin Lung's and wasn't carpeted. But the second and third floors were covered with plush navy blue carpeting, left over from the haberdashery. On the third floor, there were beautiful wood dressing rooms and mirrors, which we eventually used for storing stock and empty boxes.

Meanwhile, Dad started dividing up the merchandise with Uncle Joey. Each day we'd load up hand trucks filled with merchandise and wheel them down to our new location. My buddy Hassan must have made a hundred trips with that hand truck, back and forth and from store to store. But it was still convenient, being within walking distance. I recruited Hassan to work with us. He had gotten an early discharge from the air force. Apparently the air force promised him a certain career path, but he ended up tightening screws and performing minuscule tasks instead. Hassan only worked with us on a day-to-day basis, because he'd try and live out his dream of becoming a professional Punter in the NFL.

Howard and I had orchestrated the preparations for a big grand opening. We set up some shelves and ordered new showcases and wall cases, but they only filled out one side of the store. We'd complete the other half with cases after Chin Lung had officially closed. We ordered new types of merchandise, and not from all the traditional vendors that Dad and Uncle Joey had dealt with for all those years. We bought electronic games for the first time and stocked Simon, an electronic game of rhythm and memory skills. We carried one of the first TV-video game consoles called the Atari 2600 and all its game cartridges. Atari was a much bigger sensation than Pong ever was. We handled Mattel and Coleco electronic football games, as well as Boris diplomat electronic chess games, and we were the first store to carry Nintendo handheld LCD games in the entire city. The game hadn't officially sold in the United States yet; the instructions were only in Japanese. Digital watches considerably dropped in price, and so we displayed a whole new line with discounted prices. Because we didn't have showcases and wall cases yet on one side of the store, we ordered Sanyo and Panasonic stereo equipment and sat them on their boxes with their speakers. We lined them up in rows like soldiers and filled in all the empty spaces. We found a slew of new wholesalers to buy from, because the electronics boom was about to explode.

Then one day an Aerial truck pulled up on the sidewalk in front of the store. A man in a bucket raised a black sign that revealed bold white lettering superimposed on an aqua and green colored picture of the earth. The sign was officially installed on the roof of the store's Swiss-looking façade. Then Howard, Hassan, Mom, and I opened the doors for business at Worldwide Electronics. Dad would start working at Worldwide when Chin Lung closed its doors. We opened a month before Christmas in 1979, and the timing couldn't have been any better. The store looked half-ass, but it was challenging and fun trying to sell the merchandise that we did have. Black Friday and Christmas revenues were good, and we attracted new types of Gs.

After Christmas, Chin Lung took its final bow on F Street and closed its doors forever. We installed new carpeting at Worldwide because the floors were way too hard on our feet, and then Dad hired movers to bring over the rest of the wall cases and showcases needed to complete the interior of the store. The only other expense was a new air-conditioning and heating unit that was installed right after we opened for business. Dad brought himself and his cigars over and made it official. We carried on with many of the same traditions that Chin Lung had over the years, but we definitely took it to another level.

At one o'clock in the morning on New Year's Day of 1980, I signed off the air as a radio disc jockey forever. WNAV was a great station and a lot of fun to work at; I even signed autographs for school kids as they toured the radio station. I actually ran two stations at the same time there. I operated a five-thousand-watt, AM top-forty radio show alone, entertaining the audience with my ad-lib humor and updating my radio listeners about the time, temperature, station ID, and local and national news at the top of each hour. I played the top songs on the music charts and inserted carts at precisely the times indicated on the station log. Carts were used to play and record commercials and station jingles. It was a plastic box reminiscent of the old eight-track tape, but when played, it always came back to start and ready for use the next time it was needed. I was also the board operator, inserting recorded spots (commercials) during Orioles baseball, Colts football, Navy basketball, and football games, and I recorded the traffic reports. The intern who watched the big daddy fifty-thousand-watt, FM automated easy listening station left for the day when I started my shift. I had to update the FM station with the latest news every hour and make sure it ran smoothly. If it went off the air for some ungodly reason, a light would flicker in the AM studio. Oh yeah, I almost forgot—I had to write down meter readings from inside the transmitter room at the top of each hour, and I set up all the commercials (spots) inside the wheel on the automated FM machine for the next day. Whew! And this was all done on Saturdays, between 5:30 PM and 1:30 AM.

One evening while I was on the air, I slipped into the news booth that sat between both radio stations. I hurriedly recorded myself with a fresh newscast for use on the FM side. Someone left the volume pod on full blast, and my headphones got too close to the microphone. Well ... you do the math. The screeching feedback was so loud that it knocked me to the ground and left me unconscious for about thirty seconds. When I came to and finally dragged myself up, I noticed that both stations were off the air at the same time. The AM side was silent as a church, and the warning light for the FM side was blinking away. This was every deejay's worst nightmare, the dreaded dead air—and I had it twice! I took a deep breath, walked into the AM studio, and slipped on "Rapper's Delight" by the Sugarhill Gang. It was the first hip hop single to ever go gold. More important, it was a really long song; even the normal version was six minutes and thirty seconds, so it gave me just enough time to figure out why the FM side had gone off the air.

Unfortunately it wasn't the first time that both stations went off the air at the same time. One day during a horrendous lightning storm, the AM side went soundless during my show, and the FM warning light blinked on. I was so overwhelmed by the dead air that I ran between both studios, stopped, and looked both ways, acting like a cartoon character that repeated, "Which way did they go?"

Dad and Howard needed help desperately on Saturdays, and I knew I wanted to settle down with a family one day, which was almost impossible to accomplish while I was trying to make a name for myself in broadcasting. Brown Institute was right: I was one of those deejays they said would drop out of the business. I had a great send-off though. Several minutes past midnight, I received a phone call. I answered, "WNAV, where we bring you more."

Instantly and simultaneously, I heard a crowd of voices shouting through the end of my receiver, "Happy New Year, Ray!" It was a big New Year's Eve party that had listened to my show for the entire evening. It reminded me of *A Charlie Brown Christmas,* when the Peanuts gang yelled out, "Merry Christmas, Charlie Brown." I shed a tear that night. I tolerated the family business, but I truly loved radio.

I started working full-time again with the family. It was a Wednesday morning when a young Israeli guy pulled up to the front curb in a white van. He said that he had the latest product line of JVC boom boxes at the best prices. Dad and Howard had a tendency to buy too many of the knockoff brands, supposedly generating better PR and more opportunities to saff the Gs brains out. I hated the knockoffs; I'd rather pay extra for the name brand goods. The knockoffs were manufactured cheaply, thus generating lots of BOs (SY slang for returns), which meant more headaches for all of us. I was very happy to see that white van filled with JVC merchandise. We bought the entire JVC line, and each machine was equipped with the 110 and 220 volts needed to operate in any country around the world. A small switch inside the unit had converted the current for use in other countries. Worldwide's electronics niche was selling dual voltage, portable stereo equipment and color televisions for use in any country around the globe. It's what distinguished us from the competition. Thanks to the Israeli guy, we had the biggest selection of JVC boom boxes, sometimes referred to as ghetto blasters in DC.

Then out of the blue, we started receiving these huge boxes filled with merchandise at Worldwide. There was nothing out of the ordinary about receiving large UPS shipments. What was unusual was that we never ordered these particular shipments, and we never knew what was inside them. Eventually we'd refer to them as "surprise packages." Inside the box was a spectacular selection of the latest and greatest retail electronics. Anytime we opened a surprise package, it was like opening a huge box filled with cash. The box contained merchandise that the wholesaler had believed we'd be able to sell quickly, and it usually contained goods that no other retailer in DC had in stock yet. We never protested any of the shipments, no matter how much it cost us, and we developed a great rapport with that wholesale company. Those random shipments from New York City kept us ahead of the competition.

At three o'clock in the afternoon, a couple of young men who wore military uniforms, and who only spoke Spanish, walked into the store. Howard and Mom waited on them. We found out they were both serving in the Argentine air force. The conversion of the peso ley to US dollar was very attractive, and so they prowled the streets of DC for JVC electronics to purchase and take back home. The timing was uncanny; they were only interested in buying JVC products. The two Argentine men eventually bought two JVC dual-voltage, portable component systems. While Dad checked line at the register counter, a group of twenty Argentineans stormed through the front door, and all of them were looking for JVC products. Group after group of Argentinean air force Gs raced in all day and practically all night. Every time they entered the store, they'd hurriedly walk over to the nearest salesman and demand, *"Jota ve ce!"* (JVC in Spanish). There were only the four of us to take care of all of them, and Mom and Howard were the only ones who spoke Spanish fluently. The barrage of sales came to an end at three o'clock in the morning. A lone husho tried to sneak in at around 11:15 that evening, but we all yelled at him to get the hell out, and he quickly left. The Argentines were "Gimme I take" customers, and nobody was going to interfere with us or them. A "Gimme I take" is our slang for a G who buys without hesitation and doesn't care about the price.

The next day, more Argentinean groups came in, and more JVC electronic merchandise flew out the door. The wall cases were bare. By high noon, we accepted their Swiss francs and Diners Club credit cards as they ran short of American dollars. Howard looked in the newspaper to see what the exchange rates were. The Argentineans were completely done shopping by ten o' clock that evening. It was the most money we had ever made in a two-day period. We were exhausted but completely gratified.

The following week, Dad hired a Mexican fellow named Louie to clean up around the store. He didn't talk very much and didn't speak English, but Howard and Mom were there to help him out. I understood a lot of Spanish but never learned enough to speak it fluently. But I cursed with a perfect Cuban accent. Dad had a very special job for Louie. When there was a lull in business, Dad would tell Louie to tear up newspapers in small pieces and throw them all over the floor. Dad said it made the store look busy and gave the impression that a crowd of Gs had just left the store. After awhile, Dad told Louie to get the broom and sweep it all up. If business still hadn't picked up, he'd tell Louie to rip up different newspaper and do it all over again. On really slow days, poor Louie might have repeated the ritual for countless and tiresome hours. I think Louie finally lost it when he began mumbling to himself one day. I caught him talking to himself in back of the store ranting, "I throw the paper … I pick up the paper … I throw the paper … I pick up the paper." Needless to say, Louie quit soon afterward, but his English got a lot better.

Uncle Davey performed similar tactics to change the luck at his store on Ninth Street. He had hired several Hispanics to help him around the sales floor and upstairs in the stock room. If business was slow, he'd tell them to take all the merchandise out from one half of the store, and swap it with the merchandise from the other half of the store. If business never got any better, he'd tell them to do it all over again.

One day, the UPS truck driver delivered several large packages. I signed his clipboard for the shipment and noticed what appeared to be another surprise package along with other shipments that we had intentionally ordered. Howard walked over to see what shipments were delivered. I opened the surprise package first. As I started to stack all the merchandise up on the showcase, Howard grabbed one of the items to examine it, and then he started to open the box. Howard and I were like children playing on Christmas morning when we got to test the latest electronic devices. We'd rush to see who could put the batteries in first. The device looked like a handheld blue and silver cassette tape recorder, but it was labeled as the Sony Soundabout, and it came with tiny headphones. The electronic gadget was defined as a TPS-L2 walkman. None of us had ever seen anything like it before. The Sony Soundabout came with a cool demo cassette tape, a case, and the headphones. After Howard loaded the penlight batteries into it, he slid the small headphones onto his ears, and then he inserted the demo cassette tape into the machine and pushed play. "Wow! You got to hear this, Raymond, this is unbelievable." Howard took off the headphones and immediately placed them on my ears.

I reacted about the same. "Holy shit! Where is all that sound coming from?" At that moment, I knew this was the beginning of great and wonderful things in the world of retail electronics. After the first Sony walkman arrived, we had a hard time keeping them in stock. We marked the box as lot #92209, with a price tag of $249.95. The price we usually sold them for was $199.95. Overnight, competitors mass produced knockoffs. When we received the first knockoff walkman, it sold for about half the price of a Sony Soundabout. The manufacturer for the new knockoff was called Cybernet. We jokingly told all the Gs that the company was owned by Carol Burnett's husband.

Bernadette came back to work with us at Worldwide, and we really needed her. She had been working with Uncle Davey for awhile. Then Howard hired a black dude named Haywood away from the Radio Shack store next door. Haywood had a laid-back personality, a mustache, goatee, and a permanent smile on his face. He smoked a cigarette every twenty minutes or so until closing. Haywood had a quick wit and a knack for conversation, especially with the ladies. But it was hysterical watching him get through one of his bad karma days. Haywood never got mad or upset, and that's why it was humorous to see him have such a bad day. First, a customer with which he'd already spent countless and tireless efforts with a day earlier had decided she wanted her money back on the walkman knockoff she bought from him. The store's policy was absolutely no refunds, and exchanges were honored up to seven days only. She started to get confrontational with Haywood because of the no refund policy. After an hour, she caved in, and Haywood exchanged the knockoff for a Sanyo model. She stormed out of the store anyway, still really pissed off at him. Haywood was easygoing, and so he just shook his head and smiled. Then he decided to walk outside for a smoke, when a man sitting inside an old Lincoln Continental began muttering something at him. He told the man that he didn't understand what he was trying to say and asked him to repeat himself. But for some bizarre reason, the man in the Lincoln got really angry and began screaming at Haywood, to the point where I thought he'd jump out of his car and come after him. Haywood tried to reason with him, but it only agitated the man even further. Haywood threw his arms up in the air in disgust and walked quickly back inside the store. Then he walked up to Dad with a puzzled expression on his face and said, "I can't do nothin' right today, Mr.

S. I'm gonna sit in the back for awhile, away from people." It seemed like everyone was out to get Haywood that day.

Howard and I decided to take a little R&R away from work and fly to Las Vegas. Mom and Dad's travel agent got us a special deal, and we spent an extra night in Los Angeles. I'd never been anywhere out west before. Hair perms for men were popular, and I got one before we left. I actually resembled my cousin David. We took off from Washington National and later arrived at the Riviera Hotel. While Howard and I waited for our rooms to be ready, we tried our luck at the blackjack tables. It was my first experience in Vegas and at a blackjack table; my gambling experience had been limited to betting with the trotters at Rosecroft Raceway. I sat at the table with a freakishly tall dealer that resembled Lurch from the *Addams Family*. The deck of cards had almost disappeared in his monster mitts. I thought I was acting kind of cool until I picked up the cards and heard the dealer's Lurch-like voice say, "Don't touch the cards, sir." I wasn't sure what the hell he was talking about, so I proceeded to look at my cards again. Lurch reprimanded me a second time. "Sir, you can't touch the cards!" It took me a few minutes before I finally figured it out, but it didn't seem like a very fun game; five hands later, I lost seventy bucks. I got up from the black jack table looking like I'd just had an enema. I was pissed off already and hadn't even checked into the room yet.

Later that evening, Howard and I went to see Steve Martin's act downstairs at the Versailles Showroom and laughed our asses off. The maître d' seated us with a couple of wild girls from California. The blonde wore tight leopard print pants. Both of the women were bosomy, and I was surprised that their boobs hadn't fallen out of their blouses. Our table completely lost it when Steve Martin shaped his balloon animals on stage, and one balloon didn't shape into anything noticeable, so he looked at the audience with a stupid look on his face and said, "Hey, everybody, look … its gonorrhea!" Martin Mull was in the audience, and he took a bow.

The next night, we saw Siegfried and Roy at the Stardust Hotel. My blackjack etiquette got much better, and although I was still not happy about losing money, the free drinks while I gambled had made it easier to forget. Howard on the other hand won eight hundred dollars. He always did have better luck than I did. We flew out of McCarran International early the next morning and landed in LA, and then we checked into the Century Plaza Hotel in Century City. We had one whole day to spend in Los Angeles, and so we toured Universal Studios in Hollywood. We had a camera with us but forgot it in the cab on the way back to the hotel. We were exhausted when we got back to our room. Howard wanted to eat in and call it a night. We sat around watching TV when I noticed the local news reporter talking about a huge gala happening inside our hotel. She talked about a huge benefit with celebrities for Saint Jude Children's Research Hospital. I explained to Howard that it might be a good opportunity to see some Hollywood stars before we headed back to DC. After all, we didn't have to walk very far to look. I finally convinced him to go out and take a look around. We got all dressed up in our suits and rode the elevator down to the lobby. We looked around the lobby for awhile, but it seemed unusually quiet. We walked outside and crossed the street to the ABC Entertainment Center. It was rather late, and no one was around except for a lone black musician playing his saxophone for tips. We saw the Playboy Club, but we weren't members, and so we turned around and headed back. I started to think that we got all dressed up for nothing. When we walked back inside the hotel lobby, I noticed a fat, obnoxious kid with glasses clicking snapshots with his camera at people riding down the escalator toward him. The flash on his camera was extremely bright, and I'm sure those people had to be annoyed. Then Howard and I witnessed hundreds of people in tuxedos carrying goody bags, stepping off the escalator one by one. They were all the celebrities who attended the Saint Jude Hospital Gala. We were definitely in the right place and at the right time. Most of Hollywood shared the room with Howard, me, the fat obnoxious kid, and his mother. We didn't want to walk over and talk with any of the celebrities because the fat kid was embarrassing to everyone, and we didn't want to be associated with him in any way. Besides, we'd lost the camera in the taxicab.

A very tall and lanky Fred MacMurray walked over and stood alone right beside me. I said hello and wanted to strike up a conversation with him, but all I could do was to stare and imagine that he was still Steven Douglas as he lit up his pipe. Actor Vic Tayback, who played Mel in the TV sitcom *Alice,* came walking out quickly and was loud and upbeat. We shook hands as he shouted hello to everyone. Like my grandparents, Tayback's parents were also immigrants from Aleppo, Syria. Suddenly my attention focused on watching Kirk Douglas and Connie Stevens as they slipped out one of the side double door exits together. Most of the celebs were quickly lifted up by an escalator, and I witnessed George Burns, Vic Damone, Marlo Thomas and Phil Donahue, Rita Moreno, Linda Carter, Ernest Borgnine, Peter Falk, Robert Stack, and Red Buttons climbing slowly up the moving staircase. Danny Thomas and Frank Sinatra were at the event but never came out. Early the next morning, we took a cab to LAX and flew back home. It was definitely an action-packed, four-day trip.

Three months after Howard and I got back from Vegas, I decided to take a second trip alone. I must have caught the Vegas bug or something. I asked Iggy to go with me, but he had other obligations with his girlfriend. When I arrived in Las Vegas, I caught two shows every night, and this time I actually won a few hundred dollars at the blackjack tables. But the highlight of my trip was when I saw Frank Sinatra. I found out that Sinatra was performing at Caesar's Palace. After a few Seagram Seven and Sevens in my room, and then a few more at the blackjack tables, I decided that I was going to see Frank. I had no idea how I was getting in to see the show because I didn't have a ticket, and it was already sold-out. The Riviera Hotel staff flagged me a cab. I jumped inside and told the driver to take me to Caesar's Palace. Then I asked him what my chances were to get into Sinatra's show without a ticket. He said my chances were good because I was going alone. I stepped out of the cab and headed for the Circus Maximus showroom. A huge line of people had already formed in front of the showroom and stretched throughout the casino. It must have been the booze that took control over me next because I walked right up to the maître d' standing at the front entrance, in front of hundreds of people waiting in line. But at no point did I think that it was bad idea. I whipped out a hundred-dollar bill and flashed it to a big, tough-looking guy in a tuxedo. He stood next to the maître d' like a bodyguard.

I was buzzed and feeling quite good, so I asked him, "Can you get me in to see Frank?"

He responded in a Mafioso sounding tone, "No, I can't do that."

I said, "All right thanks," and prepared for my exit.

Suddenly he grabbed my arm and said, "Hold on, I can't get you inside—but he can," nodding his head toward the maître d'.

The maître d' summoned me and said, "Stand over to the side for a second." I stood next to his podium, not knowing what to expect next. He glanced down at a list filled with names that lay flat on the podium, and he said, "When I call you, just say that you're with the Johnson party." I don't think he wanted to piss off any of those people that waited in line for over an hour. Then I thought to myself that I may just get in to see Sinatra after all. Immediately he called, "Johnson party?"

I responded, "Yes, that's me."

He said, "Go right in, sir." I walked through the entrance door into the showroom. A third man in a tuxedo from inside the showroom approached me and asked, "Do you have the yard?" meaning the hundred-dollar bill. I snuck the bill into his palm, much like the way Uncle Joey use to pay the salesmen at Chin Lung on Saturdays. He stashed the C-note into his trouser pocket and started walking toward the stage. Then he turned around and asked me, "You want to sit front row center, right, sir?"

I said, "Of course." I felt like a real big shot. The man picked up a single chair and jammed it between two other chairs at the front center table by the stage. It was the best service I ever received. I ordered my three-drink minimum and waited for the show to start. Comedian Freddie Roman came out first, and then Sinatra strutted out on stage, looking and sounding the way he should. It was the best show I'd ever seen, and it all couldn't have been more perfect. I phoned Mom and Dad at two thirty in the morning, boasting about my Sinatra experience.

When I got back home to Alexandria, I told everybody about how spectacular the Sinatra event was. Mom and Dad had always loved Ol' Blue Eyes, and growing up I'd hear Dad playing his albums when he wasn't listening to "Om Kalsoum." But I had never really appreciated Sinatra until after that magnificent performance at Caesar's Place. I started buying Sinatra and Dean Martin albums and brought them with me every time I went out on a date. My dating skills were definitely getting more romantic. I thought I was one of the Rat Pack now; I even wore attire reminiscent to Sinatra and Martin's casual style. I started drinking Jack Daniels in honor of Frank. One thing was for sure, I never went through any of my crazy phases half ass.

Chapter Eighteen

Throwing Tomatoes for Justice

On a disturbing evening in December 1980, I had decided to watch Monday Night Football in my bedroom. John Smith of the New England Patriots was about to kick a field goal against the Miami Dolphins when Howard Cosell announced that John Lennon was shot in the back twice and then pronounced dead on arrival. I couldn't fathom what I had just heard. I rushed into Iggy's room to tell him the news, and then we both rushed back into my room to hear the news again. An ex-Beatle was murdered; we were both sad and angry. On that evening, I knew none of us were safe and anything was possible. The first thing I thought about was all the great memories the Beatles had given to me. They made headlines throughout my entire childhood. I always thought John was the coolest and preferred his singing style over McCartney's. After he released the *Double Fantasy* album, there were rumors of a possible tour. I had seen McCartney with Wings and George Harrison in concert, and I was looking forward to a possible Lennon tour. I never had the opportunity to see the Beatles play live, but I thought at least I'd get to see them all play individually. Lennon's death put to rest any chance of a Beatles reunion … forever! I met Iggy at Worldwide the next day; he was working full-time with his brother-in-law on

17th Street. I told Dad that Iggy and I were going to attend a silent tribute to Lennon at the Lincoln Memorial. Both of us wore black armbands all day as a tribute to his memory. It was the senseless act of murder that had made his death so tragic. Even if you didn't like Lennon the man, you were still saddened by the news.

Around that time, another broadcasting career bit the dust. My friend Eric from Brown Institute, who had worked at a radio station inside Luray Caverns, quit his job. The worst part of it all was that he had lost his high school sweetheart, too. Apparently every time Eric was on the radio, his girlfriend cheated on him. It was very convenient for her knowing exactly where Eric was while she made his life miserable. Eric had dated her for nine years, and he certainly didn't deserve for it to end that way. He actually caught them together one day in his apartment. I'm not sure if they were careless or if she intended for them to get caught; in either case it led to a huge brawl, and Eric got the worst of it. The guy was twice the size of Eric, and so he literally left Luray Caverns a broken man. Eric ended up moving back to Springfield, Virginia, with his parents. I knew he was in rough shape and needed a friend, and I took him out to the Bayou in Georgetown and then helped him to unleash some of his frustrations. There was a band playing there that night called The Marbles, and we thought they really sucked, so we expressed how we felt by kicking over chairs and tables, just like when we went out to those clubs in Miami. Eric came over to visit me at my place a lot, and I noticed he was usually drunk. I thought he needed a permanent distraction to help him ease his pain, so I asked Eric to come work with us at Worldwide, and he accepted.

Meanwhile, Dad hired Saul. He was a Colombian-Syrian Jew and only eighteen years old. Saul's father owned a women's clothing store down the block and catered to the local hookers. Dad hired Saul as a stockperson and to clean up around the store. Saul was definitely a nerd; he always smiled and wore thick black glasses, but he was a hell of a nice kid.

It was another typical *mejnoon* Saturday at Worldwide. I think anyone who has ever worked long retail hours eventually goes a little berserk. Our day started getting nuts at 12:30, around lunchtime. While Eric ate his lunch upstairs on the second floor, Howard and I took turns throwing pennies from the sales floor at his really huge head; it was just too tempting of a target not to aim for.

At 1:30, Bernadette came back from lunch and appeared a bit shaken. I asked her, "What's wrong, Bernie?" She started shaking, and her eyes rolled back into her head. After finally regaining her composure, she held both of her hands to her chest and said, "I ran into the man with no head by accident, and he sacred me to death." We had names for everyone; there was a man that walked around F Street over the years who always had his head bent down when he walked. He was known to us as "the headless man" because when you saw him from behind, he actually appeared to have no head.

At 2:20, I watched Eric demonstrating a 35mm autofocus camera to an African G, and Eric intentionally annoyed the crap out of the man by shooting the flash directly into his eyes. He'd repeatedly snap the shutter and made the flash go off in the customer's face, over and over again, until he finally couldn't take it anymore. The African G pitifully requested, "Please, sir, no more flash; I am going blind." The African bought the camera anyway but never figured out that Eric's true motive was to provoke him. I think his customer thought Eric was just demo happy or something.

Eric was a perfect fit for Worldwide. He picked up on our lingo really fast and even created some of his own. Eric came up with a name to classify the white government workers who wasted our time during their lunch breaks. He referred to them as the "itey-whays" (pig Latin for whiteys). They'd walk into the store eating what was left of their lunches, dropping crumbs all over our floor. Then they'd ask us to demonstrate one of the latest products they saw advertised in the newspaper for a ridiculously low price, usually at one of the suburbia catalog stores. The catalog stores didn't have salesmen to show them the merchandise and teach the customers how to use it, like we did; that's how they could afford to sell cheap. The itey-whays just wanted to bust our chops, but we were on to them. Every time they asked us to pull the goods out of a case, we'd firmly ask, "Are you going to buy one today, sir?" If we weren't convinced by their response we'd say, "Sorry, we don't demonstrate the merchandise," or, "There are no batteries inside."

At 3:00, Dad started spraying Lysol directly on Gs that smelled bad. We had a lot of foreign tourists that walked into the store, and some didn't bathe as often as they should. When an offensive visitor walked around the store, there'd be a loud announcement from Dad, "Wow, what an ell-smay!" Then, when the G had his back turned, Dad sprayed him down with the Lysol from head to toe. Dad made it a lot more tolerable for everyone, and the G remained clueless.

At 3:30, like clockwork, the old black lady with really thick glasses and her guitar peeked inside our front door and hollered, "Is this Radio Shack?" Haywood, Bernadette, and Eric all harmonized, "Radio Shack is next door!" It was probably the fiftieth time that she had asked us if we were Radio Shack, but we just played right along, as if it were always the first time that she had asked us.

At 3:45, the store got packed with customers, and everyone had a G they were waiting on. I had the wall case door slid wide open and was demonstrating a Sanyo boom box. In a flash, a husho grabbed one of the other boom boxes off the shelf and then ran out the front door and down the street. Without thought or hesitation, I ran after him. I chased him down Fourteenth Street in a very comical way. During the chase, I yelled at him, "Stop, I've got a gun!" and then pulled out my comb. I quickly drew the attention of the crowd walking up and down the city street. The husho looked back at me to see if I really had a weapon. Then I did one of the stupidest things ever. I aimed my comb at the running husho and screamed, "Bang! Bang!" After that I lost all respect from the crowd; I saw and heard their bursts of laughter, but I still continued my pursuit. Finally I did the unthinkable and followed the husho into a deserted alleyway. I couldn't see where he ran off to, but I continued to walk slowly through the alley anyway. Then, in a remarkable turn of events, I saw two black dudes walking toward me carrying the same boom box stolen by the husho. They both walked over to me, and one of them asked, "Is this your box, man?"

I said, "Yeah, I work around the corner, and the dude I was chasing stole it from our store." Then the guy holding the recovered Sanyo boom box handed it to me. Apparently, those two black dudes had stolen it from the husho that had stolen it from us. I was overwhelmed that those two dudes had returned the box over to me, especially when all three of us were all alone in that alley. I asked both of them to follow me over to Worldwide, and then I gave each one of them a Timex watch and thanked them for returning the boom box.

My chase after that husho reminded me of an incident that happened to my cousin Howard in Baltimore. Howard owned a check-cashing business on Baltimore Street, and a husho stole money from him and ran out of his store. Howard took out his gun, chased the husho down the street, and then followed him into a bank. When Howard entered the bank, he started to wave the gun over his head and shouted, "This is not a hold up! This is not a hold up!" I thought that was really funny.

At 5:15, about half of the store's overhead lights had gone out. Howard and I changed a few fluorescent tubes but still couldn't restore power, and so we decided to change the fuses. This was a first for us; we'd never had to change the fuses before. After spending thirty minutes looking around the store for a fuse box, we finally figured it out. It was located in the darkest, dreariest, and spookiest area of the store, in the downstairs cellar. No one had ever gone down there before. There were no lights, and it resembled an old dungeon. All the buildings on F Street were extremely old. Just down the block from Worldwide was the Old Ebbitt Grill. It was Washington DC's oldest and most historic saloon, founded in 1856. The F Street Restaurant and Saloon was just two doors away from the Rhodes Tavern, which had a history of its own. The bar was reportedly the site where British generals toasted one another as they watched the White House burn during the War of 1812.

Howard and I decided to change the fuses as a team effort, mainly because we were both scared to do it alone. The stairs that led to the cellar were located at the very back corner of the store. Howard and I took a deep breath and walked down the flight of stairs. I had a bad feeling, so I let Howard walk down in front of me while I held onto his shirt. Howard held the flashlight. It looked like a scene from an old Abbott and Costello movie. We hurried to the fuse box and quickly replaced the burned-out fuses. I turned around to head back upstairs and away from the creepiness when I saw several strange objects in the darkness scattering around us. My eyes quickly adjusted to the darkness, and I focused on six dog-sized rats at our feet. I immediately used my first instinct for survival and jumped on Howard's back. He didn't know what was happening until I yelled, "Huge rats everywhere!" Howard calmly ran out of the cellar and up the stairs to the sales floor, with me riding piggyback.

At 6:00, before Saul went home that day, we decided to scare the shit out of him. He was a bit naïve, and so we had some fun with him. We told Eric to hide in an empty box on the third floor, and then we sent Saul upstairs to carry that very same box downstairs. When Saul tried to pick up the box, Eric jumped out screaming. Saul was so scared that he tried to run all the way back downstairs to the sales floor, but I ambushed him at the bottom of the second floor stairway and scared the crap out of him again.

At 6:35, after we closed the store that evening, we headed for the parking garage. I told the parking attendant about our rat incident that day, and then I noticed that there were large rat traps scattered throughout the parking garage. I asked the parking attendant, who kind of looked like a skinny rat, if they had a rat problem. He remarked, "Hehe … I saw a rat the other day with a syringe sticking out of his arm."

On Monday morning, Eric, Bernadette, and I prepared to open Worldwide for business; Dad and Howard were coming in later.

Eric and I unlocked all the iron gates that protected the windows, and then we opened the final one to the store lobby. We lifted up all the gates, and I unlocked the front door. But before I could turn the lights on, I noticed that the rats were now running around freely on the sales floor. Bernadette jumped up on a chair while Eric and I climbed up on top of a showcase, and we all watched the huge rats scamper in the dark. We looked at one another in disbelief and wondered how the hell we were going to open the store for business. Well, I was in charge and wasn't about to let a few gigantic rats prevent us from paying the rent that day. I knew once the lights were on the rats would go into hiding, so I ran like the wind to the back of the store and flicked on all the breaker switches, and then we opened the store for business. Most of the day it was business as usual with no signs of the rats. Our store trash can was actually just a cardboard box. Dad liked throwing the trash into a cardboard box so that when it was full, he'd toss the whole thing out. Eric took what was left of his lunch and threw it into the cardboard trash can. When he tried to push the trash down in the box, he nervously backed away and shouted, "I touched its fur! There's a rat hiding in the trash!" It was just a subtle reminder that they were still running around on the sales floor and were still in charge.

The next day Howard called exterminators, and what an ordeal that was. First they baited the store with poison to slow down the rats. Later they confronted the rats with poisonous gas and started to hit them with large sticks. The rats were huge, and you could hear them squealing in pain after being struck repeatedly by the exterminators' sticks. All of us actually felt sorry for the rats; it was a sad display of brutality but had to be done. The exterminators finally killed them all and removed the dead rats from the store. Eric actually taped the rats' horrific squealing sounds on a handheld tape recorder.

Iggy and I shared a day off from work together, and we were just sitting around watching the news. They were talking about the Iran hostage crisis and how there were Iranian protesters in front of the White house. Iggy and I couldn't believe it. They held American hostages and yet had the right to protest in our town. Iggy got up, turned the TV off, and said, "Hey, man, let's go down there and throw tomatoes at them."

Without hesitating I said, "Let's go!" We jumped into his old, beat-up van and headed for the nearest grocery store. We bought about fifty huge tomatoes and then jumped back into his van and headed for the White house. Iggy drove slowly and carefully, directly in front of the protestors, and then he quickly stopped. Then I brought out a big brown bag that was filled with the giant tomatoes; we both stood up and squeezed through the van's tiny sunroof. We aimed and fired! The Iranian protestors were completely surprised by the attack. They were being pelted by two angry, young Americans looking for revenge. Both of us loved our country. In conversation, Iggy would always mention how grateful he was to be living in America. He'd always boast to whoever he was talking to, "This is the land of opportunity, brother; be proud." As a child, he and his family luckily escaped the clutches of Castro's Cuba to live here in freedom. I was also reminded of Abuela's peril, her liberties confiscated when the communist took over Cuba, forced to abandon her life as a prestigious medical doctor and by chance allowed to board an airplane to America, but with only the clothes on her back. I was also reminded of Dad's mother and father, Cecelia and Howard, who were Jews living in Aleppo, Syria, a Muslim land, and who immigrated to Ellis Island and began a new life free from oppression. The tomato barrage splattered our own message for freedom that day as DC police officers just stood there, watched, and smiled.

A week after our patriotic stand, Iggy had invited two of his old buddies over to spend a couple days with us. They were navy seals stationed in Hawaii. Iggy and I had been thinking of joining the navy for some time on some sort of a buddy plan. We were both getting bored with our lives and looked for some sort of a diversion. There had to be more to life than working and partying. I thought that I could use my experiences in broadcasting to work in communications, preferably on a ship. I was all set to hear about his buddies' wonderful adventures in the navy and then perhaps be psyched enough to go and visit a recruiter after they left. After talking about music and what we were going to do that night, we shifted into a more serious conversation about Iggy's and my plan of joining the navy. Their immediate reaction to our intentions was, "Don't do it, man!" Here we were, discussing our enthusiasm for joining the service to a couple of navy seals—stationed in beautiful Hawaii, no less—and they practically scolded us not to join. I was shocked. They repeated the same negative messages again and again. "You don't need to put up with the bullshit, man, don't do it." Iggy and I thought there must have been some truth in what they were saying, and their harsh message echoed in our heads. Those two navy seals had convinced us that night not to join. It was probably the only chance that I had to mimic Dad and Howard's military duty, but I guess it was not meant to be.

Worldwide Electronics had developed a strong business relationship with the National Press Corps. Marsha K, one of our favorite press Gs, invited me and a guest to one of President Reagan's inauguration parties. I decided to invite Iggy to the black tie gala. We drove up to the old and elegant Georgetown residence in my '79 black Trans Am. Military guards stood at attention as we were about to make our grand entrance. A gentleman in a black tuxedo and wearing gloves inspected our invitations at the top of the stairs. We arrived early, but there were plenty of tuxedos and gowns already mingling about. Iggy and I had put our suave and sophisticated game faces on, and we were ready to become one of the elite upper class—for one night anyway. The first thing I noticed at the party was a champagne fountain. Iggy and I walked over and filled up our glasses. We split up so to make ourselves known and popular, conversing intellectually. I started the night off by chatting with the ambassador of Ecuador. He spoke very little English, and I tried sneaking in what Spanish I knew, with my best Cuban accent. I always understood and spoke just enough to win him over. We'd talk for awhile and then dip our glasses into the champagne fountain. I think we dipped around four times. Ignacio and I had dipped at least three times earlier when we arrived. I noticed that everyone at the party was getting inebriated rather quickly, especially me. After my conversation with the ambassador,

I walked by him and spilled my entire champagne drink down his back. He was drenched, but he didn't seem to notice, so I didn't apologize and kept walking. By then, the room was getting louder; everyone was happy and getting loaded. A full orchestra was set up on a small stage in one of the rooms. The music started to play, and then I saw Marsha K, our reporter friend. She introduced me to the great granddaughter of President Franklin Delano Roosevelt. I asked her to dance. Afterward the music changed from dance to Broadway tunes, and the little girl from *Annie* came out and sang "Tomorrow."

I walked into a different room and saw Iggy; he appeared to be in deep discussion. I watched and listened to his conversation with a pretentious man. While Iggy balanced a plate filled of hors d'oeuvres with the palm of his hand, he talked some shit about how he owned a chain of jewelry stores up and down the east coast, and how he was preparing to expand his operations into several other countries in South America. He was really laying it on thick—a little too thick for my taste. I thought he looked and sounded ridiculous, and I was determined to take him down. I walked in between the conversation and knocked the plate right out of his hands. The food on his plate must have flown ten feet in the air. Iggy just stood there with a puzzled frown, and bits and pieces of food scattered all around him. When he finally spoke, he said, "Man, that was not cool." I was really drunk from dipping into the Champagne fountain and couldn't stop laughing. Meanwhile, the affluent gentleman that Iggy had gloated with for most of the evening had disappeared.

Later that evening, we had heard rumors that the Beach Boys were upstairs, and that Honor Blackman, who played Pussy Galore in the James Bond movie *Goldfinger,* was in the house. Iggy and I were already plastered, and so there was definitely a good chance that we made up those rumors. I knew for a fact that President Reagan or Vice President Bush never made it to our party; we would have remembered that. After a few more hours of mingling and drinking expensive Champagne, we decided to call it a night. Iggy and I headed for the valet. After we exited the home, I reached for the top second step and completely missed it, plummeting down the entire flight of stairs and falling flat on my face. I felt no pain but was kind of embarrassed by the incident. Iggy ran over and stood me up and then asked, "Are you all right dude?"

I think I said, "Yeah, man; do you know where my car keys are?"

Iggy looked at me as if I was a complete lunatic and responded, "You're not driving, man, are you crazy? You're wasted!" Iggy was in much better condition than I was that night, because he ate food and I hadn't. He helped me into the passenger seat and drove us both home.

Chapter Nineteen

Do You Want to Meet My Friends?

Monica gave birth to Tiffani Marie in October of '81. My brother Howard had two children now, and I was an uncle again. It was kind of ironic that Monica and her children, Sean and Tiffani, were all born on the twenty-seventh day of a month. I wondered if Bernadette had played that number.

Iggy and I met three gorgeous roommates. They lived at another apartment complex only a few minutes from our bachelor pad. Iggy was getting really serious about his girlfriend, but they fought a lot, and so he ended up dating other woman from time to time. I on the other hand had finally overcome my shyness and awkwardness around women. Lacy and I had kept our relationship—only as friends, but she was a cool girl. We went to a couple of rock concerts together, and she liked wearing the "WNAV—We bring you more" T-shirt that I brought her from the radio station. I was twenty-two years old, and for the first time in my life, I became a "player." Maybe Frank Sinatra had something to do with it, I don't know. Iggy and I took turns dating the hot roommates. Our romantic escapades reminded me of a Sinatra or Dean Martin movie from the sixties. Through high school, all I wanted was to meet a sweet and nice girl to be with, but because of my own insecurities, it never happened. Then at the clubs, I'd always be on the lookout for that special somebody, but I usually met superficial and uncaring woman. I was convinced that I didn't want to be a player for very long; it just didn't feel right.

At work, actor James Mason and his wife, Clarissa, walked into Worldwide one afternoon. They lived in Switzerland, so maybe it was the Swiss facade of Worldwide Electronics, which had enticed them to come inside and shop. In case you don't know who James Mason was, he was considered one of the finest film actors of the twentieth century. One of his most memorable roles was his portrayal of Captain Nemo, from Jules Verne's classic *Twenty Thousand Leagues under the Sea*. Mr. Mason was on a mission to find a Bone Fone. (It was really cool to hear him pronounce Bone Fone in his English accent) The Bone Fone was a personal stereo with its wrap-around design and unique speaker placement. The vibrations resonated through your ears and then into the sensitive bones of your inner ear. It gave the listener a breathtaking sound and was useful to use while exercising, jogging, or bicycling. But it wasn't a very popular item at Worldwide, and we actually thought we'd get stuck with them. We never thought it would take a famous movie star traveling all the way from Switzerland to take them off our hands. The Masons even wanted to buy two more, and we placed an order and then later shipped them to their home in Switzerland. We actually kept in touch with the Masons after that first visit to Worldwide.

After work ended that day, I decided to stop in for a quick beer at Riddles, close to home. Riddles was a very popular night spot in Alexandria. It had a nice mix of people and played great music. I stood there by the bar and took a few sips from out of my beer; all the seats were occupied and the club was packed. I felt a tap on my shoulder, and there she stood. She was beautiful and sweet. We stared at one another, and then she asked, "Do you want to come over and meet my friends?" I was charmed by her Southern accent and infectious smile. She lit up the room. What normal man could resist such an offer? I walked over with my beer in hand to a group of six giggling women. She introduced me to everyone, but I only wanted to remember one name. I primarily talked with Sharon and her friend from New York. Sharon thought I was hitting it off with her friend from New York because we chatted a lot about the same things, but I was only being polite.

After twenty minutes of hanging out in her social group, I asked Sharon to dance with me. She was like no one I had ever known or met. We chatted alone after our dance together, and she told me that she was from a small town in Kentucky. She needed a change from her small-town life and wanted to move closer to her older sister, Debbie, who lived in Stafford. Then she said that she was a registered nurse and worked in the ICU at Alexandria Hospital. Near closing time, we decided to go back to my place, and she agreed to follow me home in her little white Toyota. My townhome was directly behind Riddles and only minutes away. She liked my place but later told me that she felt a little uncomfortable. I think she was a bit spooked over Iggy's fish tanks. But we really enjoyed each other's company, and after chatting for thirty minutes, I walked her out to her car, and she headed home to Burke.

I called Sharon the very next day and asked her out on our first date. I picked her up at the townhome that she shared with her roommate, Cindy. The very first thing I noticed about her when she came to the door was the pretty red flower in her hair. Everything about Sharon was different and exciting to me. We slid into the plush red velvet interior of my black Trans Am. She wasn't so sure about those piranha fish in my townhome, but I knew for a fact that she liked my car. We drove to Kings Dominion, a popular amusement park about an hour and a half away. We took slow strolls around the park and held hands. We felt really comfortable around each other, even when she made fun of my unusually small thumbs.

Sharon had so many adorable sayings. If I asked her how she felt, she'd say, "With my hands."

If I asked her anything that had the word "see" in a sentence, she'd respond by saying to me, "See see, said the blind man." Sometimes

I'd ask her a question, and she'd answer back by asking me, "Does Carter have oats?" I never knew what the hell she was talking about, but I thought it was cute. If Sharon had her belly button exposed, she'd tell me that she worried that a frog may go inside. The same principals applied when her ears were exposed, but this time it was a fly that she was worried about going inside.

At the park, we asked a stranger to take a picture of both of us with my camera. We had our arms around each other for the first time. At the parking lot, I took pictures of Sharon posing on the hood of my Trans Am. Then we decided to head home before it got dark. I spent some time at her place and got to meet her roommate. Cindy was a cute blonde with a hot body. She had met a guy named Lee recently and was definitely gaga over him. Sharon and I had a wonderful day together; we said goodnight and then kissed for the first time.

After Sharon and I hit it off, I got calls from other girls. I had never been this popular with women before. I thought to myself, "Hmm, if I'm going to get girls like Sinatra, than I'd better live like Sinatra." I found a penthouse-type apartment and then told Iggy that I was moving out. I rented a space at the swanky Towers 2000 high-rise apartment building, only minutes from my old place. I invited Sharon to help furnish my new swinging bachelor pad. Of course at the time, I didn't reveal to her my plan of becoming 50 percent Frank Sinatra, 30 percent Dean Martin, and 20 percent Hugh Hefner. Sharon and I had a lot of fun picking out the furniture together. I made great money as a single guy working at Worldwide, and we picked out enough swanky furniture to furnish the entire apartment. When everything was finally moved in, the place looked seductive. Now I had everything I needed to lure beautiful Playboy playmates and be the ultimate player. But one thing had prevented that from happening … love! I fell in love with Sharon and didn't care about anyone else. I couldn't believe what I was doing; I canceled dates and plans with all the other women that same week, and I concentrated all my efforts into making Sharon happy and getting her to love me back. She was the love of my life.

Sharon worked the seven-to-eleven shifts at the hospital. I'd wait for her downstairs in the emergency room and watched *M*A*S*H* on the hospital TV until she got off work. Sometimes it wouldn't be until after midnight. When she finally got off, I'd follow her home. She worked as an agency nurse for awhile, which meant working at a lot of different hospitals. I waited for her inside all the emergency rooms at every hospital until she got off work. I was very protective and very much in love.

The Ku Klux Klan had decided to hold a demonstration in DC. A very small group of them showed up, and there were an excessive amount of police officers protecting them. Just about any radical group could get a permit to march and demonstrate in our nation's capital. But there were always counter groups of troublemakers that used demonstrations as an excuse to raise their own havoc on the city. The KKK held their demonstrations on the grounds of the Washington Monument. They were outnumbered and confined to a very small group and area. Sometime after their meeting broke up, Aunt Mattie called me up on the phone; she let me know that the police had warned Benson Jewelers of trouble brewing in retaliation for the KKK being in town, so we should stay alert. Mattie worked as a bookkeeper for Benson Jewelers right down the block. Immediately after I hung up with her, the phone rang again. This time she was panicky. She said there was a large group of black youths storming down the block with sticks, yelling and breaking windows.

Dad, Howard, Haywood, and I immediately ran outside to take a look, and we saw the large group marching toward us. Howard and my instincts had told us to man our battle stations. We had one G in the store, and he was black. He overheard everything that was about to happen and nervously hid in our bathroom. Meanwhile, Heywood told Howard that if the angry mob came into the store, he was going to jump on his back and say, "I got one of them!" And he wasn't kidding either. Howard grabbed the shotgun that we kept inside the store and ran up to the third floor. He opened the window and pointed the gun out toward the sidewalk, waiting patiently. I grabbed a .38mm pistol out of the drawer from underneath the cash register and released the safety. It was already loaded.

Dad and I headed for the front entrance of the store. Then Dad totally took me by surprise. After we walked outside to the store lobby, he reached up and pulled down the rolling security gate for the outside lobby, leaving him standing alone on the other side. The store's security gates were a solid sheet of iron, so you couldn't see through them. One by one, I heard him pulling down the rest of the gates that protected each of the store front windows. It took me a few seconds to digest what had just happened. Then I reacted by running as fast as I could over to the stairs that led to the third floor. I yelled up at Howard, "Dad's alone outside in front of the store!" Howard took more serious aim while I ran back to the store lobby. I had never fired a real weapon before, but I held that pistol in my hand like a soldier defending his fort. Wild thoughts started to race through my mind, like what if I had to shoot someone, or what happens if I did start shooting, and they kept on coming.

I hollered out at Dad from inside of the iron barrier. "Are you all right?" But he didn't answer. "I'm ready if you need me," I said. Howard and I were ready to defend ourselves, but dad's heroics had us both baffled. Then I heard the angry voices; they were right outside the gate. I called out a second time, "Dad, are you all right? Answer me!" He still said nothing. I was really worried. At that moment anything could have happened. It was quiet and still, but there was no hint of violence. I had to see what was happening outside. I bent down to lift up the security gate but got distracted by a loud, screeching, rattling noise. Then I realized that someone beat me to it—on the other side. After I recovered from the noise and shock of watching the gate lifting up, I quickly focused my attention on Dad, standing outside on the sidewalk—and all alone. It was like a scene right out of a movie. Dad looked like the last man standing after a huge war battle. The only thing missing was smoke clearing all around him.

I asked Dad, "What the hell just happened, and why did you pull down the gate?" He said that he pulled the gate down so they wouldn't be able to get inside the store. Then he just stood and watched the angry mob walk right by him. The occurrence reminded me of Passover, when the Hebrews were instructed to mark their doorposts to protect them from the tenth plague, and the spirit of the Lord passed over them. It also took me back to the '68 riots. Howard and I were ready for an all-out war that afternoon, but Dad used his natural instincts that he had inherited from all those years of working in the city.

There was another twist to the story. When we first saw the mob marching down the street toward us, I called 911 and told them that there was an officer down by Fourteenth and F Street. Unfortunately, it was the only way to get fast and immediate action from the DC police department. So by the time the mob had walked past Dad, the police had already started to arrive at the scene. Later, after we closed the store, we walked by the district building on the way to the parking garage. We saw Mayor Barry standing at the corner, and Dad let him have it. He scolded the mayor by saying that he was a business owner that worked in the city for more than twenty years, and that it was a disgrace to let incidents like that to happen, especially to hard-working taxpayers. The mayor just shook his head and said, "It's not my fault!"

Sharon and I had been dating for about a year when I had asked her out on a picnic at Burke Lake Park. I brought wine, cheese, and an engagement ring. The last time I brought Sharon to Burke Lake, we were startled by two huge German shepherds. They appeared from out of nowhere and seemed to be loose. They stared at us and we stared back at them. We were frozen and couldn't move a muscle. It really looked as if we were going to be their next meal. Suddenly the dogs' owner appeared with their leashes in his hand.

This time, after Sharon and I talked for awhile and had a couple glasses of wine, I finally built up enough nerve to ask her to marry me. We sat quietly on her blanket, side by side and staring at the lake, when I slowly reached into my jacket pocket and pulled out the ring. I slowly opened the tiny ring box in front of her and asked, "Sharon, will you marry me?" I immediately saw that beautiful smile, and then her eyes filled up with tears; she looked up at me and said yes. It was the happiest moment of my life.

I soon asked her dad's permission to marry her, and later I celebrated with her parents on the phone. I had never met them face to face. Lyle and Arlena lived in Henderson, Kentucky, all of their lives. They appeared to be down-to-earth and really nice people. The next step was to actually meet her parents. Our plans were as followed: Sharon was to fly out first so she could spend some extra time with her folks, and then I'd fly out five days later. Sharon's sister Debbie and her husband, Jim, were going to drive out and meet up with us a few days after I arrived. They were driving to Louisville first to see Jim's family. I drove Sharon to National Airport, and we kissed good-bye.

Five days later, I drove myself to the airport and walked to my gate. I checked my tickets; I'd have to change planes in Indianapolis before I finally arrived in Henderson, Kentucky. When I got to the gate, it was already packed. One distinctive thing I noticed about the people at the gate was that most of them were freakishly tall. After we boarded the aircraft, I needed to use the restroom. While I waited my turn, I looked back at two men seated and working together in the very back row. I peeked over their shoulder and witnessed a roster. At the very top of the page it read the Indiana Pacers basketball team. I returned to my seat, and sitting by the window next to me was Georg McGinnis. He played forward for the Pacers and was in the final year of his NBA career. I remembered watching McGinnis playing in the playoffs against the Washington Bullets. He played alongside Doctor J when he was on the Philadelphia 76ers. I introduced myself to Mr. McGinnis, and then he asked me why I was flying to Indiana. I told him I was meeting with my in-laws for the first time in Henderson, which was just over the John James Audubon Bridge from Evansville. McGinnis was born and raised in Indiana and knew all about Henderson. He was a very personable guy and gave me pointers on meeting with Mom and Pop Clements for the first time. Through the remainder of the trip, he talked relentlessly about his moose hunting adventures in Alaska.

I landed at the tiny airport in Evansville. It was the first time that I had actually walked out of an aircraft onto the runway. I had a feeling there would be a lot of firsts on the trip. Sharon met me at the gate, and we kissed. I hadn't seen her for five days, but it had seemed like forever. She laughed when we walked over to get my luggage, because it was already there waiting for me. She jokingly said, "There aren't many airports where your luggage is waiting on you." We left the airport and then ten minutes later drove the John James Audubon Bridge over the Ohio River, crossing into the Bluegrass state of Kentucky. It was a chilly autumn afternoon, and the leaves had already changed. My first thoughts of Henderson was of a Norman Rockwell masterpiece. We drove on the old, narrow streets, and I gazed at the old Kentucky homes. And I imagined the many generations of families that may have lived there. Before I knew it, Sharon pulled into Elm Street and under her mom and dad's carport. We were there, at my future wife's childhood home, and I was about to meet my future in-laws.

Chapter Twenty

Is the Grass Really Blue?

We walked through the door to Sharon's mom shouting, "Oh my ... he's here, hold on, let me get my shoes on." Arlena had pretty white hair, but she wore modern glasses. She was bosomy and tall like Sharon. Her face had smooth skin with absolutely no wrinkles. After she put her shoes on, she ran up and gave me a big, warm hug and kiss. After that, I felt like I was officially welcomed into the family. Sharon resembled her mom a lot. Some of the traits that I noticed rather quickly about Arlena was that she always thought carefully and hard about something before finally giving you her answer, and she never hesitated about throwing in her two cents. But she was a very sweet and caring lady.

Then I shook hands with Sharon's dad, Lyle. He was tall and extremely talkative, and he had a permanent smile painted on his face. I immediately knew Lyle could talk about anything to anyone. Doctor Clements was a dentist who housed his practice on Main Street in downtown Henderson. Arlena worked right alongside him in the office as his receptionist and bookkeeper. Lyle was extremely intelligent, although sometimes it was masked by his country boy persona. He was also a man's man. He served in the army in World

War II and was assigned the role of a point man, meaning that he'd position himself ahead of the patrol as a lookout. He had lost some of his hearing in Europe during the war from marching alongside Sherman tanks. Lyle was a Pac-Man game fanatic. During our stay, we'd walk over to the truck stop across the highway and play competitively for over an hour. Being around Lyle was more like hanging out with a buddy.

I knew I'd be spending time in a really small town, and so I was forewarned about my future in-laws bathroom. It may not have had all of the most modern conveniences. But the only real inconvenience was being without a shower. I admit it was somewhat of a shock, but I adjusted. I brought from home a hose attachment that allowed me to at least pretend like I was taking a shower. I really didn't want to take a bath, but I was forced to when my rubber shower device repeatedly kept squirting off. In years to come, they built a second bathroom in their basement with a shower. I think they built it for Sharon's and my convenience because we always stayed in the basement when we came to visit. The shower was located under the basement stairs, so you had to bend over and crouch as you showered. It was much better than my rubber hose device, so I dealt with that just fine. But the toilet that they installed was horrifying. We called it the toilet from hell. When you flushed the toilet, it swirled around violently and then it made a loud and terrifying screeching sound. Sometimes the contents in the bowl would fly out unto the carpeted floor. After several mishaps, I avoided using that toilet all together, and so I'd walk up the steep creaky wooden stairs, no matter what time it was, and used the upstairs bathroom.

I felt a little uneasy in the upstairs bathroom too, mainly because of one of Sharon's amusing stories. When the bathroom door was shut closed, it still left an opening where someone could see in. Sharon told me when she was a kid, she and her older sister Debbie would take a peek through the doorway just for fun, especially when their brother Larry was in there. I'd always try and block the tiny opening with a towel when I did my business in there.

Sharon's brother Larry was killed when he was only twenty-five. He was sitting in the back of a pickup truck, helping a friend move, when all of a sudden they hit a bump in the road. Larry flew off the back of the truck and hit his head on the roadway. The freak accident left him in a coma, and he later died. He was going to school to become a dentist like his dad. I was sorry that I never got to meet Larry, but I'm sure we would have been close. Arlena said he was very pleasant and always made people laugh. She'd compare Larry to the *Three's Company* star John Ritter and his portrayal of Jack Tripper. Sharon said that Larry always had lots of girlfriends because he was handsome and had a wonderful personality.

Gayle, one of Sharon's best friends, attempted to make me think that Henderson was a hillbilly town. Before I left DC, her friends would get on the phone and talk to me about how they all had outhouses and how they all married their cousins. One evening, Gayle came to the front door dressed in big baggy overalls, oversized rubber boots, a straw hat, and a corn pipe held between her teeth. After I opened the front door for the planned visit, I excitedly hollered, "Hi, Gayle, it's great to finally meet you!" and I gave her a big hug. I always considered myself to be like the chameleon, able to adapt to any situation, and so I had no reaction when I saw her standing there in that goofy costume—though I thought to myself, "I guess that's how they really dress around here."

Poor Gayle; she was so disappointed when she didn't get a rise out of me. She looked around at everyone watching us and explained in her sad little voice, "It took me all day to put this outfit together, and I got nothing!"

We said our good-byes after Debbie and Jim had arrived in Henderson. They spent half of their trip in Louisville visiting Jim's mom and dad and his three brothers and three sisters. We had a great time; my future in-laws were wonderful, and Sharon's uncles, aunts, cousins, and friends had all accepted me. And yes, Henderson did kind of remind me of Mayberry. But you know, it was nice to be able to call a locksmith on a Sunday, or for everyone in town to know your name, and I really enjoyed seeing the name Clements on a rural street sign named after Sharon's family. It was definitely a nice change from the hustle and bustle of DC. Lyle and Arlena were going to make plans to visit everyone in Virginia around Christmastime, and then we'd all be back in Henderson for the wedding in February. The four of us pulled out of Lyle and Arlena's carport waving good-bye, and then we headed for Louisville.

We spent only one night in Louisville, but I got to meet most of Jim's family. Sharon's Aunt Lois and Uncle Walter lived right down the street from Jim's parents. It was Uncle Walter who actually introduced Jim to Debbie. When they first met, Debbie was wearing beer cans in her hair for hair rollers. After getting married, they moved to Virginia. They finished school, and Jim went to work for the FBI, while Debbie became a school teacher. The first time Sharon introduced me to her sister and Jim was at their home in Stafford, Virginia. I expected this macho government stick in the mud and was somewhat nervous about meeting him. When we got there, I was greeted by the complete opposite. I wasn't worried about meeting Debbie; I knew she was a lot like Sharon. But when I met Jim, I immediately thought of Baloo the Bear from Disney's *The Jungle Book,* and it wouldn't have surprised me if he had danced and sang "The Bare Necessities." Jim was a very personable guy who laughed and joked a lot. One of our first conversations was about how he got bald. Jim said his hair rubbed off from banging his head on their headboard from having so much sex. He'd always bullshit like that. He even told me that he and Debbie had a trampoline and used whips and chains in the bedroom. I was totally taken by surprise when he said that and wasn't really sure on how to react. After all, it was only the first time that I had met him. But later, I got to know him, and then I realized he was just Jim being Jim. He would sarcastically refer to Sharon as a bad influence and the troublemaker of the two sisters, only because of Sharon's disco outings at a nightspot called Funky's in Evansville; Sharon and her wild buddy Anna were permanent fixtures there. But I'd retaliate with comments about old pictures that I had seen of Debbie wearing hot pants and go-go boots. Debbie actually told Sharon that she could get pregnant while sitting on the commode, so I didn't worry too much about Sharon's past—Debbie had spooked her pretty good.

I first met Sharon's wild friend Anna at a big party that Anna threw in Virginia Beach. Anna was in the navy and stationed there. Sharon; her roommate, Cindy; and I drove down to visit her in my Trans Am. On the way down, Cindy wanted to drive my car, so I let her. While she drove, Sharon and I got cozy in the backseat. When I was first introduced to Anna, she acted like I was invisible. Her main focus was on entertaining her best friend at this wild party, which happened to be loaded with single navy seals. I don't think she liked the idea that Sharon was in a relationship, and I didn't like being jilted. Needless to say, we both had unfavorable first impressions of one another. Sharon knew I was uncomfortable and didn't want my feelings hurt, so we left the party and spent the night on the beach. It turned out to be a romantic evening.

The next morning, Sharon, Cindy, Anna, and I headed to the beach. When Anna finally realized that Sharon was in a serious relationship, she started to be nicer to me and treated us as a couple. Anna had wild, crazy eyes, and she always looked antsy and ready to party. We flopped on the beach with our cooler filled of Coronas and began spreading out on the sand. Then Anna immediately took it to another level. She pulled out the bottle opener and pretended it was a microphone. I thought it was funny when she started asking Sharon, Cindy, and I questions with her pretend microphone, but then I became concerned when she tied a beach towel around her neck like a superman cape and started interviewing random beachgoers with it. Despite our precarious first encounter, we eventually became really good friends, and I fondly refer to her as Anna Banana.

We were fixin' to leave, and so we said our good-byes to Jim's kin and then headed back to DC. After we visited Kentucky that week, I had already started to talk like they do. Somewhere in West Virginia, Jim's car broke down. We were towed to a gas station and then found out that it may take several days to repair. Jim and Debbie encouraged Sharon and I to call for a cab and go to the airport. We didn't want to leave them alone, but I think Jim wanted some more headboard action. A taxi cab picked us up and drove us to the airport in Charleston. Sharon had dressed comfortably for the long car ride back to DC. She wore nursing scrubs that were all wrinkled up and tennis shoes. She got plenty of stares from the locals while we bought our airline tickets. We got lucky and caught a flight out within an hour, and then we landed back home safely at National Airport.

The competition on F Street had changed a bit. Douglas Stereo had changed its name to the Wiz. And remember Fat Bobby? Well, he opened a store across the street from the Wiz. He walked around in slippers and smoked cigars while he waited on Gs all day. He also lost a lot of weight, and so his nickname hadn't made sense any more. We all had our regular and faithful customers, and there wasn't any need to get into serious price wars.

I got a call at one o'clock in the morning from Dad. He said the alarm company had contacted him about the store's alarm going off, and he asked me to go check it out because I lived only fifteen minutes away. (Actually, I could get there in ten minutes without traffic in the Trans Am.) I called up Iggy and asked him to go with me. We met at the parking lot in front of his townhome. He brought the .45mm pistol that he kept stuffed underneath his mattress, just in case. When we arrived at Worldwide, the alarm guy was there waiting for us, but there was no police. I anticipated a false alarm, but then I saw that the heavy padlocks that secured the protective gates were cut in half. The lobby gate had been raised halfway up. Iggy and I pushed the gate the rest of the way up and entered the store lobby. The alarm guy waited on the sidewalk in front of the store. We noticed that the left side window had been broken into. There was merchandise scattered everywhere mixed in with chunks of broken glass. While Iggy and I were inspecting the damage, the alarm guy said, "Why don't you guys check inside to see if there's anyone hiding out in there?" There were no cops to back us up, and the alarm guy bravely waited outside. He did let us use his flashlight, though. I wasn't even nervous about lurching in the dark and anticipating a struggle of some kind. It was sort of a relief knowing that Iggy was packing heat, but for me, this was just another day of working retail in the city. Iggy and I carefully patrolled all three floors inside the building. While looking around for possible thugs in hiding, we hollered out obscenities and hoped they would nervously reveal themselves. Luckily the extent of the damage was limited to the outside window in the lobby. Our insurance company would cover the loss, but how the hell did they break through those huge locks? The hushos were getting way too smart.

The next day we took everything out of the windows and swept up all the glass. We used the break-in as an opportunity to change all the windows around, filling them up with the latest and greatest merchandise. Dad was an expert window dresser; he had organized storefront windows since his days of working on East Flagler Street in Miami. The window display was probably the most important aspect to an SY's store. It's the store's big chance of exhibiting power and deflating the competition. The SY window dresser is an unsung hero; he is the ultimate salesman because he handpicks and displays the most seductive merchandise and then portrays them for all to see, like an artist painting on his canvas. When he finally completes his painstaking craft, his achievement resembles a masterpiece. His sole objective is to allure the G into walking inside the store. If he accomplishes the task, he is like a great artist who captures someone's soul. All that's left is for someone inside to sell the painting.

The windows were more than halfway done, and so I decided to go take a walk. It was not uncommon for each of us to escape the store for awhile and take a walk. And you never knew what you were going see on the streets of DC. As I walked down G Street, I turned to look across the street and saw a dead white man sprawled out on the cement pavement directly in front of the bank. There was thousands of dollars in loose cash scattered all around him. Everyone assumed that he was just a bank robber and continued on their way like no big deal. Then I spotted a *mejnoon* harassing two foreign teenage girls. They were clueless to the man's character and could have easily been ripped off. I ran over to the lowlife and shouted, "Take a walk!" into his piratelike mug. He mumbled something at me and scooted away. After all the years of working downtown, it became easy to spot the scoundrels from the genuine homeless. There were always the street bums that would walk up to you and ask for money; you'd see them later scoring a bottle at the corner liquor store.

After lunch, a limousine pulled up in front of Worldwide. Usually that meant a diplomat or ambassador from an embassy was coming inside to shop. An elegant blonde woman, completely dressed in leather, got out and walked next door to Radio Shack. A few minutes later, I got a call from the manager of Radio Shack. He asked me if we sold binoculars. We did of course, and so he said he was sending us a customer. When she approached the store lobby, I could see it was the elegant blonde from the limousine. And as she walked inside to greet me, I knew instantly that it was Dinah Shore. She was in her late sixties but looked fantastic. She was looking for compact Zeiss binoculars. We didn't carry Zeiss, but we sold the entire Nikon line. I grabbed each pair from out of the wall case and laid them down gently on the showcase in front for her. She picked one up, aimed across the street, and gazed through the eyepiece. While she looked through each pair of Nikon binocular, I told her that I thought she looked even more beautiful in person. She quickly laid down the pair that she was looking through and formed a great big smile on her face and said, "Aw, you're so sweet." I could tell that she really liked my compliment, but she had to have Zeiss, so I didn't get the sale.

Howard got lucky, though. His favorite customer walked in just minutes after Dinah left. One of our loyalist Gs was Captain Najjar from the Kuwaiti air force. We carried a 220-volt wireless phone that claimed to work up to a thirty-mile distance. The phone had an optional antenna that could be used to double the signal strength when mounted up high, like on a rooftop. The phone could never be tested in the United States because the voltage was suitable for overseas usage only. Every once in a while the captain would pay us a visit, and we were always glad to see him. We'd usually keep two phones and two antennas in stock. The captain always bought both phones and antennas when he dropped in. The phone cost lot

#913009, and we sold them for $1299.00 each. We sold the external antenna for $250.00.each. It was a good ale-say and great PR. We assumed the phone worked in Kuwait because the captain always came back to buy more. It was a very specialized product that no one else carried.

After the captain left, business slowed down, and then the phone rang. Howard answered it behind the register counter. Everyone's attention focused on Howard after his conversation turned loud and desperate. "Calm down, Joaquin, and tell me what happened." Then Howard repeated those same words again in Spanish. Joaquin was the companion that Mom and Dad hired to help Abuela out during the day. Howard quickly hung up the phone and announced, "Joaquin said Abuela passed out on the floor. He said he called 911, and they were on the way."

Mom glanced over at me and said, "Raymond, you go with me and drive." We left the store immediately; Dad and Howard followed after they closed the store.

Mom and I pulled up to the front of her house, and there was already a police car and an ambulance there. We rushed inside and ran upstairs toward the kitchen where all the excitement seemed to be. It was too late; Abuela had already left us. Mom immediately fell on top of her and cried. Then she grabbed her hand and said, "Mama, you're so cold already." I was heartbroken watching Mom's sorrow. I began to weep and then repeated what Abuela had always said to me every night before I went to sleep. I got on my knees and whispered over her, "*Sueño con los Ángelitos,*" which meant "dream with the angels," and then I kissed her forehead as she lay on the kitchen floor. Dad and Howard arrived at the house twenty minutes later. Abuela died while she was cooking, what she loved doing more than anything. She was standing on a chair and reaching for something out of one of the kitchen cabinets when her heart gave out. Abuela had lived with us since our Johnnycake Road days; we never prepared or even thought about the day when she'd no longer be with us. It was almost as though we thought she'd live forever.

Howard had to sign the final paperwork so that the body could be removed. It was both sad and Ironic. Abuela had brought Howard into the world, and now he helped her to leave it.

Abuela did get to spend quality time with Howard's kids, her great-grandchildren, and I'm grateful for that because she adored children. Mom canceled my engagement party. Abuela was so excited about our engagement party; she even picked out a new dress. She and Sharon loved each other very much, and it was so funny to hear them try and communicate with each other. Sharon sorta had a little girl's voice, combined with her Kentucky accent. When Sharon telephoned Mom's house, Abuela usually answered the phone. Sharon would say, "Hi, Abuela, how are you doin'?

Abuela would answer, "You have the wrong number, little girl," and then hang up on her.

Abuela was buried in the same dress that she picked out for my engagement party. During and after the funeral, Howard and I had noticed that every time we spoke about Abuela, a light flickered. We interpreted the flickering as her message from heaven, letting us know that she was all right and would always be with us.

Chapter Twenty-One

Hail to Mr. and Mrs. Shashow
… and the Redskins

My bachelor party ended in mayhem. The invite list included, Howard, Eric, Monica's brother Ricky, and Jim (my future brother-in-law), and they all participated in a long evening of carousing inside the trashiest nudie bars of Washington DC. We should have called it quits, but someone suggested ending the evening at a joint on Fourteenth Street. I was traditionally disorderly when we entered the bosom palace. After we walked inside, I staggered to the front of the stage and demanded seats up close for my entire party. When the waitress said it wasn't possible, I may have responded belligerently. A bouncer appeared and began threatening me, even after I explained to him that we had a bachelor's party. Hey, I knew I was the antagonist, but I was also a Shashow! No one talked to me that way. I grabbed his shirt, and he reciprocated by grabbing mine. Then his posse arrived, and mine escaped out the back exit, all except for the two dauntless souls that watched my back. In a matter of seconds, there were ten able-bodied men pushing up against me, Howard, and Ricky. Someone swung an arm toward Howard and knocked off his glasses. Howard tried reasoning with the embittered swarm by commenting, "This is not necessary!" But they kept on coming. The situation appeared hopeless. It was the three of us against the entire strip club.

I was buried somewhere in the middle of the huge mob when a hand clutched the left side of my chest and hurled me from out of the crowd and into a wall. Then I was manhandled and pushed out the front door onto the pavement adjacent to Fourteenth Street. After I came to my senses, my eyes were fixed on a short and stocky DC cop. He stated, "I think you boys should go somewhere else." He said that we were lucky that someone hadn't pulled out a knife or even a gun. I think God was watching over me that night.

Eric waited for me the next morning in his VW Bug in front of my high-rise apartment building. We carpooled to work every morning and usually took turns driving. His car didn't have any heat. I could see him from my tenth-floor window, crunched over behind the steering wheel in his pea coat and wool knitted cap, probably freezing his balls off. Maybe his beard provided some warmth. Eric was a good friend; he was sarcastic and cynical but had a good heart. He was a hard worker, and if Dad asked him to do something, no matter how crazy it was, he'd always do it. I remember when a bum took a crap in our store lobby, and Dad asked Eric to clean it up. Eric threw buckets of water at it and flushed the human feces into the city street. Then there was the time I decided to take off in January of '82. That day an Air Florida Boeing 737 crashed into the Fourteenth Street Bridge over the Potomac River, killing all but four passengers and a flight attendant. The accident killed seventy-eight people, including four motorists on the bridge. The bridge carried traffic on Interstate 395 between Washington DC and Arlington County, Virginia. It was Eric and my daily roundtrip route together from Alexandria, Virginia, to Worldwide in DC. On that day, Dad and Howard decided to close the store early because of poor weather conditions. Eric's usual twenty-minute drive home turned into a six-hour pilgrimage on that tragic day. It was extremely rare to find good people like Eric to work for us.

I finally made it to the elevator and pushed "L" for lobby. I walked outside and jumped into Eric's frigid cold car. I was still hungover, but Eric didn't seem affected by our big night out. I brought a big suitcase with me because later in the afternoon, I was flying out to Evansville. There were only two days left before I got hitched. I drove Sharon to the airport on Monday morning before work. She needed to get to Kentucky for those last-minute wedding details. Sharon and I were already living together at my high-rise apartment, but she kept her furniture and continued paying rent to Cindy for the townhome they shared in Burke. She didn't want to give her place up until we were married. When her mom came to visit us in Virginia, she wanted to see where I was living. Sharon never wanted her folks to know that she was living with me, so we hid all of her clothes underneath my bed when her mom came.

The first time I spent the night with Sharon at her townhome in Burke, she led me downstairs into an unfinished basement. There was a queen-size bed and six alarm clocks down there. I asked her why she was sleeping down there when she had a fully furnished bedroom upstairs. She said it reminded her of her mom and dad's basement back in Henderson, and she also liked how quiet and dark it was. She always slept down there when she had to go to work the next day. When she turned the light off, I immediately sat up in the bed and started getting panicky. There was absolutely no light in the room, and it felt as though I'd gone totally blind. I freaked out! She had to turn the lights back on and then find some kind of nightlight for me before we went back to sleep. I was woken up the next morning to an alarm clock buzzing at 5:00 AM. Sharon turned off the clock and went back to sleep. At 5:15, I was woken again by another alarm clock, this time it was an excruciating beeping sound that appeared to get louder and louder. Sharon turned that one off and went back to sleep again. At 5:30, a third alarm clock began to buzz. At that point, I was already awake; I never went back to sleep in anticipation of the next alarm to sound. At 5:45, the fourth alarm clock rang. This time she woke up and stayed awake. While she was in the bathroom, the fifth alarm clock went off. She yelled through the door for me to shut it off. After she took her shower and got dressed upstairs, the final alarm clock kept beeping downstairs, so I ran back down to shut it off. Sharon and I left the house together.

I walked Sharon to her car; she was in her nursing uniform and had a stethoscope wrapped around her neck. I kissed her good-bye and asked, "Do you go through that routine every time you go to work?"

She just laughed and said, "Those are my backups, it's the only way that I can get up in the morning."

While inside Eric's VW, I could see my breath blowing out smoke. "Eric, when are you going to fix the heater in this car, man? It's cold as shit."

"Why should I? It gives the car character. Would you rather take your car today?"

"Nah, I'm already inside."

"Then stop complaining." As always, we hit a huge traffic jam on Interstate 395. Eric always brought a couple of sixteen-ounce beers for our snail-paced journey into DC. We approached the parking garage on Fifteenth Street and gulped what was left in the cans; I looked over and saw two motorcycle cops slowly passing by me and glancing inside my window. They kept going and were followed by a very large black limousine. I peeked inside the darkened rear window, and it was President Reagan. Eric and I were gulping down beers on the way to work and drove right by the president—it could only happen in DC.

Later in the day, a package was delivered with Sharon's and my name on it. After opening the package, I pulled out a beautiful set of gold spoons and a very special card from James and Clarissa Mason. I had sent out a wedding invitation to the Masons at their home in Switzerland. I didn't think they would come, but I really liked them and wanted to let them know that I was getting married. Then I walked over to G Street to pick up my tuxedo for the wedding. All the men were going to wear white tuxedos with tails; I got the idea from watching the Beatles perform "Your Mother Should Know," from the *Magical Mystery Tour* video.

After I got back to the store, I heard WPGC playing through the lobby speaker and telling everyone about the huge parade going on down Pennsylvania Avenue, honoring the Super Bowl champions. The radio announcer said the city estimated over five hundred thousand fans at the event. Last Sunday, the Washington Redskins had beaten the Miami Dolphins, 27–17, and won their very first Super Bowl. We had all become Washington Redskin fans since the Millers had given us tickets to every home game, on the fifty yard line. Colonel Dave and Charlotte Miller lived across the street from Mom and Dad in Camp Springs and were very dear friends. Our tickets were right behind the Redskins bench. The Millers religiously attended every home game and cheered for their Skins, regardless if they were good or bad, for over thirty seasons. They were true Redskins fans. Dave and Charlotte were in their midseventies. Dave was a retired air force coronel. Charlotte always brought her flask filled with whiskey and shared it with the rest of us. It really came in handy, because at most of those games you froze your balls off. Charlotte always screamed at the top of her lungs, "Mafia!" Her outrage was usually directed at the referees when she thought they made a suspect call.

I snuck out and walked down to the district building a few blocks away, and I witnessed Redskins head coach Joe Gibbs raising the championship trophy over his head. It was pouring down rain, so I didn't stay very long. On the way back to the store, I stepped into a really large pothole and was almost completely submerged in water. After I got back to the store, I took out the blow dryer from my suitcase and dried my pants. Time flew by, and I got ready to leave for the airport. I said good-bye to everyone and then hailed a taxi cab to National Airport. Lyle, my future father-in-law, waited to pick me up in Evansville.

The next day, Mom and Dad, Howard and Monica (with their latest addition, baby Tiffani), Sean, Aunt Mattie, and Eric flew into

Evansville, and I picked them all up at airport. An hour earlier, Tony and Gigi flew in from Miami. It was everyone from my side of the family who were coming to the wedding. My nephew Sean was the ring boy, Howard was the best man, and Monica was a bridesmaid. We all gathered for the rehearsal dinner that night at the Ramada. The evening wound down after we received our traditional toasts and finished several glasses of champagne. Sharon and I kissed goodnight. We both knew that the next time we'd see each other would be inside the church, where we would become husband and wife. I went back to my hotel room at the Ramada. Eric's room was next door to mine, and we had a couple of drinks together. It was only 11:30, but I was already tired. Tony came into my room with a drink in hand. Laughing, he said, "Come on, it's your last night as a single man; I have to take you to the strip club … Let's go!"

"No way, Tony, I'm going to sleep."

Then Tony warned, "Okay you better not go to sleep tonight, because I'm going to sneak into your room and paint your *juevos* blue." That kind of worried me, because I knew he was capable of doing that.

On the eve of my wedding day, Tony and Gigi. along with their newfound friends Gayle and Ed, ventured out of the Ramada hotel to experience the nightlife of Henderson Kentucky. Everyone else had already retired to their rooms; even Eric went to sleep. But the groom laid in bed cautiously, with one eye opened and both hands cupped over his crotch, waiting for Tony to sneak into his room in the middle of the night with a brush and a can of blue paint.

By the next afternoon my emotions ran rampant when I witnessed how beautiful Sharon looked, dressed in her angelic white gown. With her dad at her side, they started their walk down the aisle toward me. My new father-in-law gave his daughter away, and now it was my duty to watch and protect her. I had plenty of practice taking care of Sharon, since the first day I told her that I loved her. Several moments later, we spoke our wedding vows, and Father Willett pronounced us husband and wife. The wedding party marched down the aisle and out the church doors. The poor bridesmaids shivered endlessly while they waited outside on a frigid Kentucky winter day. We took lots of pictures afterward and then headed for the reception, which was held at a place that resembled a fancy ski lodge.

Lyle and Arlena hired a piano player who played mostly Sinatra tunes. Tony was the life of the party; all the woman wanted to dance with him. Sharon and I had such a wonderful time at the reception, and we didn't want to leave. Finally, Sharon's mom made us leave, and we slowly headed for the door. We were both pelted by rice as we exited the reception hall, especially by the handfuls thrown by Jim's mother. We drove Lyle's car back to their house and then changed our clothes. Then drove out of Henderson and headed for Louisville with one quick stop at a Burger King; we didn't eat much at the reception. Our first night together as Mr. and Mrs. Shashow was spent at the Executive Inn Hotel, just a few minutes away from Churchill Downs, the home of the Kentucky Derby. We awoke the next morning to snow on the ground and then drove to Louisville International Airport, where we caught a flight to Chicago's O'Hare Airport. We arrived late in Chicago and then rushed to our gate, which was positioned on the other side of the airport. We were exhausted once we got there, and they had already started boarding the plane. We climbed aboard and prepared for the eight-hour flight to Honolulu, Hawaii. After landing on the island of Oahu, our eight-day honeymoon stay at the Sheraton Waikiki had commenced. The trip was Mom and Dad's wedding gift to us … *Mahalo!*

1983 was definitely a great year! And it finished up strong when the Baltimore Orioles won the World Series on October 16. How many people can say their favorite football and baseball teams were world champs on the same year they were married? Sharon and I also bought our first home that year in the Saint Charles neighborhood in Waldorf. Howard suggested that we look for a home in that area because the prices were so reasonable. Our first home together was brand-new and had a manmade lake in the back yard with lots of ducks. We bought way out in southern Maryland because it was affordable; we really wanted to stay in Virginia but couldn't find any good deals. Our new home looked like a great place to raise a family.

Washington DC was still buzzing over the Redskins, and street vendors sold Skins paraphernalia on every block. By now, the entire block that stood across the street from Worldwide Electronics had been demolished to the ground. There were plans in the works for something completely new on F Street. It was very sad to see Chin Lung Art Gallery reduced to dust.

Every Saturday after we closed the store, we'd bump into a sweet, middle-aged black lady with a huge smile. After we locked up the store and began our journey toward the parking garage, we'd see her scamper over to greet all of us with that truly sincere smile she possessed. She'd talk about Jesus and hand out pocket-sized Christian leaflets. Her spiel only lasted about twenty seconds, and then one of us would slip her some money. On the last Saturday before Christmas, we'd slip her extra cash, and if business was good she'd get more. We never knew her real name, and so we referred to her simply as Dolly. She was always so thankful for the money and never ever glanced at it or counted the bills in front of us. She said her good-byes by repeating, "God bless you." When she tried to pass out her leaflets, only the non-Jews would accept them. Her Christian leaflets were never accepted by Dad, Joey, or any of my cousins; they acted like it was against their religion if they even touched one of them. The Dolly-Saturday ritual started way back in the Chin Lung days and continued when she found us at Worldwide. Dolly was like a good luck charm, and if we didn't see her after we closed up on Saturday, we all got worried.

It was January of 1984; Dad, Howard, and I had just finished watching the Redskins get destroyed by the Oakland Raiders in Super Bowl XVIII, by a score of 38–9. There was just way too much Marcus Allen for the skins to handle. Howard and I always let the Redskin defeats get to us mentally and physically. We'd actually get a stomach ache anytime they'd lose a big game. But we always bonded during football season. Howard and I were years apart in our ages; it never seemed like I saw him very much when we were kids, and while I was growing up, he was travelling all over the world with the United States Air Force. We spent more time together at Worldwide than we ever had.

I remember the day when we both laughed our asses off nonstop for thirty minutes. Howard, Dad, and I were in the basement watching the *Tonight Show Starring Johnny Carson*. On that particular night, Joey Bishop was the guest host, and he was chatting with actress Connie Stevens. She was telling Joey how she'd sometimes receive strange gifts from men admirers. On one occasion she received a llama, a gift from a gentleman from Peru. Ms Stevens explained that she had lots of animal furs hanging up in her closet, which were also gifts from her many suitors. The llama wandered off one day and was later found in her closet among the furs. Joey Bishop stared into the camera with a dumbfounded look on his face and said, "Who knows, you might find an extra pair of gloves in there one day." Howard and I lost it! I didn't think Dad thought it was that funny. It was a simple punch line but very clever. We had never laughed that hard before.

The construction of the Shops at National Place—a mall project bounded by Pennsylvania Avenue and F Street, between Thirteenth and Fourteenth Street NW—was almost completed. It was going to be a three-level, indoor shopping mall and eventually house over seventy-five specialty shops. The mall would also connect to the new JW Marriott Hotel. If you rode their elevator down to the bottom floor of the Marriott, you'd see their spectacular ballrooms. A short escalator ride down from the lobby let you exit through the Pennsylvania Avenue entrance and arrive at the National Theater within seconds. It was also a short elevator ride up to the National Press building. The hotel consisted of 15 floors, 737 rooms, and 35 suites. The first phase of the Shops was to open in May. It was an exciting project, and we wanted to be part of it, so we signed a seven-year lease to open another retail electronics store on the block. It would be the first time we'd have two fully operational retail stores running at the same time. We selected an 1100 square-foot space located in the lobby of the JW Marriott Hotel. The rent was $7,000 per month. All of the stores at the Shops had to look upscale and high tech. SYs would usually try to open their new businesses as cheap as possible, but the new store was definitely not going to be a typical SY store, and it was extraordinary when we hired an architect to design it, which was definitely a first.

I got really involved with the new store project and decided that I wanted to work there permanently. I also wanted full control of buying the merchandise. I was definitely unhappy with the relationship that had developed between me and Dad and Howard. They were making most of the business decisions together at Worldwide and had left me out of the loop. I never understood why. It even took me awhile to earn Uncle Joey's respect at Chin Lung, and I was a damned good salesman. If it weren't for the new store, I would have probably ended my association with Dad and Howard for good. I disagreed with a lot of their vender purchases. They continued to buy the knockoffs that later got returned by the Gs, especially the cordless phones. I told them, "If you continue to buy junk … then you sell it!" I wasn't going to sell it because I knew it was going to come back anyway.

Chapter Twenty-Two

Sight & Sound Camera and Electronics

After the new store was completed, it resembled a pinball machine. All the showcases and wall cases were a shiny black laminate. There were two slanted wall cases at the very front of the store that angled toward the front entrance and actually resembled flippers on a pinball machine. We had a small office, shelves for stock, and a private bathroom in the back of the store. The private office was located behind a glass door with a two-way mirror. But what created the store's state-of-the-art ambience were the three-tier colored neon lighting tubes that wrapped around the entire shop. It was a small store, but we had plenty of showcase and wall case space to display the merchandise. We brought some merchandise over from Worldwide to start filling up the shelves, and we named the store Sight & Sound Camera and Electronics.

We bought an advertisement in a book called the Guest Informant. The publication would be placed in all the hotel rooms around DC. It told travelers about the finest restaurants, shops, and attractions around town. We never liked to advertise, but it seemed like a good idea in this case. When the salesman first introduced us to the publication, it was a few weeks before Sharon and I got married. He was a really tall man, basketball player tall. The salesman knew I was getting married soon. He looked down at me and said, "You know, you need to know who you are before getting married."

I looked at him and thought, "I don't know you; why don't you mind your own fucking business!"

He was adamant about getting his message across to me, though. He said, "Do you truly know who you are? If you don't know who you are inside … don't get married! I made the mistake and was miserable; I had to get a divorce." Why was this guy telling me this, and when do you truly know when you know yourself? I'll admit it; I didn't really know who I was. I'd been trying to figure it out my whole life. But getting married was not going to stop me from figuring it all out—if anything, it would help. Marriage would add structure and keep me focused on things. And I always heard that behind every great man, there was a great woman. This guy was just bitter because it never worked out for him. Someone always wanted to rain on my parade, because their life sucked! The same thing happened when I was at WNAV. One of the other deejays told me that I should quit radio and work full-time in the family business, because I'd never amount to anything in broadcasting. Why can't people just mind their own business?

During the first year of business at Sight & Sound, Dad sent Bernadette or Haywood across the street to work with me as needed, but Mom worked with me for the majority of the year. I only needed one other salesman because it was really slow. Mom liked the class and elegance of the JW Marriott. She also got to wear fancier clothes and had brand-new boutiques to shop at. I was happy to work there too; it felt right, and we definitely didn't have to worry about rats or *mejnoons* anymore.

But the hushos were still around, and these ones were a lot craftier at their trade. Two black guys walked into the store and stood by the showcase filled with Seiko watches. I asked if I could help them, but they answered, "We're just looking … thank you very much anyway." All the showcases had locks on them, and they weren't leaning on the case, so I didn't pay much attention to them. After a few minutes they walked out. I started to clean the showcases and slowly made my way over to the Seiko watches. I gazed into the case and noticed two rows of watches were gone, about forty watches. The hushos used a crowbar that was hidden under their shirt and then pried open the top showcase glass, easily lifting out the watches. Unfortunately the architect designed the showcase tops to be totally unglued. Hushos could no longer be easily singled out. They camouflaged themselves in expensive clothing, behaved intelligently, and were even polite. It was a new day for the husho.

Our neighbors directly to our left were Melart Jewelers; across the lobby to the left was a Colombian leather goods store, and a B Dalton bookstore was directly across the lobby. We received minimal foot traffic from the mall. Most of the Gs that entered the mall came inside through the F Street entrance. We were positioned in the hotel lobby, and so shoppers that entered through F Street couldn't find us. It was very frustrating. Our hope was to attract those reliable Gs that we knew so well over the years. We looked to bring in the foreigners, Gs from the National Press building, and ambassadors and diplomats stationed at the various embassies around town. But I thought, "Will that be enough to survive? And how do we lure them inside a hotel lobby?" Sales were dismal; all of us thought that we had made a huge mistake. The stagnation was unbearable, and so we took lots of walks around the mall and the hotel. We made a lot of friends, though. Some of those walks ended up at the bar near the front entrance of the hotel.

Around Christmastime the store should have been packed with Gs, but instead Mom and I went stir crazy. We were mentally exhausted from not doing anything. I couldn't stand it anymore, so I asked Dad to watch the store for awhile. I had never sat down at a bar with my mother before, but it was one of those days where we both needed a pick-me-up. I ordered a Jack Daniels with a splash of water, and Mom ordered a Fundador brandy. We had several cocktails together. If we had a friendlier bartender that afternoon, I'm sure the both of us would have spilled our guts to him. After thirty minutes, we got up from our barstools and walked from the ill-lighted watering hole to a luminous hotel lobby. As we headed back to Sight & Sound, Mom looked up at me and mumbled, "Boy, I'm bombed!" We were both lit up good, and it was a perfect ending to a crappy year of business. Christmas sales were the worst we'd ever seen. We weren't operating on the street anymore where everyone could see us; we were buried inside a mall, and people were going to have to find us. The highlight of the year was when the US gold medalist team from the summer Olympics shopped at Sight & Sound.

Howard and I carpooled together to Mom and Dad's house every morning from Waldorf. We all stood around in the kitchen waiting for Dad to finish his coffee. Howard started to gaze through some insurance paperwork that Dad had lying on the kitchen table. He read something on the document that left him with a devastated expression. He held the document in his hands, looked up at Dad, and asked, "You were married once before you married Mom?"

Dad responded without a hint of emotion and said, "Your mother was married before she met me also."

Howard and I looked at each other as if we had been betrayed. Then Dad added, "It was before both of you were born, so what's the difference?" Not only were we both shocked to find out our parents were married before, but finding out so many years later added salt to the wound. I asked, "How long were you both married to your first spouses, then?"

Dad said, "I don't know maybe a year; it was a mistake, and we were both young."

Of course it didn't stop us from joking around about it. Howard and I made wisecracks to each other, like, "You must have been conceived during the first marriage."

We left for work in Dad's black Lincoln Continental. On the drive in, I changed the subject and asked Dad, "How come we never merged as a family to create a chain of retail electronic stores? You know, the New York Shashows with all of us in DC and Baltimore.

We could have been a chain of stores like the Wiz; the owner is an SY like us, right?"

Dad said, "Forget it, we'd never get along with each other. Everyone's too greedy." I always wondered how life may have been if our family had united and conquered the retail electronics market together. After all, they were all shrewd businessmen, and everyone worked extremely hard. I don't think anyone had ever discussed the possibilities of a merger, and I think it was a damn shame.

I remember talking with my younger cousin Howard, Uncle Sammy's only son, when we visited Bensonhurst. I asked him the very same question. He agreed that if the family had put all of their heads together, we would have been huge. My world seemed tame compared to my cousin Howard's, but it was like we were both living in parallel universes. Howard started working with his father when he was six years old, too. He even had a black Trans Am like mine. But his life of growing up around the family business turned out a bit different than mine. Howard was always quiet. Someone once told him, "The less you say, the more mysterious and intelligent you become. People will wonder about the secrets and knowledge that you conceal. And you'll become more interesting than the guy that can't keep his mouth shut and talks aimlessly about nothing." Howard practically grew up in Times Square and came to know all the drug dealers, undercover cops, and hookers on the street. He was only allowed to venture out alone within a three-block radius of the store, but he was recognized as a popular icon on the street. Hookers flagged him down to buy them cigarettes while they waited for business, and he always got to keep their change. Howard spent much of his early teenage years getting blowjobs and snorting blow inside the infamous Studio 54 discotheque. He hobnobbed with Hollywood and became good friends with actor Matt Dillon. Howard later distinguished himself from all the other Howards in our family by referring to himself as simply "Son of Sam." Uncle Sammy had to close Victory Camera to make room for a Marriott Hotel. His store had been a mainstay on Broadway since the early

1960s. He reopened under the name Lewis and Clark Electronics, near Wall Street in lower Manhattan.

We arrived at the parking garage and then strolled down F Street. Howard and I unlocked the locks and pushed up the security gates at Worldwide. Then Dad unlocked the front door and turned on the lights. I didn't have to open Sight & Sound for another hour yet. Later in the day I got a call from Howard. Apparently, a developer visited Worldwide earlier in the day and then made Dad and Howard an offer to dissolve the lease and vacate the premises. He wanted to knock down several stores and put up a parking garage. Hypothetically, Worldwide Electronics would get paid enough money to cover sales for the remaining term on the lease, and then some. Howard said he and Dad were seriously considering the offer.

Throughout the following week, we contemplated the possibilities of closing Worldwide Electronics. Howard said he would call it quits if Worldwide closed. He believed that the three of us could never work peacefully together at Sight & Sound, a considerably smaller working space than Worldwide. He said there would be too many captains trying to run one ship. Howard was definitely showing signs of aggravation and frustration from working in retail. Lately he'd lose his cool more easily and frequently. It wasn't his nature to let anyone get to him, especially when a *mejnoon* tried his patience one day by banging on the front windows over and over again. Howard ran outside screaming at him to stop, but the louder he screamed, the more the guy banged. I think the straw that broke my brother's back was when a G returned an off-brand piece of crap wireless phone. The G ate a cup of yogurt while asking Howard for a refund. Howard offered to exchange the item, but the G was persistent about asking for his money back. Then the G threw a rolled-up, dirty Kleenex at Howard's face. I saw a big change in Howard after that incident. He definitely lost his passion for retail.

A week later, Howard and Dad snuck out of Worldwide to meet with me at Sight & Sound. Howard said, "We signed the deal." I admit I was disappointed, mainly because of Howard's previous announcement of quitting the business once Worldwide closed its doors. Monies received from the developer were to be divided between Dad, Howard, and myself. The majority of the funds went to Dad and Howard, and I'd become the president of Sight & Sound Camera and Electronics. Worldwide Electronics immediately ran a going-out-of-business sale, and all the leftover merchandise was sent over to Sight & Sound. The developers construction crew started demolishing some of the stores around us. They kept their machinery on the sidewalk directly in front of Worldwide's lobby, making it extremely difficult for Gs to enter the store. The Gs almost had to squeeze through to get inside. But somehow the bargain hunters found their way inside, and 90 percent of the merchandise was sold.

After Worldwide closed its doors, Haywood decided to pursue other opportunities. We offered him a job at Sight & Sound, but I think he thought the store was way too small to support a large sales staff. Eric decided to go back to school and enrolled at George Mason University. He got married to a girl that he met at Riddles in Alexandria, a truly magical place. I was Eric's best man at his wedding. He married his new bride, Jenessa, at the Washington navy yard chapel. Eric later came back to work on Sundays at Sight & Sound. Bernadette went to work at my cousin Seth's store in Baltimore; it was closer to her home. Not having Bernadette around really broke tradition. Howard left the business for good and eventually obtained his real estate license. He started out selling homes and later became a commercial realtor.

As for the original sales crew of Chin Lung Art Gallery ... well, we hardly ever saw them anymore. Uncle Joey and Roland were still working together in downtown Baltimore. Cousin Seth found his niche selling beepers, even though it was David's idea, and he played the stock market religiously. Seth originally thought his father and Roland were going to sell household items like sheets, towels, pillows, and comforters, but they ended up selling electronics like he did. Uncle Joey's store was located directly across the street from

Seth's store. Seth got pissed, and they stopped talking to each other. Cousin David struggled with drug addiction and was eventually admitted into rehab. Uncle Abe still came around, though; he even helped us stock the shelves when Sight & Sound was getting ready to open. Uncle Davey's store was a permanent fixture on Ninth Street, but he'd enjoy spending more time out hanging with his cronies. Evan the engraver set up another jewelry repair shop in DC, and I'd bump into him on the street every once in awhile, but his dad, Seymour, had passed away. My ex-roommate and confidant, Iggy, decided to move back to Tampa, Florida, where his parents lived. His many years of painstaking tutelage and hard work had finally paid off, and he opened his own jewelry store on South MacDill Avenue in Tampa, naming it Gold Palm Jewelers.

Hassan eventually went to work with his dad at their wine and sub sandwich shop in Crystal City, Virginia, with the hope of taking it over one day. He got really close to fulfilling his dream of becoming an NFL punter. He signed on with the Washington Redskins and Philadelphia Eagles but never made the final cut. His best shot was with the San Francisco 49ers, when Joe Montana was the quarterback and Bill Walsh the head coach. Hassan's agent got him to sign with the team, and he really caught the attention of the 49ers' special teams coach. Hassan was pure muscle; he played linebacker and punter for our high school and for the Chargers, a semipro football team. One drawback was that he didn't graduate from college, or he would have gotten drafted by the pros with ease. He was a hell of a punter, though, and was not afraid to hit anyone hard. His only weakness was that he loved women … a lot! Things were looking good for Hassan; the special teams coach felt that he was going to win the starting punter position for the team. Then one day in the team's lunch room, Hassan flirted with one of the girls that served the players. I think he may have even sat her on his lap. He was kicked off the team the following day and blacklisted for the rest of the season. Hassan had his shot and blew it. His infraction seemed minuscule compared to today's standards. I think the league missed out on a great athlete, and I can honestly say that I've never witnessed a punter in the NFL who had his toughness. The majority of punters in the NFL are just a bunch of wimps.

The sales lineup at Sight & Sound was me, Dad, Mom, and Saul. Saul was promoted to sales and did a great job. Our accountant was Aunt Mattie, who still worked on F Street as a bookkeeper with Bensons Jewelers. The tone and tempo of checking the Gs had completely changed now. Dad wasn't his usual crazy self anymore. Those days of ringing the bell and shouting, "Don't push that lady, there's plenty of room for everybody!" and "Everything must be sold to the bare walls!" were just an echo from the past. We all got very serious, and our clientele was much more upscale and knowledgeable, meaning we had to be polished too. We couldn't get away with some of the things that we had done in the past. But thinking about the past and what was ahead for my future reminded me of a lyric by Ian Anderson of the rock group Jethro Tull: "It was a new day yesterday, but it's an old day now."

Ever since I had taken over Sight & Sound, I'd hoped for a professional running operation without the usual maniacal practices that I grew up with. But just for kicks, Dad would revert to his old ways. A couple of French Gs walked into Sight & Sound, and Dad asked, "Where are you from?"

Smiling, they responded, "We are from France." I thought to myself, I have a really bad feeling about this.

Dad remarked, "Ah … you speak the *oui, oui!*" I thought, maybe I was wrong; he was trying to banter with them in their native tongue. I guessed that was okay.

But Dad continued his bantering with the French Gs. "Do you speak *oui, oui* or do you make wee-wee in your pants?" He just had to do it, but I still had to laugh anyway.

I loaded Sight & Sound with the highest quality merchandise, and it had the best look of any store that we'd ever had. Our prices were marked higher and our profits skyrocketed. By the end of our second year, the business had a complete turnaround, and we started to make money. My secret to success was carrying the very latest products before anyone else did, displaying a huge selection of merchandise to choose from, keeping plenty of goods in stock, providing exceptional customer service, and most important ... saffing their brains out on every item. But our customers bought the latest and greatest quality merchandise. We didn't sell any knockoffs or crap. The merchandise cost us more, but we made more! The Gs expected to pay higher prices because we were in the lobby of a high-class hotel. This time we used the concept of being inside and not outside on the street to our advantage.

Dad still looked for the hot gimmicks to sell, though. He bought hundreds of dancing Coca-Cola cans. The cans wore dark sunglasses and headphones. We completely filled up one of the show windows with them. They were voice activated, so they'd start dancing in the window when there was any kind of noise. The dancing Coca-Cola cans were a hit, and we sold a ton of them.

Business was kind of slow one day when I walked out the front door and leaned on the ledge that stood several feet from Sight & Sound's entrance. I glanced to my right and witnessed a huge crowd entering the hotel lobby from the mall entrance and walking slowly toward me. In the middle of the crowd was Muhammad Ali. When people noticed Ali walking around inside the mall, they immediately crowded around him. As Ali made his snail-paced stroll through the hotel lobby, the swarm of people moved alongside him. It reminded me of the crowd of people that walked with him during his ring entrance, when he made the long trek into the boxing ring before a championship bout. Back in April of 1976, Dad and I had watched Muhammad Ali fight Jimmy Young, live at the Capital Centre. We paid fifty dollars apiece for tickets in the nosebleed section. The fight lasted the whole fifteen rounds. After seeing Ali in the mall, I didn't have anything better to do, and so I jumped into the crowd and followed right next to him. I kept tapping him on his hard, rocklike shoulder, trying to get his attention so he'd sign an autograph. An old lady was in the crowd, and she dropped her pen; Ali immediately bent down to pick it up for her. Bernadette was in the store and came running out with a Polaroid camera in her hands. I finally got his attention. He signed an autograph for me, and then I asked if he'd pose for a picture with Bernadette. Ali had been moving very gingerly through the crowd, and I noticed his hand was shaking, but when he saw Bernadette, he wrapped his arms tightly around her and smiled like the Muhammad Ali of yesteryear. I snapped the photo.

On September 30, 1985, Sharon and I had our first child, Michelle Marie. We named her after the Beatles tune. We already knew that we were going to have a little girl, but I always wondered how and when it would happen. When our baby was ready for its arrival into the world, I always pictured myself reacting much like a certain *Dick Van Dyke Show* episode, in which Rob Petrie slept in his suit in preparation for his wife's "The baby's coming" announcement. I was at Sight & Sound when Sharon called me the first time. We all carpooled together, so I had to close the store when I got her call. It turned out to be a false alarm, though. But on Monday morning and on her exact due date, Sharon's water broke. I anxiously picked up her bag and gathered everything else we needed to take to the hospital, and then I nervously walked her outside to the car. We headed for Southern Maryland Hospital about thirty minutes away. There was a considerable amount of traffic because everyone was headed to work. It was still dark outside, and everyone had their lights on. Sharon looked at me with a baffling look on her face and asked, "Why does everybody have their brake lights on?" I guessed her mind was already in baby mode.

After I checked her into the hospital and they gave us a room, it took hours upon hours for Sharon to be ready for birth. Sharon and I played cards while we waited for Michelle to arrive. But then after awhile, our friendly game turned sour. Her contractions had been painless, and we actually thought, "Hey this wasn't so bad after all; what's all the fuss about?" Then reality struck! While we were playing cards, the pain started getting intense. Sharon threw her cards up in the air and screamed, "I want my epidural, now!" I ran out of the room and called for the nurse. While she waited for the shot, I was stayed against the wall, and I started feeling queasy. The doctor came in to give her the injection, and I left the room. Sharon looked much better when I came back inside; I wish I could've said the same about me. One of the nurses said I resembled a ghost, and she force-fed me orange juice. Then after one more examination, I was told to put on my scrubs, booties, and mask, and into the delivery room we went. The doctor needed a little help and used the tongs. A last push … a tug … and out came little Michelle. The doctor made me cut the long umbilical cord, and I was a bit uneasy when it didn't cut so easily. Then he cleaned her up and placed baby Michelle with her mommy for the very first time. Sharon was surprised and astonished to finally see what had been inside her for the past nine months. It was the most beautiful and spiritual event that I had ever witnessed. Sharon said it was a miracle. I thought to myself, there really was a God.

Chapter Twenty-Three

Farewell to a Friend

By the fourth year of business, life was good. I made the most money that I had ever made, and at the end of the year, Dad and I took hefty Christmas bonuses. The store became familiarized globally. Most of our international clientele had difficulty speaking English, and so we had to learn bits and pieces of their language to make the sale. Mom learned enough Portuguese and Italian to sound credible. My Spanish skills improved tremendously, and I was close to actually having normal conversations with the French and Arabs. Even Dad communicated with confidence to the Arabic Gs, and his pronunciation was excellent. Saul spoke fluent Spanish and could easily converse with the Israelis, he had actually spent some time in Israel living in a Kibbutz. Sight & Sound resembled the United Nations. We even displayed miniature flags that represented all the countries from around the world; we had actually bought the set of flags from the United Nations gift shop. International Gs were so intrigued by our display of global representation that they were lured into the store. They'd spend countless moments hunting for their native flag. Once it was located, there was acclimation and then inspiration to buy.

I decorated the store for President Reagan's second inauguration. I went out and bought buttons, pennants, and photos of the president. If there was a big event in DC, then Dad and I liked to dress up the windows with the theme of the event.

A frigid-looking businesswoman walked into the store and headed directly for me. She said, "Take that picture of Reagan out of your window, and I'll buy something from your store."

I stared at her like she was some kind of nut or something. Then I responded, "You're kidding me, right?"

She said, "Hey, it's a political town, what can I say."

Now I was pissed. That wasn't a picture of Adolf Hitler in the window; it was the president of the United States. I thought Reagan was a damned good president and a decent human being. She was out of her mind to think that she'd shove her political views into my store and get away with it. I told her, "The picture stays, so I guess you'll have to take your business somewhere else."

She abruptly turned around and sarcastically declared, "Your loss." Actually; I won one for the Gipper. We never expressed our political views inside the store; we always remained neutral. Why piss someone off who had the potential for spending money? And we certainly had a lot of controversial Gs walk through our doors over the years. If they would mouth off about a certain political stand that was against our beliefs, we'd simply saff their brains out! But I wasn't about to change our window display around to appease a cocky G.

Mom and Dad were old-school Franklin Delano Roosevelt faithful. While growing up they would refer to FDR as one of the greatest presidents ever. Mom switched to the Republican party when Barry Goldwater ran for president, and she was determined to stay a Republican after the Kennedy debacle with the Bay of Pigs Invasion in Cuba. Dad on the other hand had never voted in an election. He always said that if he registered as a voter, than he was liable to be called for jury duty. That meant time off from work, and he wouldn't allow it.

We were so busy at Sight & Sound that we were forced to hire someone else, and it also helped to give everyone else a break from working so many long hours. Mom suggested hiring Arturo, who worked at the Colombian leather goods store across the lobby. Arturo had a heavy Mexican accent, but he spoke and understood English perfectly. His father owned and operated radio and television stations in Toluca, Mexico, and so they were definitely in the upper class. Arturo was a funny, likeable soul with a charming personality. He worked hard to make a sale and never gave up easily. He was also a womanizer and was never reluctant about asking a woman out on a date. He even copied down women's phone numbers off their credit card receipts for dating opportunities. I think the thing that surprised me the most about Arturo was how intelligent he was. He would talk about any topic with substance. The fact that he was bilingual was also a huge bonus. Arturo's personality was a perfect fit for Sight & Sound, and eventually we'd turn him into a Mexican SY.

Sight & Sound had a good feel to it. The harder I worked, the more I enjoyed it. I constantly searched for the latest electronics to sell and ordered mostly top-of-the-line goods. I'd order expensive items that no one had the balls to order in the past, in fear of getting stuck with it. And those surprise packages were coming in more frequently now. The electronics boom was in full swing, and there were plenty of new high tech gadgets to display on the shelves. I kept the store spotless; I figured if we were going sell the merchandise at a higher price, then the place had better look sharp. I constantly changed the look of the store, always keeping a fresh look. And it was always gratifying when celebrities accepted my advice. Like Art Buchwald, an American humorist who had a long running column in the *Washington Post*. Mr. Buchwald liked state-of-the-art tape recorders. We had a fantastic selection of standard size and micro recorders. He walked in and asked for the best. As soon as I presented him with my recommendation, he'd say, "I'll take it, and let me have some extra tapes and batteries." Not only was Mr. Buchwald an interesting man, but I think he and Dad had a few things in common. He grew up in New York, and like Dad he quit school to join the marines. He served in the Pacific in World War II and moved to DC in the early 1960s like Dad, and he was also Jewish. Dad always asked me to wait on the celebrity Gs, so he never got to know Mr. Buchwald like I did.

Another regular celebrity G who took my advice on high-end tape recorders was Dick Gregory. He only bought the best. Dick Gregory was a comedian, social activist, and writer. One evening I watched an old *Rowan and Martin's Laugh-In* rerun on Nick at Nite, and Dick Gregory just happened to be on the show. When I went to work the next day, Mr. Gregory walked into Sight & Sound. It was a bizarre coincidence.

A lot of professional athletes stayed at the JW Marriott, and they usually found their way into our store. I posed for a picture with the center from the Boston Celtics, Artis Gilmore. It was his last season in the NBA. I was six foot tall and felt like a little kid standing next to him—and when Arturo was ready to snap our photo, Mr. Gilmore shouted, "Cookies!" Larry Bird came in about twenty minutes later. I mentioned to Mr. Bird that I had recently sold one of his ex-teammates a pair of Porsche Carrera sunglasses. As soon as I mentioned the player's name, his attitude quickly turned from passive to peevish, and then he blatantly accused the former Celtic player of stealing money from the team. I was quite surprised by his willingness to share that information with me.

Arturo worked full-time, and Saul was reduced to working on Sundays for now. He started working at another SY store with his brother Eddie during the week. He had an opportunity to become a manager there. The Shashows always paid their sales staff well, and every year, everyone got a huge Christmas bonus and a paid vacation. But no one had ever got benefits, until Sight & Sound. It was really something to watch Saul mature into a decent salesman. He'd come a long way from that naive kid that we'd scare the shit out of. Dad and I took turns working Sundays. Most of the time, we'd wait all day for a good G to walk inside. And sometimes we'd only get a handful of people in. But we always at least broke even, and then sometimes we hit it really big, like when Gs from Abu Dhabi or a prince from Saudi Arabia walked in and bought everything in the store that I suggested. It was nice to ring up a ten-thousand-dollar sale on a Sunday, and it definitely made working on Sundays worthwhile. During those long Sunday lulls, Saul and I usually got into a beer-drinking contest. I always had the tiny fridge in the back office stocked with cold beer. We'd see who could guzzle their beer down the fastest. I don't know how he did it, but the kid beat me every time!

We had just enough help at the store so that everyone could take their vacations. Mom and Dad went to Aruba with Uncle Davey and Aunt Jeanie. They always had a good time together. Sharon and I took two trips. First we flew Michelle to Kentucky to visit with her grandparents. Sharon's mom stayed with us when Michelle was first born; Arlena's mission was to stay with her daughters and help out when they had their baby's. I thought I was the perfect new dad and wanted to show her mom that I was always one step ahead of the game. I had all the baby bottles lined up in the refrigerator like soldiers. But when Arlena took one of them out to feed the baby, the nipple was way too big. I was so disappointed!

The three of us flew to Evansville on Michelle's very first flight. There weren't any direct flights, and so we had a forty-five minute layover in Dayton, Ohio. Michelle was having fun on the trip until she developed a strange look in her eyes. The no seat belt sign was lit, and Sharon stood Michelle up in front of her. Michelle walked over, stood directly in front of me, and vomited. It was almost like she had made it a point to puke on me and not on her mom. Michelle's lunch completely covered my pants. I had to fly all the way to Dayton covered in kid vomit. As soon as we landed, I ran for the bathroom. When we finally arrived in Evansville and met with Lyle and Arlena at the airport, I had this huge stain on the front of my pants. Sharon was impressed, though; she said I was really calm about the whole thing. I just chalked it up to another day of daddyhood.

For our second vacation, we decided to take Michelle to see Mickey Mouse at Walt Disney World. Our big mistake was taking her into a fancy restaurant with a violinist that played from table to table.

We had just been served our dinner. Michelle was in her high chair and made a huge mess with her crackers. Then all of a sudden, she began shouting, "Burp ... Excuse me! "Burp ... Excuse me! Burp ... Excuse me!" She repeatedly shouted it, louder and louder, and wouldn't stop. The ambience inside the restaurant was extremely quiet until Michelle's comical outburst, so I flagged down the waiter and asked him to box up the expensive dinner. We finished our cold meal in the hotel room. On the same trip, Michelle got her head stuck between the bars of a metal railing waiting for the monorail to arrive. I panicked of course and tried to pull her head back out without thinking of the consequences. Sharon and the Disney staff finally freed her by lubricating her head. Later that same day, Michelle ran off after Donald Duck, and we almost lost her. The terrible twos were definitely apparent on our Disney trip.

Arturo was a huge Dallas Cowboys fan, and because I was a Redskins fan, it led to many heated discussions at the store. Arturo was visited by his two all-time heroes. First, the Cowboys had arrived by bus to the JW Marriott, and he watched the entire team unload and parade into the building. An hour later, Arturo's eyes were glued on the ex-Oakland Raiders football coach and CBS color commentary announcer John Madden, who walked around the hotel lobby smoking a huge cigar. Arturo came back inside the store extremely excited and began rattling off all the Dallas Cowboy player names and coaches that he had observed. A couple of hours later, safety Bill Bates of the Cowboys walked into the store. I sold him several Nintendo handheld video games to help him pass the time during those long plane rides. Then one of Arturo's football heroes, running back Tony Dorsett, walked by. Arturo asked to get a picture taken with his idol, and I hurriedly grabbed a Polaroid Spectra camera off the glass shelf and snapped a few photos. I never saw Arturo so happy.

Later in the week, the Hall of Fame quarterback from the Dallas Cowboys, Roger Staubach, wandered into Sight & Sound, and I found that to be a strange coincidence. Roger Staubach had been retired from the Cowboys since 1979 and was CEO of the Staubach Company, a commercial real estate business. But he was also Arturo's number one football hero. It was really something to see all of his heroes visiting him at work.

One morning a month later, Dad and I had just opened the store. We both wondered where Arturo was; he was supposed to be with us when we opened for business. I was just about ready to go and get our coffee when the phone rang. I picked it up and it was Arturo's roommate. The first sentence out of his mouth was, "Arturo will never be coming to work again."

I asked him, "What do you mean by that?"

He said, "Arturo died in a fire last night." Apparently he fell asleep with a cigarette in his mouth and may have been drunk. Mom told me that she had witnessed Arturo sitting at the bar inside the mall during working hours. Apparently he had a drinking problem. He'd stop at the bar every day at lunchtime and guzzle down a few. I had no clue. Ironically the day before, Dad had announced that there would be no more smoking inside the store. Arturo had smoked cigarettes quite heavily; Dad and I both smoked our cigars inside the store, but we were finally taking notice that it may not be good for business. Dad and I were shocked and stunned; we had become very close to Arturo. We changed the displays in the windows all day to keep our minds occupied.

The hardest part was notifying his parents in Mexico. I thought it be better that Mom did it, coming from another mother and from someone else that spoke Spanish. When Mom informed his mother that her son was dead, she cried out and screamed, "Why?" We were all heartbroken that evening. We prayed for Arturo's soul to go straight to heaven and to provide comfort for his grieving family. Mom and I met with all of his many friends at the Shops, to organize a ceremony for Arturo at a local church in DC. We had a huge turnout, and even his brother flew in from Toluca, Mexico. I think I cried more than anyone at the ceremony, and Arturo's brother embraced me as I wept. I'd lost a good friend; we worked many hours together and laughed a lot. When business was slow, we'd get out the electronic golf game and play championships against each other, and he'd always win. I don't believe it was a coincidence that all of his heroes came to visit him that week. Maybe God wanted Arturo to visit with them before he died. We were never able to replace Arturo with another salesman as good as he was, and it never felt the same working there after he was gone.

The next month, my encounter with a legend transpired when I spent several hours with the Splendid Splinter. One morning an older gentleman in his mid to upper sixties walked into Sight & Sound Camera and Electronics. He wore a gray wool sport coat with a white pullover shirt underneath and some gray slacks. He was really tall and appeared to have a big beer belly. He inspected our wall case filled with 35mm cameras and asked me to take out the latest of the Minolta Maximum series. I immediately pulled it out and placed it in his hands. He told me that he already had one but had a few questions on how to operate it. As he asked me questions, I started to notice that he looked very familiar. Finally, I looked up at him and asked, "You're Ted Williams, aren't you?"

He quickly responded, "That's right." I told him that we missed him in DC. Mr. Williams said, "You know, I miss Washington." Besides being one of the greatest baseball players in history and the last one to bat over .400 in a single season, he was once the manager for the Washington Senators. Then I asked him if Washington would ever get another baseball team; the Senators had moved to Texas in 1971. Mr. Williams said, "Not as long as Baltimore had a good ball club and draw people in the stands like they are." I answered all of his camera questions, and then he asked if we carried shortwave radios. I told him that we carried the Sony ICF 7600A (W), a nine-band radio that was actually compact enough to travel. Mr. Williams quickly walked over to the shortwave wall case to take a fast peek. He said, "Thank you," and then walked swiftly out the door. Dad and I were excited to have Ted Williams in the store, but we wondered if he still had any *fuluus* left after all those magical years in baseball.

Later that evening, Ted Williams and his friend Sam Tamposi rushed back into Sight & Sound. Mr. Williams led him over to the shortwave radios displayed in the wall case. An animated Ted Williams barked at me, "Show us that shortwave radio you were talking about earlier." I quickly opened the wall case and took out the radio. Mr. Williams was excited; I had shown the radio to Gs hundreds of time, and it had been one of the most popular items in the store over the years. Then he asked Tamposi if he wanted a radio too. "Come on, Sam, I'll buy you one," he said. Samuel Tamposi was one of New Hampshire's largest commercial real estate developers and was a limited partner in the Boston Red Sox. He rarely missed a game and occasionally traveled with the team. Mr. Williams wanted cases for his shortwave radios, and Mom quickly hunted for a case that would fit snugly. After several minutes, she found two identical cases that fit the radios perfectly. I retrieved two new Sony radios and took them out of their boxes to load up with batteries. At that time, an excited Ted Williams asked me, "When do you close?"

I said, "Mr. Williams, I close when you're all done shopping."

He laughed and said, "Son, you should be a God damn politician!" I'll never forget the way he recited that magnificent sentence to me. While I rang up the two radios and cases with his credit card at the register counter, Mom asked to take a picture of him. We had already gotten a great photo of Mr. Williams earlier holding the Minolta Maximum camera with me by his side and my hand on his shoulder. He posed and Mom took his picture. After the Polaroid snapshot developed, Mr. Williams examined the photo and excitedly reprimanded my mother. "God damn it, little lady, you cut my God damn head off!" He was right; it was a lousy picture, and we all laughed after he had said it.

Ted Williams said it like it was. He reminded me a lot of actor John Wayne, a real man's man. You either loved the way he was or hated the way he was. At Sight & Sound, we all loved him. I'll always remember Ted William's enthusiasm that day inside the store. I'll quote Mr. William's hero, General Douglas MacArthur, and say, "Years wrinkle the skin, but to give up enthusiasm wrinkles the soul."

Chapter Twenty-Four

Celebrity Gs and Almost the Pope

We were good friends with Pete, the engineer of the JW Marriott Hotel, and he ran a special cable to our TV in the back office so that we could watch the hotel pay-per-view channels for free. Dad, Mom, and I took turns watching movies when business was slow. I was in the back watching *The Delta Force* starring Chuck Norris. I was caught in a stupor watching the movie when I heard Dad shouting, "Check the G!" I shook off my trance, got up from my chair, and headed for the sales floor. When I finally reached the G, I focused my eyes on actor Chuck Norris. At first I thought he was my brother Howard's friend Jimmie, who looked somewhat like Chuck Norris. When my head finally cleared, I finally realized that it was *really* Chuck Norris. I had to admit I was freaked out, and I thought he had popped out of the Sony television set in the back office. I sold Chuck Norris the last 8mm Sony Handycam. He was a "Gimme I take" G; he knew exactly what he wanted, no salesmanship required. While we posed for a photo together, it felt like he was feeling around the middle of my back for a pressure point. I was worried he'd use one of his martial arts moves on me. I'm glad he changed his mind, though ...whew! An hour after Chuck Norris left the store, boxer Sugar Ray Leonard walked into Sight & Sound. Coincidentally, he too wanted to buy the Sony Handycam. I told him that Chuck Norris was in earlier and bought the last one. Mr. Leonard said, "Man, I'm gonna get that Norris!" I responded I'd like to see that; it'd be a damn good fight."

Actress Sally Struthers walked in about thirty minutes after Sugar Ray Leonard did. She looked stunning; I complemented her on the performance she gave as Florence (Felix Unger) in a female version of *The Odd Couple*. All of us had gone to see the play at the National Theater less than a block away. We had three celebs in one day. DC was turning into Hollywood, thanks to President Reagan. I heard President Reagan's booming voice every time he gave a speech downstairs in the grand ballroom. Pete the engineer used to ride the elevator with the president just in case it got stuck. He told me that Mr. Reagan had always come up with a good joke or story while on the short trip.

President Reagan's advisor Lee Atwater was a regular at Sight & Sound. He'd buy the top-of-the-line Sony Pro headphones. I always kept the best in stock just for him. I enjoyed talking with him about guitars and the blues. Mr. Atwater was also quite a musician; he briefly played backup guitar for Percy Sledge in the 1960s and played with bluesmen such as B. B. King.

Anton's 1201 Club, a swanky new establishment, opened downtown a few blocks from the store. It was a marvelous place to dress up, eat, drink, and watch a show. It resembled a Las Vegas showroom. Downtown Washington hadn't housed an elegant restaurant with a showroom since the sixties. I was excited when I convinced the whole family to go. It was pricey but I could afford it. I even wore a Rolex, but I was definitely not a yuppie. At this point Howard's new career in real estate had begun to flourish. I selected a show that I thought everyone would enjoy. We all went to see American jazz and pop singer Jack Jones, who was especially well-known for singing the *Love Boat* theme.

We got all spruced up for our big night out on the town. Sharon dressed in a black leather outfit, and Mom dressed in her white leather outfit. After a superb dinner and a fabulous show, Howard and I headed for the restroom. It was in there that I spotted Speaker of the House Jim Wright. I followed him out of the restroom. After I caught up with him, I introduced myself and we shook hands. Howard harassed me about shaking his hand later at the table. He said, "He just came out of the bathroom, and you shook hands with him?"

I said, "So what? He's the Speaker of the House."

Howard responded, "So what? You don't know if he washed his hands, do you?"

I said, "Whatever."

Mr. Wright was as enthusiastic about Anton's as I was. I asked him if he'd seen the show schedule for all the performers who would be appearing at the club. He hadn't, and he invited me to his table to discuss the upcoming schedule. On the way to his table, I grabbed Sharon. We spent a half an hour with the Speaker of the House and his wife talking about anything but politics over cocktails.

A few weeks later, Mikhail Gorbachev was in town for the summit. The press set up their headquarters downstairs in the JW Marriott. During the event, Russians frequently visited Sight & Sound. They relentlessly negotiated with me and tried to barter caviar for Sony electronics. At that time, we started receiving Sony portable stereos manufactured in Korea. The Russians were adamant about purchasing Sony products made only in Japan. Andy Warhol was correct when he said, "Everyone will be famous for fifteen minutes." The press found their story: "Russians trading caviar for electronics." The news media raced upstairs to Sight & Sound Camera and Electronics. Before I knew what was happening, there was a microphone in my face with an ABC news logo on it. This would actually be the second time that I was interviewed inside the store.

The first time, I was interrupted by news reporter Del Waters while I ate my lunch in the office. He asked me what I thought about a comment Mayor Barry had made on national television. Barry and a welfare mother of fourteen children had appeared on *The Phil Donahue Show* together. Barry told the welfare recipient, "Why don't you stop having all these babies?" I think it was the first time that I ever agreed with the mayor.

Anyway, ABC News asked me about my experiences with the Russians. I talked about their tendency to barter caviar and vodka for retail electronics, and within minutes I was on ABC radio coast to coast. Sharon's relatives in Kentucky even heard me on the radio. I guess I got my fifteen minutes.

The JW Marriott became the key to our success. If there were conventions and large events booked, then business was good. We became very dependent on the hotel's ability to bring in customers, and we never knew who was going to walk through our doors. An anonymous gentleman walked in with four bodyguards carrying automatic weapons resembling Uzis. Immediately after entering, his guards deployed throughout the 1100-square-foot store. The men stood at attention holding their weapons and wore secret service–type earphones in their ears. The mystery man was Caucasian and appeared to be an American. He looked like he was in his early thirties and about five feet six inches tall. None of us could identify the man of importance. He browsed around the store for several minutes. I asked him if he needed some help finding anything, but he said, "No thanks, just looking." I whispered to one of his guards, "Who is he?" After all, there were four armed body guards surrounding me inside my store carrying automatic weapons; I think I had the right to know. The armed guard answered, "Sorry, I'm not at liberty to say." The anonymous man finished gazing at our merchandise, and then he and his outfitted entourage raced out the front door.

On the following day, a well-known actress made her way inside Sight & Sound. I asked her to leave the store rather angrily, so the celebrity G in mention shall remain nameless. She was rude and appeared to be intoxicated. She came in looking for a light meter for her camera. We didn't carry them because we weren't a full-service camera shop, and besides, no one had ever asked for one before. I was extremely courteous and offered to call Ritz Camera a block away to see if they had them in stock. She refused to accept the fact that we didn't carry light meters. She belligerently remarked, "What kind of damn camera store doesn't have a light meter?" I explained to her that we carried a variety of electronic merchandise and were not just a camera store. I called Ritz Camera anyway, and they confirmed that they had several types of light meters in stock. However, she just wouldn't let it go. She said, "It doesn't make any damn sense not to carry a damn light meter." That was it for me; I told her to get out of my store. She appeared surprised by my suggestion and responded, "You're nothing!"

I retaliated, "You're a nobody!"

As she headed for the front door, she shouted back at me, "No, *you're* a nobody!"

She stormed out of the store and walked right by Terrell, one of the JW Marriott security guards. Terrell walked inside Sight & Sound after hearing my confrontation with the famous actress. He looked confused; we were all good friends, and he understood our demeanor. He knew it was uncharacteristic for the store to be involved in any kind of conflict, but he was especially bewildered over the fact that a famous actress had just been asked to leave an establishment inside his hotel. Terrell asked me, "Do you know who that was?"

I said, "Of course … a big-mouth nobody!"

We had our share of celebrities walk into Sight & Sound, and I hung pictures of all our famous customers around the store. Some of the notable Gs to walk through our door were John Candy, Clifton Davis, Dionne Warwick, The Temptations, Jon Voight, Gregory Harrison, Alex Haley, Didi Conn, George Kennedy, Tom Poston, Kid 'N' Play, Marvin Hamlisch, Stan Shaw, CNN's Bernard Shaw, Leslie Uggams, General Colin Powell, Senator John Warner, and Governor Bill Clinton. We also had the cast members from various stage productions at the National Theater. I watched movie crews shoot scenes for the picture "Broadcast News" on the ballroom level inside the JW Marriott. I could step out of Sight & Sound's front door and walk a few feet forward to the ledge and then look down to see all the action.

One of our most faithful Gs was a priest. Father Albacete walked in occasionally and studied our newly arrived electronic gadgets. He always called them gadgets. The father's Achilles heel was surely technology. It made sense; he was also a physicist. I'd pull out something brand-new and exciting from out of the showcase to demonstrate it for the father. I knew instantly when he was hooked. First his eyes got really big, and then he'd say, "That's obscene!" After he got familiarized with the item, he'd calmly remark, "I must have it!" The father was Puerto Rican, and so he and Mom always conversed in their native tongue. He was probably the coolest priest that I'd ever met. He was extremely intelligent, but I could tell he could talk to anyone on any level. To me it was apparent that he liked to laugh and enjoyed life. He was a really funny guy. One day he came in, and his blood sugar had dropped. He looked white as a ghost. Mom had to rush out and get him a coke while he sat down to revive himself. Father Albacete was also a close friend to Pope John Paul II. I asked the father, next time he was at the Vatican, if he'd snap a photo of the Pope holding one of our shopping bags with the Sight & Sound Camera and Electronics logo on it. He said he'd do it, but it never happened.

We never did find a decent replacement for Arturo. It became extremely difficult to find good help. Saul quit permanently, and luckily Eric decided to work on Sundays with me. Eric's father-in-law became our new accountant. Mattie said she was overloaded at Bensons and asked to step down from her bookkeeping responsibilities at Sight & Sound. Eric and I had a blast during those short five hours we spent together every Sunday. We'd reminisce about the good old days in Fort Lauderdale and Mister S. work ethics at Worldwide Electronics. Eric liked mimicking all the Gs that he waited on, like the lady that came in and asked him for ear heads instead of headphones. He sarcastically asked the lady, "What size ear heads do you want—the ear heads that stick in your ear, or the ear heads that go around your head?" I wondered if that poor lady ever figured out that Eric was just messing with her. When I worked with Eric, I was instantly transported to my past. He was the final connection to my carefree, rebellious days. The family business wasn't the same anymore. Sure, Mom and Dad were still there, but they were way too complacent now. Dad either sat on his stool behind a showcase smoking a cigar, or he'd be watching TV in the back office. I had no one to connect with anymore or to share camaraderie with, and I missed that.

It was April 3, 1988. Sharon and I rendezvoused with Mom and Dad at Southern Maryland Hospital, where we handed over a sleepy three-and-a-half-year-old for them to watch. Baby Raymond was almost two weeks late, and so Sharon had to be induced into labor. I wanted my son to be named after me, and Dad wanted his name on the birth certificate too, so we compromised by naming the baby Raymond Abraham. Sharon and I walked the hospital floors for hours upon hours, waiting for the baby to "drop." Both of us were exhausted and had run out of things to keep our minds occupied. We waited through the night and into early afternoon. Michelle's birth had been a piece of cake compared to this one. I started watching the first game of the baseball season on the hospital room TV. A nurse hurriedly walked into the room and seemed alarmed. She said it appeared that the umbilical cord may be wrapped around the baby's neck, and they needed to take Sharon into the delivery room immediately. I didn't have time to blink. They wheeled Sharon away and told me to quickly get on my scrubs. I had a difficult time putting on the scrub booties, and I said screw this, and rushed into the delivery room anyway. Within a matter of seconds, the doctor pulled out baby Raymond with the tongs, and again he made me cut the umbilical cord. Doctor Amiri was the same doctor who had delivered Michelle. My son was born on the first day of the baseball season, and of course I took it as a sign that my son would grow up to be a major league ballplayer. Sharon had two epidurals before she gave birth. After she gave birth, she was wheeled to a permanent room. There were at least six other beds in the room, but they were all empty. She couldn't feel or move her legs from all the injections, and I started to get worried. If there was a fire or something, she wouldn't be able to get out of bed. My second fear was getting our baby mixed up with someone else's, but there weren't any other babies in the nursery yet. I had made sure that I could identify Michelle when she was born because there were plenty of babies in the nursery on that day. When I finally left the hospital after Raymond was born, I'd been awake for more than twenty-eight hours. We had a girl and now a boy ... we're done!

Chapter Twenty-Five

Everything Was Sold to the Bare Walls ... Even the Toilet

Sharon and I sold our home in Saint Charles, and we spent the first few weeks after Raymond was born living with Mom and Dad at their home in Camp Springs. The construction of our new home in White Plains was near its completion. White Plains was only minutes away from the Saint Charles neighborhood. Sharon, Michelle, baby Raymond, and I slept in my old bedroom downstairs in the basement. It was actually kind of fun. I got to watch Mom pamper Candy and Brandy, her two toy poodles. Mom cooked special meals for the both of them, usually consisting of chicken gizzards. For snacks she'd feed them cheese. Brandy and Candy were so spoiled that Mom tore the cheese into very small pieces and then organized each piece in separate rows for them to eat. The dogs wouldn't consider eating the cheese until Mom walked completely away from them. After that, they took their time eating each piece of cheese, one by one from each of the rows. It was quite a ritual and something to watch. Dad on the other hand fed the dogs peanuts while he sat in his recliner drinking scotch. Most people referred to their dog as doggie, pooch, pup, puppy, or mutt. Not Dad though—he called them woo-woos.

After spending a couple of weeks with Mom and Dad, we finally moved into our beautiful brick home on Foxhall Place. The home sat on a one-and-a-half-acre lot with a woodland backyard. There were an abundance of deer and rabbit that frequently scampered across our yard. I bought a white deer statue and sat it in front our home. I thought it looked really cool between our two front trees—but I had to get rid of it. I kept finding broken arrows and shotgun shells in my front yard. I guess it looked like a real deer at nighttime, and hunters tried to kill it.

The people that lived on our street were young like we were, and they all had children. Our neighbor next door to us had eight kids. Raymond was nicknamed Ray-Ray, just like I was at his age. Both of our children had blonde hair and blue eyes. Ray-Ray learned to talk by shouting, "Charge!" Sharon or I would provoke him by pretending to initiate the historic bugle call that usually played at baseball games. Raymond first learned to stand up when he heard a song being played on an *I Love Lucy* episode. He was leaning on a table and began bouncing up and down to the beat of a rumba song called "*El Cumbanchero.*" Sharon, Michelle, and I would motivate him by singing, "*A cumba, cumba, cumba, cumbachero … A bongo, bongo, bongo, bongocero …*" After that, he started walking. Ray-Ray never pronounced Michelle's name correctly; he always called her Cha Cha. It's a name that will probably stay with her forever.

Of course we brought up our kids the traditional way, with Disney's *Sing-along Songs* on video tape, and *Sesame Street, Teenage Ninja Mutant Turtles*, and then the *Mighty Morphin' Power Rangers*. But somehow, I just had to sneak in some rock and roll too. So Ray-Ray got in the habit of falling asleep with the band "Yes" playing through his portable stereo in his bedroom, and Michelle listened to "The Dogs of War" by Pink Floyd with me. She was kind of scared anytime I played that song, but she was always curious too and asked me to play it anyway. She'd battle her uneasiness during the song by repeating, "Wassat dogs of war, Daddy?" throughout the entire song. Michelle's favorite rock tune became "Got My Mind Set on You" by George Harrison. The WPGC radio magic of yesteryear was replaced by music videos on MTV and VH1. It was like The Buggles said, "Video Killed the Radio Star."

Sharon was a stay-at-home mom now. We agreed that she'd stop working at the hospital when we had kids. Once the kids were in school, then she could go back to work if she wanted to. A few hours after Dad and I opened up for business on Monday morning, I received a phone call. It was the Charles County sheriff's office. "Is this Mr. Shashow?"

"Yes, it is, can I help you?"

"Yes, sir, we found your wife's pocketbook in the middle of the road. It appears as though all the contents are still inside. We tried contacting her at home, but your answering machine picked up. We got your phone number off a business card we found in her purse."

I got really nervous when I heard that. "Okay … where's my wife, then?"

"We only found her pocketbook; do you know where she is right now?"

"No, I don't; I tried calling her a few minutes ago, and I got the answering machine too."

"Well, when you reach her, tell her she can pick up the pocketbook at the sheriff's office on Leonardtown Road."

"Thanks for your help, officer, good-bye." After I hung up, a thousand different thoughts raced through my mind. I was losing it, and couldn't think straight anymore. I told Dad what the police had said, and of course he remained calm, but I was still a young and inexperienced husband. I kept trying to reach Sharon at home, over and over again, but I kept getting the answering machine. I probably left her twenty messages over the next hour. I had that nervous, worrisome sensation in the pit of my stomach, and I hated it. Then I thought about driving home to look for her. But Dad said to give her some time to call first.

An hour later, she finally called. "Hi, sweetie, how are you doing? Are you busy today?"

"Honey, are you all right?"

"Yes ... why? Do you know that our answering machine has over twenty messages on it?" I could hear her playing the messages back while she was talking to me.

"The police called me and said they found your purse on the road."

Then she said with a laugh, "You know what, I'm always so concerned about getting the kids into their car seats, I must have left my purse on the roof of the car and then drove off."

All I could think about at that moment was that my wife was the real Lucy Ricardo. And you know what, I think I was Ricky: *"Aye yai yai yai yai!"*

Competition became a legitimate concern at Sight & Sound, especially from discounted catalog stores like W. Bell & Company. They were always a thorn in our side. What angered me the most was how they'd advertise the latest model video camera, costing them $1000.00 wholesale, and then they sold it for $1050.00 retail. Why would you invest that kind of money to make a $50.00 profit? They never tried to make up the difference by marking up their accessories, either.

The Shops complex wasn't unique to Washington DC anymore; there were other mall complexes that had opened all around DC. There was the Old Post Office Pavilion on 1100 Pennsylvania Avenue, the new Union Station on 50 Massachusetts Avenue NE, and the Georgetown Park Shopping Mall on M Street NW. All three locations were loaded with specialty shops and restaurants, like us. In addition to all the new competition that we dealt with, it had looked more and more like the country was falling into a recession. Sales dropped considerably and business was awful. Hotel conventions declined, and foreign tourist weren't spending their money. To make matters worse, Mayor Barry made national news when he was arrested for crack cocaine, and Washington DC was dubbed the murder capital of the United States. My cut for selling Worldwide Electronics wasn't looking very good.

One day I decided to take a walk around the mall. On the way back to the store, I passed by what use to be a vacant store, just yesterday. The retail space was only two doors down from Sight & Sound. I peeked inside their window and saw various displays of retail electronics that were identical to ours. All the manufacturers that we carried at Sight & Sound over the past six years were now duplicated less than twenty feet away. They must have loaded the store up overnight. Besides selling related merchandise, they flaunted price tags advertising unusually low prices. Every item revealed a discounted price. I thought, "How can you lease space to a direct competitor of another tenant less than twenty feet away?" It was wrong and I was pissed!

I later found out that our landlord had decided to lease the space temporarily, but they still had a two-year lease. The landlord never gave us advance notice; they filled the space without thinking twice and never thought about how it may have impacted us directly. There was absolutely no loyalty; we were among the first-phase tenants to open at the Shops, and we signed a seven-year lease at top dollar. Dad and I marched upstairs to the leasing office and let the landlord know how we felt. The landlord's response to our dissatisfaction was, "Well, at least the new store doesn't carry cameras." But they eventually did.

Later in the week, I received a phone call from someone on Madonna's touring crew. They wanted to trade concert tickets for a brand-new Sony 8mm video camera. I said no. It may have been a huge mistake because her concert tickets were in high demand. Then I got a call from the television show *America's Most Wanted*. They wanted to film a segment for the show at Sight & Sound. The filming would take an entire business day and featured a dramatization of a man purchasing wires and accessories from our store to build a homemade bomb. They would have compensated us for the business downtime up to one thousand dollars. Again, I said no. I just couldn't think out of the box anymore. Ever since the landlord planted a direct competitor less than twenty feet away from us, it was all I thought about.

With business slipping, Dad and I reverted to old-school tactics for attracting business, like flooding the store with sales signs and banners. I'm sure if Louie was still around, Dad would be telling him to rip up newspapers and throw them on the floor. I sent out weekly flyers to all the offices in the Nation Press building, we created our own retail catalogue, and we were more willing to negotiate for a potential sale. I didn't want any G to leave the store and buy from a competitor because of pricing. We'd match or beat anybody's price—it was uncharacteristic of Sight & Sound but we had no choice; we did it just to ring up the register. Sight & Sound had to make a decent profit on the merchandise to cover the higher overhead costs, and getting into a price war with the competition was detrimental to our business. I stopped buying merchandise until sales had routinely increased to normal business standards. I even stopped the surprise packages from coming in. Sometimes they were shipped anyway, but we refused the order when the UPS guy delivered it.

Our sales lineup was the worst—Dad, Mom, and an Ethiopian guy named Assefa. Eric had quit working on Sundays with me. It just wasn't fun anymore after he left. Dad and I had minor conflicts and started to get on each other's nerves. He wasn't as active in the store anymore either; he'd just follow through with the natural motions of the day. Mostly he'd sit in his chair, smoke his cigar, and wait to go home. He took an unusual amount of days off, and I'd mostly drive downtown alone to work alongside Assefa for most of the week. I tried desperately to find someone else to fill the void left by Arturo, but every applicant had spoken horrible English and had absolutely no sales experience. I didn't want to run the store alone without a trustworthy and dependable right-hand man, someone I could eventually proclaim as the manager. Dad's mood was more like a song penned by Rick Darnell and Roy Hawkins: "The Thrill Is Gone." I seriously wondered whether I should keep Sight & Sound alive after Dad finally called it quits, but my heart said no. Mom and Dad were the last ties to the past, and I'd already been through too many changes and seen too many faces come and go.

I brought my daughter Michelle to work with me for the first and last time when she turned five years old. Michelle strutted around the store like she owned the joint. I gave her Windex and paper towels and told her to clean the showcases. A G walked in, and Michelle's tiny head peeked over the show case. She smiled at the lady and surprisingly asked, "Can I help you?" It immediately took me back to my first day at Chin Lung, so many years ago. After I closed out the register that evening, I let Michelle count the *fuluus,* and she was a natural. But sadly it would be the only time any of my children would be associated with the family business.

After forty years of running successful businesses, Dad said, *Hadje!* (SY slang for "enough already"). He told me that he was ready to retire. Dad and I walked upstairs to the leasing offices and attended a scheduled meeting. I told them that we weren't renewing our lease. Of course they acted coy and wondered why. I gave him my blunt answer: "Because you screwed us!" The landlord tried to offer us several months of paying only half the rent and then a slight decrease for the ongoing monthly rent payments. They even offered to renew the lease for a shorter five-year term or simply to go on a year to year basis. But I said no. Dad and I walked out with the same "kiss my ass" attitude that we had when we walked in, and it felt great! The landlord was unethical and couldn't be trusted. The only other thing to do was to go out of business, for the very last time. The signs went up immediately; our intention was to sell everything to the bare walls—all the merchandise, wall cases, showcases, stock shelves, neon lighting, and even the bathroom fixtures. We didn't want to leave anything behind for the landlord

The going out of business sale went well; we made a few dollars on some items and lost a few on others. If it appeared like we'd get stuck with any merchandise, we'd pack it up and ship it back to the wholesaler. I advertised in the paper and sold all the store fixtures, even the toilet. I wanted to leave the store as clean as possible and without owing anybody anything. Dad wanted to close up shop without paying some of the wholesalers, but he wouldn't need a good credit rating like I would. I was full of adrenaline; all I thought about was selling everything we had, paying the bills, and splitting what we had left with Dad. I wanted to keep my reputation clean because I was already planning my next business venture. I was in discussions with a dry cleaning franchise and a small community bank to help me in securing financing. It would be a move extremely out of the ordinary for a SY. The nation was still in a recession because of steep oil costs, higher unemployment, government deficits, and slow gross domestic product growth, not to mention the beginning of the Gulf War. I did the research and thought a dry cleaning business would be recession proof. After all, everyone still needed to have their clothes cleaned for work. Because I had no clue how to start one, I had requested the help of a franchise.

I never did have much time to reflect and finally admit to myself that it was over. It was the end of an era. Where did all those years go? My whole life revolved around the family business. I had a lot of good times and survived through the bad ones. My family was definitely different to say the least, but I wouldn't have wanted it any other way. There was a special bond that we all shared. I learned things that could never be taught in colleges or by corporate trainers. One of the most important traits that I mastered and demonstrated through the years was the act of becoming a chameleon, having the ability to adapt. Over the years, the business taught me to be many things—a salesman, an entrepreneur, a diplomat, an actor, and a clown. But more important, it taught me to be a man, and it gave me the strength and courage to not take any shit from anybody.

I locked the front door to a depleted Sight & Sound Camera and Electronics store that evening for the very last time. The only thing that remained was the black wall-to-wall carpet. Dad slowly made his way through the lobby of the hotel puffing away at his cigar while

I stood there and stared at the memories through the glass window. I saw Dad ringing the bell behind the register counter hollering, "Buy now and save … Don't push that lady; there's plenty of room for everyone." I watched Uncle Moey waiting on the Nigerian and breathlessly lifting out the two shortwave radios from out of the wall case. I saw Fat Bobby strolling around the store with his huge stomach and baseball bat–size cigar. There was Uncle Joey parading up and down the center aisles, straightening and feather dusting the souvenirs. I noticed Bernadette quietly writing down the numbers she'd play on a small brown paper bag while she caught a glimpse of her favorite story on a display model TV. There was Tony standing in front of the wall case and inspecting the latest model 35mm camera while puffing away on his cigar. I could see Roland wearing his head magnifier while trying to fix a broken radio. Cousin David was banging a beat on the showcase with his nervous energy, and his brother Seth laughed hysterically. Seymour, Evan, and Iggy were collaborating behind the engraving counter. My brother Howard is opening up a huge box that just arrived via UPS, possibly a surprise package filled with the latest state-of-the-art merchandise. Uncle Abe just popped in, wiping his brow with his handkerchief. There was Mom dressed stylishly and chatting with Arturo in Spanish, Haywood was smiling while he took a drag off his cigarette and then sipped his coffee. There was Eric making faces at his customer while they pointed for him to take an item out of the showcase. I noticed Saul plugging in the vacuum cleaner to clean the rug before closing time. And then I saw myself, proudly walking through the front door of Chin Lung Art Gallery to start my first day of work back in 1965.

After seven years of running a successful business, I had to shut it down. Sure, it brought back painful memories from Johnnycake Road in Baltimore; it was like my sunflower getting chopped down again, after I had worked so hard to preserve it. But I didn't care anymore, because I had the ability to grow a bigger and better business. Was I afraid of my future, without the family business in my life anymore? You bet I was. I never got a college degree. As a matter of fact, no one that worked in the family business had one.

And even though I didn't attend college, I knew I was going to make it, because I attended the school of hard knocks, and I learned to check the Gs!

The end